D0436069

THE TALIBAN REVIVAL

THE
TALIBAN REVIVAL
VIOLENCE AND EXTREMISM ON
THE PAKISTAN–AFGHANISTAN FRONTIER

HASSAN ABBAS

YALE UNIVERSITY PRESS
NEW HAVEN AND LONDON

For information about this and other Yale University Press publications, please contact:

U.S. Office: sales.press@yale.edu   www.yalebooks.com
Europe Office: sales@yaleup.co.uk   www.yalebooks.co.uk

Set in Minion Pro by IDSUK (DataConnection) Ltd
Printed in Great Britain by Gomer Press Ltd, Llandysul, Ceredigion, Wales

Library of Congress Cataloging-in-Publication Data

Abbas, Hassan, 1969-
    The Taliban revival : violence and extremism on the Pakistan-Afghanistan frontier / Hassan Abbas.
        pages cm
    Includes bibliographical references and index.
    ISBN 978-0-300-17884-5 (hardback : alkaline paper)
    1. Pakistan—Politics and government—1988- 2. Afghanistan—Politics and government—2001- 3. Taliban. 4. Pushtuns—Politics and government. 5. Borderlands—Pakistan. 6. Borderlands—Afghanistan. 7. Political violence—Pakistan. 8. Political violence—Afghanistan. 9. Islamic fundamentalism—Pakistan. 10. Islamic fundamentalism—Afghanistan. I. Title.
    DS389.A225 2014
    954.91'1053—dc23

                                                                                    2014002669

ISBN 978-0-300-17884-5

A catalogue record for this book is available from the British Library.

10 9 8 7 6 5 4 3 2 1

Sow flowers to make a garden bloom around you,
The thorns you sow will prick your own feet.

. . .

Humanity is all one body;
To torture another is simply to wound yourself.[1]
Rahman Baba (1653–1715),
the popular Pashtun Sufi poet buried in the city of Peshawar, Pakistan

Injustice anywhere is a threat to justice everywhere.
We are caught in an inescapable network of mutuality, tied in a single
garment of destiny.
Whatever affects one directly, affects all indirectly.[2]
Martin Luther King (1929–68)

Contents

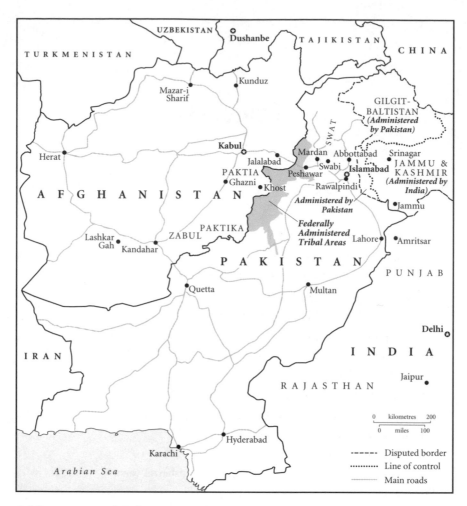

Afghanistan and Pakistan

Former North West Frontier Province (now Khyber Pakhtunkhwa Province) and Federally Administered Tribal Areas, Pakistan

Introduction
Setting the scene

In October 2001, a swift military campaign led by the Americans drove the Taliban government out of Kabul, decapitating its command system and demoralizing its cadres. But now, more than a dozen years later, as NATO troops are gradually leaving Afghanistan, the Taliban are resurgent – not only in Afghanistan, where they claimed the lives of nearly 3,000 Afghan and international security personnel in 2013 alone, but also in neighbouring Pakistan, where militants are engaged in a fierce struggle for control of the country's remote northwest tribal region. The Taliban, aided and abetted by many affiliates, including criminal networks, have shown that today they are capable of hitting anywhere across Afghanistan and Pakistan.

The Taliban arose quite mysteriously in the early 1990s, initially with a focus on stabilizing the war-torn land of Afghanistan. While in power in Afghanistan in the second half of the 1990s, the Taliban did create a fleeting sense of security for some Afghans, but overall poor governance and retrograde policies defined their reign. Built around a nefarious node, where power, dogma and money intersect, the revived Taliban movement is shaky on its religious foundations, but as a resistance movement is quite robust. Gradually it has become a marketable brand name among the militants and radicals of South Asia, especially in the south and east of Afghanistan and the tribal borderlands of Pakistan.

In Afghanistan and Pakistan alike, the group owes its strength to a reactionary zeal that is now equipped with the deadly tools of violence – especially human bombs that require no advanced technology. The core membership of all types of Taliban together is estimated to be in the thousands – not the *hundreds* of thousands – but they have a wider circle of sympathizers who look the other way when they find Taliban in their midst. Even more dangerous is the Taliban's uncanny capacity to bully and browbeat a much larger population through terror tactics. To be sure, they cannot win elections; but they can manipulate the electoral processes by creating fear and dread. As a result, the Taliban today are a formidable force, and one to be reckoned with.

This book investigates how today's Taliban have succeeded in spreading so much violence and terror. It also looks at what inspires and mobilizes them. This is also a story of their lethal renewal after their debacle of late 2001. How they regrouped, expanded their reach and fused seemingly disparate insurgent and criminal networks in their fold is a fascinating episode in modern history.

The word 'Taliban' is increasingly used as a loose term – just as the term 'Al-Qaeda' was used initially – to identify a host of groups in South Asia, including some that represent criminal enterprises and drug cartels, as well as various religious groupings. This laxity of use contributes to an ignorance of the workings and activities of the real Taliban. This book unravels this perplexing world by first telling the two distinct stories of the genesis of the Afghan and Pakistani Taliban, and then by following their tracks in parallel. The narratives then converge in the later part of the book to shed light on the resurgence of the Taliban.

For some time at least, the fashionable diagnosis in some Western circles was that the problem was Islam itself, the professed religion of these extremists and terrorists. The fact that the Taliban phenomenon has parallels in other religions as well, especially in historical terms, was either forgotten or ignored. After 9/11, the West embarked on a steep learning curve; ultimately common sense prevailed, but not before some damage was done. Many progressive Muslims who could have helped stop the Taliban momentum in its tracks stepped back so as not to be identified with the perceived Western agenda, which was seen as demeaning towards Islam. Where religious sensitivities are trampled upon, emotions run unusually high and often result in deadly outcomes. Many Pakistanis and Afghans also remained in denial – partly because of a lack of awareness and partly because of the state propaganda that had glorified the Taliban as guarantors of peace in Afghanistan in the 1990s.

I approach the overall topic as an academic. Nevertheless, I must disclose that, as a Muslim, I am deeply concerned about the challenge that the Taliban pose to mainstream Islamic discourse. A small minority of extremists have always existed within the fold of Islam, challenging the spirit and essence of the egalitarian and spiritual precepts of this great religion. At times they have risen to power; when this happened, their reigns were built on tyranny and repression. There was nothing Islamic about them, but the regimes claimed otherwise, so as to bolster their legitimacy. The Taliban worldview is certainly stimulated by such legacies, and this book discusses some of the relatively modern Muslim movements that fashioned the Taliban outlook. However, it would be a mistake to assume that the Taliban's practices are invariably motivated by conservative Islamic dictates: various ethnocentric, socio-political and criminal influences also rally this group. During my travels to the region to research this book, I came across intriguing information and insights from those who deal with the Taliban at various levels – both friends and foes. Many a time I was taken aback by the stories of the Taliban and their worldview – their waywardness, naivety and igno-rance of the world around them.

Particularly insightful was a conversation I had with a Pakistani army brigadier who led operations against the Taliban and other mili-tants in the Swat Valley in 2009.[1] Astonishingly, his interrogation of a captured man revealed that militants were sharing their wives – a prac-tice that has no basis whatever in any Islamic teachings. When ques-tioned further, the militant referred to his local leader, who had not only sanctioned the practice but had also decreed that there was no need to perform the obligatory five prayers a day because 'during Jihad they were exempt from praying'. This is yet another misplaced innovation that has no parallel in Islamic history. When I heard this, it occurred to me that if these highly controversial practices had come to light sooner, they could have had a devastating impact on the image of the Taliban and would have helped Pakistan shun extremist trends.

To explain why it did not happen, I must refer to another set of interviews, this time in Islamabad, with officials from Pakistan's Ministry of Information who were tasked with developing the counter-extremism narrative.[2] The dedicated team included a brilliant lady with media experience, a bureaucrat who was an accomplished poet and a thoughtful political activist. These were creative young people and were committed to making a difference. However, they lamented the fact that, in spite of the umpteen presentations they had delivered to local and foreign teams in a quest for funding and support, their efforts had borne little fruit.

I shared this experience with a senior official from the Pakistani government to emphasize the importance of the issue. He alerted me to the fact that all international funds that had anything to do with the counterterrorism effort were channelled to the security and intelligence agencies in Pakistan. As a consequence, many creative ideas put forward by civilian strategists and civil society actors remained unfunded. The military's domination over the country's Afghan policy – at least since the early 1980s – and everything that could be even remotely linked to it was also responsible for this policy orientation, if it can be called such. To evaluate these aspects in depth, a chapter of the book is dedicated to Pakistan–Afghan relations and to unearthing how Pakistan's role in openly supporting the Taliban during the 1990s brought the Afghan Taliban and Pakistan's security and intelligence establishment closer together in the long run. Most Afghans I interviewed placed the blame for the genesis, growth and revival of the Taliban in their homeland squarely on Pakistan. They included many young people who had been educated in Pakistan, where they had lived as refugees in the 1990s. In response, Pakistanis point to the troubles they endured as a result of the perennial instability in Afghanistan and to the economic cost of hosting millions of Afghan refugees over the past three decades. This mutual antipathy has now assumed a life of its own, which does not bode well for future relations between the two states.

Can the Talibanization trends be reversed? Yes, they can; but not until the root cause of the problem is understood and certain nuances comprehended – nuances that are embedded in the historical and cultural history of the region, particularly the Pashtun lands, which produce a major chunk of the Taliban. A majority of Pashtuns in Afghanistan and Pakistan are not attracted by the Taliban way of thinking, and indeed are the worst victims of the series of wars that have been fought on their land over three decades. The Taliban, however, quite routinely use and misuse Pashtun cultural codes (known as *Pashtunwali*), making that an important topic to cover in this book. There is no dearth of historical literature on the subject; but what is different here is a focus on the contemporary meaning and impact of this practice. The initial chapters of the book also trace the Pashtun history in parallel with the formation of the state of Afghanistan and the emergence of Pakistan, in order to compare and contrast the socio-political developments and state policies that have shaped the present.

The varieties of Taliban make it difficult to generalize about their potential, and so the shades of darkness and murkiness in their views and methods merit deeper examination. This book attempts just that. It tries to help the reader navigate the tribal borderlands, which the Taliban call their home – but without compromising the nuances that are often overlooked. It is about the historical legacy of the Taliban, their inspiration and their view of a future they want to build. To understand the Taliban variations, conflict zones from Kandahar to Waziristan, and from Peshawar to Karachi are surveyed. This is no mere narration of events: it is about ideas and the people who have adopted this worldview, as well as about those who oppose and challenge them.

The story of the Taliban is also intrinsically linked to the governance challenges in Afghanistan and Pakistan, where elites who are cut off from their own people often push for policy prescriptions that are not appropriate to the situation. The book explains how the introduction of

Western models without any local modification proved counterproductive in some instances. The impact of the so-called 'nation-building' endeavours in Afghanistan is also dissected in this light.

We approach this overall complex subject by trying to answer some fundamental questions, posed throughout the book, in order to bring out the socio-political, economic and ideological variables at play. We delve deeper into post-9/11 history to grasp what it was that turned a movement into an insurgency in Afghanistan, and we strive to explain the rise of the Pakistani Taliban in the Federally Administered Tribal Areas (FATA) and their expansion in the adjoining Khyber Pakhtunkhwa Province (KPK). The puzzling public policy choices made in Kabul and Islamabad are appraised in the light of interviews with many insiders in the two capitals.

In a way, this book also presents my personal journey from being a police officer in the Pashtun areas near the Pakistan–Afghanistan border to becoming a professor in the United States. My early education in Peshawar and Abbottabad in the 1980s and then my years in the police service in the 1990s developed my perspective of the area and its ethos. Having spent a lot of time among Pashtuns, and having benefited from their selfless hospitality, I learnt many local theories as to how the Taliban initially emerged out of this ethnic group and heard many stories about their survival tactics. My scholarly voyage in the West, first in the UK and then through the American 'power elite corridor' from Boston to New York and onward to Washington, DC, where I now reside, provides me with another lens through which to view the same developments. These are two different worlds, and I aspire to explain and compare the perspectives and the outlook for the reader. In pursuit of this goal, over the past four years I have interviewed dozens of government officials and politicians in Afghanistan, Pakistan, Europe and the United States, plus many in India, Iran, Iraq, Saudi Arabia and Turkey. I also cherish my discussions with ordinary Afghans, Pakistanis and Americans, whose insights I have found to be no less valuable.

The story of the Taliban revival is as much embedded in the cultural legacy and political history of Afghanistan as it is linked to security factors and broader regional and global developments. For the next layer of analysis, the sequence of events is as significant as the ideological mind-set of the key Taliban actors. The account nonetheless must begin with the socio-political history of the Pashtuns, the group that principally constitutes the Taliban cadres in both Pakistan and Afghanistan.

CHAPTER ONE

'Intruders are always unwelcome'
Pashtun identity, culture and political history

In the early 1980s, growing up and studying in Peshawar, the once vibrant capital of Pakistan's Khyber Pakhtunkhwa Province (KPK), then known as the North West Frontier Province (NWFP), I sometimes heard a Pashto-language proverb: 'Intruders are always unwelcome'. Thinking it was yet another 'pearl of wisdom' type of quotation, intended for students to learn and use in school essays, I was not intrigued enough to search for its 'hidden' meanings. Later my family moved back to Punjab Province and I nearly forgot the saying.

In the mid-1990s, I returned to the heartland of the Pashtuns as a young police officer, after joining the 'central superior services' of Pakistan – a brand name for prestigious bureaucratic positions borrowed from the British colonial era. On my very first day on duty as a sub-divisional police officer (equivalent to chief of police in a mid-sized town in the United States), I encountered a distressed young woman wailing in the police station of Swabi, a small town about an hour and a half's drive from Peshawar. She had come to the police to complain that her neighbour had severely beaten her after she had snubbed him when he tried to make a move on her. The man couldn't take the 'insult' and had responded brutally. When I asked the police official on duty about her complaint, I was told that this appeared to be a 'domestic issue', implying that it was an internal family matter, in which the police should avoid interfering. Being energetic and further buoyed by the new rank insignia on my shoulder, I decided to go to the scene of the crime and deal with the man myself. My staff warned me that the woman's home was far away in a mountain area, but I decided to proceed nonetheless, along with three guards and the woman who had made the complaint.

The journey was indeed hard and tiring. Around 8 p.m. on a dark, cold night, we reached the spot and the woman showed us her neighbour's house. I knocked on the entrance gate twice before my police guard told me that I was being too polite and we must break the door down, since the person we were looking for was unlikely to welcome us. Not knowing what was 'customary' for police in the area, I agreed. As soon as we forced our way in, we were met with a volley of Kalashnikov fire. My armed colleagues took cover quickly. All I had was an old Webley and Scott revolver that I had received from my father and was wearing proudly, not realizing that it was almost useless in a Pashtun land where everyone, irrespective of status and resources, was armed with rifles and machine guns.

Soon other villagers turned up in support of the culprit, and someone shouted that a newly arrived 'Punjabi' police officer had intruded into a Pashtun's house. Khyber Pakhtunkhwa's much larger and dominant neighbour, over the centuries Punjab Province has often provided safe passage to warriors from Central Asia on their way to Delhi – warriors that the Pashtuns almost always resisted militarily. Most Pashtuns are not overly fond of the people of Punjab . . . My police team members could see the dilemma and wasted no time in advising me that we must retreat, because soon the whole village would be surrounding us. We sent an SOS call via our wireless equipment, but the culprit had vanished from the scene by the time reinforcements reached us. The incident helped me learn early on that, as a non-Pashtun, I was viewed as an outsider and I should be careful how I approached my responsibilities. I was not treated as an enemy or as an 'intruder' per se, but as an outsider it took time and effort for me to develop credibility and trust.

Another experience soon afterwards showed me the other side of Pashtuns. In a police raid in pursuit of a car thief who was fond of stealing Mercedes Benz vehicles, we again had to break into a fortress-like house in a nearby district, in the general direction of the Pakistan–Afghan border. An old man, the father of the criminal, informed us that his son had not visited for many months, but quietly watched us as we searched his home. We first requested the women of the house to gather in one room, respecting their *purdah* (veil), and as a result there was no retaliation of any sort to our search. Any perceived disrespect for women can have disastrous consequences. The way in which 'women's rights' are defined very restrictively and trampled upon menacingly, often within the tribal segments of Pashtun society, is both tragic and appalling.

Failing to find our target, we were about to leave when the old man asked me where I was from. I told him I was the new police chief of the nearby town, but he repeated his question, this time specifically asking me about my ethnic background. Rather reluctantly, I gave him the answer, to which he immediately responded 'Oh, so you are our guest, then!' Seeing my amazement, he explained: 'Well, sir, you have done your job of searching my place, and now I must treat you as my guest and there is no way you can leave without having a cup of tea.' I was about to reject the offer out of hand, but one of my local police colleagues whispered in my ear that a refusal would be regarded as offensive. I was left with no option but to enjoy tea and *parathas* (tasty local oily bread) and to absorb yet another lesson that was not in any police academy textbook – Pashtuns are very hospitable and friendly if you are mindful of their customs and traditions.

It is often said that not all Pashtuns are Taliban, but all Taliban are Pashtuns. This is no longer strictly speaking accurate, as new Taliban types are being produced by parts of Punjab and Sindh provinces in Pakistan, as well as by non-Pashtun areas of Afghanistan; but still more than 80 per cent of the Taliban are ethnically Pashtun. It is also an undeniable fact that the Taliban initially surfaced from Pashtun-dominated areas in both Afghanistan and Pakistan. How and why is an intriguing story. This chapter briefly explores the history of the land and people from which the Taliban emerged in the 1990s.

Location matters and identity counts

The Pashtuns are the largest tribally organized group in the world today.[1] Though more Pashtuns currently live in Pakistan than in Afghanistan, they have historically played a more dominant role in Afghan politics and state structure. Kandahar and Peshawar are the two most important Pashtun-populated cities in the region, but there are more Pashtuns living in Karachi (capital of Sindh Province and the major port city of Pakistan) than in any other city. Some Pashtun families moved far into what is today India's heartland, and a vibrant Pashtun diaspora also exists in Europe and North America. The ethnic group is identified (and its name pronounced) in a variety of ways: in Afghanistan, most use the term 'Pashtun', whereas in Pakistan they mostly identify as 'Pukhtun', although many Pakistanis, especially in Punjab and Sindh provinces, follow the British colonial-era designation 'Pathan'. In Afghanistan, other ethnicities (especially Persian speakers) historically referred to Pashtuns as 'Afghans', but gradually the latter name became used for all citizens of the country.

I am reminded here of one of my Pashtun friends, Abdur Rauf Khan, a senior bureaucrat in Islamabad, who in a lighter vein used to say: 'Pashtun is not an ethnic identity; it is a state of mind; and anyone can transform into a Pashtun under certain circumstances!' Among friends we interpreted the saying as: 'Losing one's cool and acting a bit wildly is a common Pashtun trait.' I often shared this with Pashtun friends as a joke; but more recently, while researching the subject, I have learnt that this closely resembles a serious statement from one of the best of the modern Pashtun intellectuals – Abdul Ghani Khan, son of the legendary Abdul Ghaffar Khan ('Bacha Khan' – known in the West as 'Frontier Gandhi' on account of his close political and social ties with the great Mohandas Karamchand Gandhi). The exact quote of Ghani Khan goes: 'Pashtun is not merely a race but, in fact, a state of mind;

there is a Pashtun lying inside every man, who at times wakes up and overpowers him.'[2] Here the inference is positive and is meant to inspire young Pashtuns, among whom Ghani Khan's poetry is increasingly popular today. A Pashtun music group in Pakistan – Yasir & Jawad (Y&J) – has brought Ghani Khan's poetry into the mainstream; its rendition of his 'Reidi Gul' became one of the most viewed videos on YouTube in Pakistan (before the website was blocked in the country in late 2012).[3] This song focuses on *khudi* – a broad concept that denotes a process of introspection, leading to inner strength and achievement of high moral standards. A majority of Pashtuns earnestly aspire to reclaim their *khudi* today more than anything else.

What defines Pashtun identity is a question that deserves some attention. The Pakhta, the early ancestors of Pashtuns and Afghans, inhabited the region between the Hindu Kush mountain range and the Indus River between the second and the first millennium BC. The area is known for its rugged mountains and barren slopes, as well as for its picturesque valleys and rolling steppe. Over the centuries, the Pashtuns expanded and thrived in this beautiful but tough terrain. Most of it is beautiful to view, but requires indomitable courage to inhabit. Without enormous physical energy it was impossible to travel through its steep passes and barren deserts. The harsh weather in the area further made Pashtuns hardy and resilient.

There are various popular traditions about Pashtun lineage: some claim links with Arabs (including directly to Prophet Mohammad) while others emphasize Greek descent (with reference to campaigns of Alexander the Great in the area).[4] Interestingly, there is also a strong tradition suggesting a link with the Jewish people, first written about by the Mughal Emperor Jahangir's record-keeper, Naematullah Harvi, in the early seventeenth century.[5] Some Pashtuns hailing from the tribe of Yusufzai (Sons of Joseph) reportedly preserved copies of the Hebrew Bible, handed down to them by their forefathers, up until the early twentieth century.[6] In most local tribal lore there is specific mention of a person by the name of Qais, who is the legendary ancestor of all Pashtuns. Qais is believed by Pashtuns to be a descendant of the Jewish

King Saul; he supposedly went to the holy city of Mecca, where he embraced Islam at the hands of the Prophet himself and took the name Abdur Rashid. According to legend, he returned to his own land and converted his people, who became strong defenders of the faith.[7] Though the story defies historical fact in various respects, it suits proud Pashtuns today, as they cherish their Islamic identity and claim that they accepted Islam before other groups in the South Asian region. In fact, the message of Islam gained currency in the Pashtun areas in a slow and gradual process from the seventh to the fifteenth century.[8] Along the way, various factors – regional and global – influenced the religious practices and culture of Pashtuns. Meanwhile many smaller ethnic groups assimilated and merged with the larger, dominant communities.

Interestingly, I heard another version of how Pashtuns were introduced to Islam (though, despite my best efforts, I have been unable to find it in any written history of Pashtuns in either English or Urdu). During a *jirga* (meeting of local elders to resolve a dispute as per customary law) in the town of Swabi, a local politician narrated the story in front of many other people and no one challenged him.

First of all, I need to provide a little context. At the time, I was representing the local police organization. We were trying to gain support from local tribal leaders in order to secure the release of a woman who, we believed, had been kidnapped by a local tribesman and was being kept at an unknown location. In the absence of hard evidence, the only option was for us to reach out to the community through the local elders. Knowing full well that the 'rule of law' argument would not get us very far in the situation, I invoked religious values about humanity and explained what Islam expected us to do in such a situation. The politician who had arranged the gathering interrupted me and explained that Pashtun honour was at stake – the claim was that the lady in question had voluntarily married her alleged kidnapper. He continued:

When some Arab preachers came to introduce Islam to the area centuries ago, the Pashtun leadership responded by presenting the central features of the *Pashtunwali* code and asked them if Islam was compatible with these values. It was only after the preachers agreed not to interfere with *Pashtunwali* that Pashtuns joined the fold of Islam.

I didn't think much of the story at the time, but over a period I learnt that the practice of Islam among Pashtuns, especially in tribal and rural areas, is quite unique in more ways than one. A Pashtun saying perhaps explains matters better: 'Pashtuns accept half of the Koran.' Some experts interpret this as indicative of an age-old struggle between two important institutions – mosque and *hujra*, the local Pashtun guest-house that operates as a discussion forum.[9] Educated Pashtuns seldom fall for such myths, but the prevalence of the theory among ordinary people has certainly had an impact on society.

Before delving into what *Pashtunwali* stands for, it is important to mention the Pashtun tribal configuration and its demography. There are four descent groups among Pashtuns, all of which originated in biological or adoptive descendants of Qais. These are a) the Durrani, located in the south and southwest of Afghanistan, and adjacent parts of Pakistan; b) the Ghilzai, located in the east of Afghanistan and the largest group in the country; c) the Gurghusht, located on the southwest edge of the core Pashtun region (bordering the Baloch tribes in Pakistan), and also in the east (around Kunar in Afghanistan); and d) the Karlanri, straddling the Afghanistan–Pakistan border in the east and also located in the KPK. The total Pashtun population is estimated to be between 40 and 45 million, of whom Pakistan is home to about 28 million (KPK – 20 million; FATA – 6 million; Karachi city – 2 million). Afghanistan hosts around 15 million, and around a million live outside the region, including in Europe and North America.[10]

To say that relations between these groups are very complex and complicated would be something of an understatement. For instance, the mutual hostility that persists between the two Pashtun tribal confederacies of the Durrani and the Ghilzai goes back centuries. In total, the four groups comprise around 60 major tribes and over 400 sub-tribes.[11] Those in rural and mountainous areas stick religiously to their tribal identity, but urban areas are much less conservative in this sense. The Pashto (or Pukhto) language provides a natural bond between Pashtuns. Given the historical and cultural links between Persia and Afghanistan, many Pashtuns in Afghanistan speak Dari, a Persian dialect.

The urban–rural distinction is a tangible factor in the Pashtun areas of both Pakistan and Afghanistan, and is also expressed by the difference between *nang* (honour bound) and *qalang* (tax bound).[12] *Nang* Pashtuns are members of tribes that are relatively independent, and most reside in mountainous areas. *Qalang* Pashtuns, in contrast, are actively involved with the state authorities and either pay or collect taxes. For instance, for Pakistani Pashtuns living in the KPK, also known as 'settled areas', respect for the state authorities – the writ of the state – is tangible. Before Talibanization gained traction in the Pakistani area, the KPK used to be the preferred destination for members of the principal federal public service groups, such as the Police Service of Pakistan or the District Management Group, since the service conditions there were better than anywhere else in Pakistan. It sounds unbelievable today.

Pashtuns also constitute a little over a third of Pakistan's troubled Balochistan Province, and they are both comparatively better off economically and more stable than their Baloch neighbours.[13] There is hardly any insurgency in these areas, though Pashtuns generally stand by the Baloch in their demands for more rights.[14] This group of Pashtuns has more in common with the Pashtuns of the settled areas in the KPK. Over the decades, hundreds of thousands of Pashtuns have also migrated to Pakistan's port city of Karachi in search of better economic prospects. Assimilation has been a test for Pashtuns, but other ethnic groups in the city have also eyed them with suspicion and alarm. This city's burgeoning population problem and resource constraints have added fuel to the fire of ethnic tension.

Pashtuns are often depicted as belonging to a warrior tradition – hence the saying that 'Pashtuns are never at peace unless they are at war.' This perception is an outcome of the dozens of major battles in which Pashtuns have participated actively over the past couple of centuries. It is forgotten, though, that both regional and global politics played a critical role in these wars. The reality is that Pashtuns were forced to interact with all manner of invaders, warriors and even proselytizers from Central Asia, Turkey and Iran, who used their territory to move towards Punjab and Delhi. The Pashtun gateway has been accessible to all. However, no outsider has either settled in the area or controlled it effectively for long. The area's unforgiving terrain has also played its part in this scheme of things.

Tribal ethos and mutual rivalries similarly define Pashtun culture and tradition in significant ways. Some tribes are more prominent than others in this regard. Mehsuds and Wazirs, both residing in the Waziristan area of Pakistan's FATA, are very proud of their formidable reputation as warriors and are known for their frequent blood feuds. In the past, when one tribe decided to support the Pakistani Taliban, the other opted to cut a deal with Pakistani security forces to support their military campaigns. It was less an ideological preference and more a continuation of an old tribal rivalry.

Another important example is the Afridi tribe, which is the most powerful and dominant tribe in the Khyber agency in FATA. The tribe is known as the guardian of the Khyber Pass and is identified within Pashtun tribal lore as one of the most courageous. While known to be short-tempered, Afridi are admired as good fighters who are pragmatic in picking their battles and making alliances.[15] Of course, it all depends on one's perspective: for British historians, Afridi are remembered as a rebellious and treacherous tribe. However, few foreign historians or analysts know of two additional traits of this tribe. They are known for respecting Sufism – a mystical dimension of Islam that advocates love of humanity – which intellectually aligns them with broadminded Muslim groups.[16]

Secondly, the Afridi tribe has also produced great men of literature. Their rivals, however, project them as skilled smugglers. The stereotyping of Pashtuns, even within the Pakistan–Afghanistan region, is a serious issue.

Traditions associated with Sufism are not very popular in the Pashtun region today – in contrast to other parts of Pakistan, especially Sindh and Punjab provinces, which host the shrines of some of the greatest Sufi saints of South Asia. Historically, however, Sufism had a deep influence on Pashtun society, and a large number of Sufi shrines dot the landscape of Pashtun areas.[17] Tolerance, pluralism and selfless-ness define the Sufi ethos. It is often said that the reason this message is now eluding a significant segment of Pashtun society is the rising popu-larity of the Deobandi school of thought in the area. A late-nineteenth-century revivalist and anti-imperialist movement, this offered some conservative prescriptions to save 'real Islam' – and challenging Sufi practices was one of the important features of this message. How it gained a foothold in parts of Pashtun-dominated areas is an issue to which I return later.

The *Pashtunwali* (Way of the Pashtuns) and its impact

The somewhat controversial (as well as defining) feature of the Pashtun culture, *Pashtunwali* is a much broader concept than is generally under-stood. It evolved over a period of centuries, and is a social, cultural and quasi-legal code – largely customary and unwritten, partly cliché ridden and open to a variety of interpretations. For many Pashtuns it is a chiv-alrous code of honour that guarantees their survival; for critics it attests to the group's backwardness. Pashtuns claim that it has a 5,000-year history, but there is virtually no evidence to support this. The modern world was introduced to the idea through the memoirs and travelogues of Westerners in the eighteenth century, but the elements of the code were mentioned in local languages hundreds of years before that. The legendary Pashto warrior-poet Khushal Khan Khattak referred to an overriding concept of honour, arguably the foundational concept of *Pashtunwali*, in a famous seventeenth-century poem: 'I despise the man who does not guide his life by *nang* [honour]/the very word *nang* drives me mad!'[18] It has various sources – ranging from Sufi poetry and folklore to epic romances and various *mataloona* (proverbs), and remains the collective wisdom of Pashtuns down the ages, providing a set of principles and guidelines for both individual and communal conduct.

The major components of *Pashtunwali* are quite reflective of the Pashtun worldview. First and foremost is *melmastia*, signifying hospitality and profound respect for all guests, regardless of race, religion, national affiliation or economic status, and offered with no expectation of reward or favour.[19] Historically, even enemies are afforded this privilege if they come to one's house under certain circumstances. *Badal* stands for avenging a wrong, and is seen as an individual obligation among Pashtuns. This requirement has no time limit and there are many recorded cases of Pashtuns taking revenge after decades. An oft-repeated Pashtun saying goes: 'A Pashtun waited a hundred years before taking his revenge and it was quick work.' Those who fail to follow this custom are ridiculed even by their own families, and are often ostracized by society. Long-running blood feuds are an inevitable consequence of this provision. The concept of *nanawatay* denotes that protection is given to a person who requests it against his enemies. That person is protected at all costs and in all circumstances. However, this was originally meant for intertribal harmony; as time passed even non-Pashtuns were allowed to claim this privilege in cases of dire need.

Another one of the main features of *Pashtunwali* is *zemaka*, which inspires Pashtuns to defend their land and property against incursions and to consider this a binding obligation. Lastly in this category comes the fundamental principle of *nang*, which means safeguarding the honour of the family in terms of independence, culture and religious traditions. This can be interpreted widely or narrowly, depending on the education and exposure of a person. In a patriarchal society, where women's rights are very limited, the provision has deadly implications when a dispute is brought before a traditional *jirga* for resolution. In certain instances, 'a typical modus operandi to settle feuds by *jirga* is to make the offender yield his womenfolk to the aggrieved party'.[20]

Through such marriages, enmities between families and tribes are expected to be resolved for good; but tragically, the women are not asked if they are prepared to be sacrificed in this manner.

The story does not end there. There are many more features of *Pashtunwali* that are seldom given due importance by Western observers.[21] One important feature pertains to the idea of *hujra* (sitting place or community hall). This is a guesthouse or private assembly hall, where any member of the local community can come and discuss cultural or political issues. It also acts as a forum for conflict resolution and negotiation. It is a very well-defined concept, and even imposes specific responsibilities on the host of the *hujra*, especially regarding the safety of all visitors. Various other key aspects of *Pashtunwali* include: *jirga* (decision-making through an assembly of elders); *roogha* (need for reconciliation or compromise); *barabari* (equivalence); *ghairat* (pride); *gwanditob* (regard for neighbours); *oogha warkawel* (giving a lift to persons in need); *ashar* (encouraging collective work); *zhamena* (standing by a commitment); and *hewad* (loyalty to the Pashtun nation).

Seldom mentioned in Western analysis are a refusal to accept outside interference in internal matters, reluctance to be governed by a distant 'central authority', and an amazing confidence in the ability of local leaders to provide protection. In brief, *Pashtunwali* guides, governs and shapes the character of Pashtuns and, though dogmatic and conservative in certain aspects, it is constructive in other areas and aspires to instil discipline in its adherents.

It is difficult to generalize, but my observation has been that many of the constructive aspects of the *Pashtunwali* code are only practised by educated Pashtuns, living mostly in the urban centres, whereas the most notorious elements of the code are widespread among the uneducated, usually based in distant rural and underdeveloped areas in both Pakistan and Afghanistan. The impact of literacy rate and economic development on the prevalence of a certain norm in an area cannot be underestimated.

There are a few noteworthy Pashtun customs that are practised across the board. For instance, one (which is quite uncommon in the rest of Pakistan) is that, irrespective of social status, political stature or government rank, Pashtuns almost always eat at the same table or on the same carpet while at work. Even in private settings, the same decorum is observed. This egalitarian approach distinguishes Pashtuns from the various other ethnic groups in the adjoining areas, which are highly class-conscious. Among them, for a boss to invite his lower subordinates or staff to join him for a meal would be inconceivable.

Pashtuns are by no means homogeneous. Invasions, brutal competition between tribes, peculiar political developments, forced migrations and, most importantly, conflict have engendered many distinctive trends in the different Pashtun groups – Afghan Pashtuns, Pakistani Pashtuns and, even more starkly, in the third category of Pashtuns living in the mountainous tribal belt that was artificially and arbitrarily carved up by the 1893 Durand Line. For British colonialists on the Indian subcontinent (today's Pakistan and India), this was an administrative action designed to secure the border with Afghanistan and keep the warring Pashtun tribes in check. However, the area is more of a frontier – an elastic boundary line – than a border, and is hardly the buffer zone that was originally intended. State control in the 'unsettled' Federally Administered Tribal Areas (FATA) was always weak and vulnerable, as the people of this area took pride in being seen as autonomous from direct state control.

Similarly, in the case of Afghanistan, the central government in Kabul has historically been seen by Pashtuns in the south and east as intrusive and interfering – but when it comes to the question of who is to control Kabul, and by extension Afghanistan, Pashtuns claim that they deserve the biggest piece of the pie. Such contradictions reflect their ambitions, as well as historical memory.

Lessons of history

Many South Asians believe that British colonialists successfully implemented a special social engineering formula to dominate and control what is today Pakistan and Afghanistan: namely 'rule the Punjabis, intimidate the Sindhis, buy the Pushtun, and honor the Baloch'.[22] Irrespective of whether the British actually followed such a governing principle, the ruling elites in Pakistan since 1947, especially military dictators, pursued this model almost religiously – except, that is, for the 'honor the Baloch' part (as is evident from the restive Balochistan Province, where an insurgency is brewing). In any case, the 'buy the Pushtun' ingredient of the 'recipe', though often jokingly referred to among the non-Pashtuns in the region, is a controversial one. If this dictum were in fact true, it could have made life much easier for all those who have ever tried to rule, control and manipulate the Pashtuns. But history tells a different story.

All those who failed to govern and micromanage the Pashtuns would like the world to believe that the Pashtuns are indeed devoid of any sense of proportion, and that their tribal baggage and misdirected religiosity make their worldview incompatible with the modern world. That is simply not true. Even if (for the sake of argument) the Taliban worldview represented a significant section of Pashtuns today, this is a recent phenomenon and it needs to be seen in the context of geopolitical and security developments in the late twentieth century. Regional rivalries and consequent proxy wars only exacerbated the challenges. In the midst of it all, the distortion of Islamic beliefs provided space to extremists who employed religious fervour to sanctify their violent and brutal actions. This cycle has repeated itself periodically, to the detriment of Pashtun identity and ethos.

A perusal of history textbooks is not enough to grasp the nuances and comprehend the prevailing insurgency, the violence and especially the motivations of those who are challenging extremist tendencies in society. Moreover, the Afghan, Pakistani, British and many post-9/11 Western histories of the Pashtuns and Afghanistan often offer selective and conflicting narratives. The historical events and trends covered below are crucial in understanding the flow of history up to the present day. I have given equal weight to the written word of credible scholars, to oral history and to the personal narratives of those who love to talk about their history, culture and politics.

The rise of Ahmed Shah Durrani and the birth of Afghanistan

The Turko-Persian cultural influence over the various ethnic groups that constitute the Afghanistan of today is palpable. The administrative institutions introduced by the Mughal and Safavid empires in the broader region also generally shaped the thinking of the ruling elites in the country.[23] The Mughal Empire (1526–1857), which roughly covered present-day India, Pakistan and Bangladesh and had its capital in Delhi, extended up to Kabul, while the Safavid Empire (1501–1722), with its base in what is today Iran, competed with the Mughals for control over the region surrounding today's Kandahar, the Pashtun heartland in Afghanistan. As Kandahar changed hands between the two great empires of the era, the Pashtun tribes exploited the situation to extract concessions from both sides. The tottering Mughal Empire, which was in a downward spiral after Emperor Aurangzeb's death in 1707, and the collapsing Safavid Empire in the eighteenth century opened the way to a new empire builder – a Pashtun by the name of Ahmed Khan Abdali (1722–73), who established his reign at the young age of 25 in 1747 at a *loya jirga* or gathering of all prominent tribal leaders, at which he received the full support of united Pashtuns. Pir Sabir Shah, the spiritual guide of the Pashtun tribes, validated the selection by showering praise on the young Ahmed Khan Abdali and declaring him *Durr-e-Durran* (pearl of pearls). This led to the name Durrani.[24] His middle name Khan gave way to 'Shah' (leader). This was the first time a local leader had successfully consolidated his power across the traditional Afghan cities and beyond Kandahar, and while South Asians still know him mainly by his original Pashtun surname – Abdali – Afghans also remember him as Ahmed Shah *Baba* (meaning 'father').

According to history books popular among the Muslims of South Asia, Shah Waliullah, a well-known Muslim scholar turned activist of Mughal India, invited Ahmed Shah 'Abdali' to invade the Mughal territories and restore Muslim pride.[25] Hardliners among the Muslim clergy did not appreciate the tolerance and inclusivity practised by the Mughals, and in fact it caused them considerable rage (an emotion that their training did not equip them to keep to themselves). But the Mughal Empire was also already fracturing when Waliullah made his request around 1760. Ahmed Shah responded to the call and defeated the Hindu Marathas at the epic battle of Panipat, 60 miles north of Delhi, in 1761. He was particularly brutal towards the Sikh. This story is part of the legend among the Muslims of South Asia and Abdali is depicted as a great Muslim hero in the region.[26] (Pakistan has even named a short-range nuclear-capable missile after him.)[27]

The Durrani Empire, at its zenith under Ahmed Shah, included parts of modern-day Iran, Afghanistan, Tajikistan, Uzbekistan, Turkmenistan, Western China, almost the whole of Pakistan and Northern India. The Durrani Pashtun family survived in power (in one form or another) until 1973, which explains the Pashtun claim to leadership in Afghanistan. The Ghilzai, the most influential rival confederation of tribes, also played an important role in the region's history, but leadership positions eluded them after 1747. To be fair, it is important to point out that Mirwais Hotak, chief of the Ghilzai tribe, had revolted against the Safavid rulers in the early eighteenth century and had declared the Kandahar region an independent Afghan kingdom in 1709. The Hotaki dynasty ruled the Kandahar area until 1738, but this remained a limited exercise in 'nation-building', to borrow a modern term.

The Durrani Empire, by comparison, started off as a loose confederation of tribes, with a decentralized power structure; but gradually it built a more cohesive country. Nevertheless, the Durrani kings relied on a diverse group of power brokers to rule over Kabul, the new capital of their empire. For instance, Ahmed Shah and his descendants relied on the Persian-speaking *Qizilbash*, or 'Red Heads', for the administration of their armed forces. The fact that this group belonged to the Shia sect of Islam had little or no impact, as the scourge of sectarianism had not yet tainted the identity of Muslims in the region.

The Pashtuns were the most privileged in this empire, and especially those living in the Pashtun heartland of Kandahar and its adjoining areas were exempt from paying any taxes (the residents of FATA in Pakistan continue to enjoy similar fiscal freedom!).

Ahmed Shah Durrani not only consolidated his base through such 'tax breaks', but also expanded his territory, benefiting from the loyalty of his core Pashtun constituents. He reigned for over a quarter of a century – enough time to lay solid foundations for those who inherited his seat of power. He is buried in the city of Kandahar, just beside the famous mosque and shrine where the cloak of the Prophet Mohammad is to be found. In fact, he it was who brought the ancient sacred robe to Afghanistan, and this alone would explain his standing in the eyes of the people.[28] Pilgrims from all over Afghanistan journey to the shrine. Kandahar has always had a special significance for Pashtuns, emerging as their cultural capital as well as a trading hub; but it is nothing less than ironic that the city should later have emerged as the spiritual heartland of the Taliban. Historically, whoever secures Kandahar controls the rest of the country.[29]

Historians often emphasize the importance of the bitter rivalry between the 'elitist' Durrani and the 'egalitarian' Ghilzai within the Pashtuns. The Ghilzai are more numerous and have a weaker economic base, whereas the Durrani are generally better educated and better placed in Kabul's corridors of power. Taliban leader Mullah Mohammad Omar and many of his top lieutenants, including Jalaluddin Haqqani, happen to be Ghilzai, as were many of the Afghan communist leaders who grew powerful in the late 1970s. Some important warriors of the 1980s Afghan Jihad era, such as Gulbuddin Hekmatyar and Abdul Rab Rasul Sayyaf were also part of the Ghilzai tradition.

Durrani Pashtuns, who practically ruled Afghanistan from 1747 to 1973 (though not as part of a single dynasty), are more open to alliances with other ethnic groups and to cultural diversity – as is evident from the fact that many Durrani Pashtuns speak Dari. Afghan President Hamid Karzai is a Durrani Pashtun, and he has certainly shown some of these traits during his years as leader (though arguably this might have had more to do with political compromises he was forced to make, rather than with his Durrani roots).

Afghan politics today is not, as it is generally perceived, defined and energized by a class war, in terms of a Durrani versus Ghilzai power struggle. Many years ago, I casually asked an Afghan official about the impact of the perceived tussle on the Afghan polity, and he responded a bit curtly that 'for ordinary Pashtuns this is merely a western construct meaning "divide and rule".[30] As the noted analyst Joshua Foust forcefully puts it:

> One of the most frustrating things to read in the shallower punditry and scholarship on the conflict in Afghanistan is the assertion that the Taliban insurgent groups are being driven by tribal loyalties – that, because Mullah Mohammad Omar is a Ghilzai Hotak and Hamid Karzai a Populzai Durrani, that they are somehow magically compelled toward war since their tribes have historically struggled for control of the country.[31]

In reality, the breakdown of tribal authority was one of the most potent factors behind the rise of the Taliban. Tribal identity and ethos continued to matter, but the controlling structure and the driving force changed.

Impact of the Great Game and British colonial rule

The internal and external pressures on Afghanistan increased significantly as the nineteenth century wore on. The Russian Empire began expanding southward into Central and South Asia, and imperial Britain, already entrenched in India, was extending northwest into modern-day Pakistan, in the process surrounding and isolating Afghanistan. The two Anglo-Afghan wars during this period stemmed in part from British concern about stopping Russian influence in Afghanistan and protecting British India. The 'Great Game' was the name given to this rivalry. It was about power, prestige and keeping the other players in check. The game had its own rules, rhetoric and style, and was not confined to corridors of power and military headquarters: scholars, writers and travellers were also drawn into it. On occasion it was played in a subtle manner; at other times it was brutal and ferocious, and had deadly outcomes. The heightened external interference in

Afghan affairs also increased the complexity of the internal political environment, as more actors – including various Pashtun tribes and religious figures – started to take an active interest in the policies emanating from Kabul.

Though the British East India Company had been engaged in diplomacy with Durrani rulers since the late eighteenth century, its relations with the Pashtun tribes soured as it started acting aggressively in the early nineteenth century, in an effort to insulate areas under its control against Russian machinations in Afghanistan and against recurring tribal raids. The company achieved this by balancing the use (and misuse) of economic subsidies and force to control strategic roads and passes with a move to grant the tribesmen autonomy in their affairs. The British did attain a measure of stability in this area for a while, but their rule never went unchallenged: 62 military expeditions were mounted between 1849 and 1889 alone.[32] British anxiety about Russian expansion into Central Asia and potential Russian–Afghan collaboration against the British compelled them to wage war on Afghanistan twice: in 1839–42 (when the British forces were pushed back) and in 1878–79 (when they fared better and attained some of their goals). In both cases the Pashtun tribal belt was caught in the middle.[33]

British policy oscillated between a more defensive 'closed border' policy (which advocated hanging on and retreating to the banks of the Indus) and an aggressive 'forward policy' (which called for these areas to be incorporated into the British Empire and for neutral buffer zones to be created). Negotiations between Russia and Britain finally led to the tentative demarcation of a boundary with Afghanistan after the 1878–79 war. Over the years, the British failed to bring Afghanistan under their direct control, but they did succeed in designating the tribal belt a 'buffer zone' between the 'troublesome' Afghans, who were seen to be fond of flirting with the Russians, and British India. The 1893 Durand Line was conceived as a strategic move, and the Afghan leader of the times, Abdur Rahman, agreed to the arrangement, though not before he was promised a subsidy by the British. Some historians maintain that Rahman only signed the English version of the Durand Line agreement, even though he could neither read nor write the language.[34] He reportedly also refused to sign the map attached to the agreement. He certainly had issues with demarcation in certain areas, but there is little doubt that he agreed to the project; and all subsequent Afghan leaders, including his son Habibullah, continued with it.

For Pashtun tribes, the partition – via the newly labelled 'frontier line' – was highly controversial, as it divided the community and was seen as a devious move to undermine Pashtun unity. Understandably, Pashtuns refused to treat it as a border – particularly as this 1,519-mile line is poorly demarcated in most places and not demarcated at all in others.[35] In a revised agreement between the British and more independence-oriented Afghan leaders in 1919, the division was simply referred to as a 'frontier'. The deletion of the word 'line' was an attempt to downgrade its border status. An administrative vacuum and lawlessness in the area were by-products of this controversial exercise. No wonder the tribes living in the buffer zone – the FATA – continued to cause the British administrators sleepless nights right up until they departed in 1947. Pashtuns are quite proud of their reputation, notwithstanding the colonial efforts to portray them as brutal and predisposed to a culture of violence and religious fanaticism.

Modernization efforts and their consequences

Abdur Rahman Khan, a Durrani Pashtun who ruled Afghanistan from 1880 to 1901, is considered the founder of the modern state of Afghanistan. He is known for his political sagacity in balancing British and Russian interests. He happily received an annual grant from Britain, though what exactly he received from the Russians is not recorded! Perhaps his 12-year exile in Russia, from where he rode back to Kabul in Russian army uniform (under cover) to take over the reins of government, was sufficient Russian investment.

He was as ambitious as he was adventurous, but his attempts at modernization were haphazard at best. He circumscribed the power of tribal and religious leadership, but at the same time ensured that the

British could not extend the railway and telegraph from India into his area. Meanwhile a perverse social engineering agenda – the forced migration of 'rebellious' Ghilzai to weaken them, the massacre of Hazaras in response to their demand for independence, and the forceful conversion of Nuristanis to Islam – tainted his reign. Yet despite this mixed record, Abdur Rahman is credited with the consolidation of the Afghan state in settled frontiers.

Though Afghans never forgave him for accepting the Durand Line, he did introduce some modern administrative and legal reforms, with the aim of centralizing power and weakening regional power centres. He encountered resistance on all sides, but his remarks about Muslim clerics are insightful and relevant:

> More wars and murders have been caused in this world by ignorant priests than by any other class of people . . . the great drawback to progress in Afghanistan has been that these men, under the pretence of religion, have taught things which were entirely contrary to the principles and teaching of Mahomed . . .[36]

In reality, Abdur Rahman himself used religious slogans when it suited his political goals. For instance, he declared the defence of Afghanistan to be a religious necessity and hence 'Jihad' (understood as armed struggle). He was not doing anything unique here: many a Muslim and a Christian leader had done the same thing before. His real crime, in the words of Barfield, was that he 'linked elements of Islamic belief with Afghan tribal customs in ways that convinced his largely illiterate population that the two were identical'.[37]

Amanullah Khan, the grandson of Abdur Rahman, held similar views, but his initiatives during his ten-year reign (starting in 1919) were far more aggressive. In fact, bearing in mind the conservative reality of Afghanistan, he went too far. He did win complete independence from British control, which could only raise his stature among his people at the time; but when he called tribal leaders to a *loya jirga*, insisting that they should 'appear with beards and hair cut, and dressed in black coats, waistcoats and trousers, shirts and ties, black boots and homburg hats', this was seen as disrespectful to the culture and beliefs of his people.[38]

A glance at the other measures he took is instructive. The introduction of a written constitution, inspired by Mustafa Kemal Ataturk's Turkish secular model, was indeed a novelty, and he also instituted a system of courts and a secular penal code as an alternative to the traditional *jirga* – a step that required both vision and courage. Establishing a chain of schools (including some for girls) run by teaching staff brought in from France, Germany and India was a much-needed initiative. He also abolished *purdah* (the veil) and laid much emphasis on women's rights – a hard act for his successors to follow.

For Afghans this was truly revolutionary; but little thought had been given to implementing the agenda gradually and in a realistic way: some common sense, after all, needed to be applied when copying Turkey's modernization. Hence mullahs and tribal leaders had little difficulty in arousing severe opposition to these ideas, on both religious and cultural grounds. So sharp was the reaction, and so fierce the resistance, that Amanullah had to abdicate in 1929. Alarmed at his connections with the revolutionary Bolshevik leadership in neighbouring Russia, the British had also embarked on a campaign of defamation against him.[39] His attempt to centralize decision-making in Kabul was a further complicating issue: distrust of central authority is the most emphatically recurring theme in the history of Afghanistan.

Mohammad Zahir Shah, the last Afghan king, ruled the country from 1933 to 1973, displaying rather better judgement. A new constitution in 1964 was one of his most significant contributions. Drafted by a French constitutional lawyer, it promised the transformation of the state into a democracy by providing for elections, a parliament and civil rights. There was a specific commitment to the emancipation of women, and above all there was to be universal suffrage. This was by no means just a paper exercise in state-building. And while the king co-opted progressive elements into the process, he also involved the traditional and conservative elements of society by convening a *loya jirga* to consider and approve the draft constitution. This was the high-water mark of consensus between the traditional and liberal sections of Afghan society. However, the foreign aid that flowed in during his reign, from both East and West, was mainly invested in developing infrastructure that only benefited the urban centres, and so the urban–rural divide worsened.

Soviet funding increased substantially on his watch, empowering a new class of technocrats and politicians. They ultimately ousted him in 1973, in a move orchestrated by his own cousin, Sardar Muhammad Daud Khan, whose Soviet-leaning views were well known. The gradual rise of the communists since the emergence of the People's Democratic Party of Afghanistan (PDPA) in 1965 also alerted religious circles. The clerics had hitherto enjoyed limited public support, and this was their chance to project their cause by condemning the 'faithless' communists.

Interestingly, a new breed of university-educated religious activists – smarter than the traditional mullahs – first emerged in Afghanistan in the late 1950s in the intellectual setting of Kabul University, rather than in the country's religious seminaries. After his return from Egypt, Dr Ghulam Mohammad Niazi, dean of the Faculty of Religious Sciences, became an important proponent of Islamic ideals. He inspired the creation of Jamiat-i-Islami (Islamic Society), an Islamic party that was to play an important role. Niazi was one of many educated Muslims who were searching for 'a modern political ideology based on Islam, which they see as the only way to come to terms with the modern world and the best means of confronting foreign imperialism'.[40] This trend produced a new religious zeal, though one that was relatively measured in tone – in comparison to the fanatical outbursts of mullahs who, in cahoots with tribal leaders, mostly operated on the periphery of the state.

Most of the stalwarts of the PDPA, such as Nur Mohammad Taraki and Babrak Karmal, were on the payroll of the notorious Soviet intelligence agency, the KGB.[41] They also acted as silent kingmakers when Daud Khan assumed the leadership of Afghanistan in 1973. In a move that was all too familiar to students of history, Daud embarked on the dangerous path of ditching those to whom he owed his rise to power. He also grew very close to the shah of Iran, a staunch Western ally, receiving a ten-year aid commitment from Iran worth $2 billion. But the PDPA could not stomach such a thing, and in the ensuing struggle he lost both power and his life.

The PDPA came to power in a coup in 1978. Moscow was clearly jubilant to see Taraki and Karmal in leading roles: in a Cold War setting, nothing could be better than having its loyal agents in top positions in a contested country. Now, inspired by the ideals of social justice, the PDPA challenged archaic tribal traditions and conservative clergy, but a deadly internal power struggle was to dilute its vigour.

Earlier, in the late 1960s, the party had undergone a split between the Pashtun-dominated and largely rural *Khalq* (Masses) faction and the urban, Persian-speaking *Parcham* (Banner) group. Moscow had brought about a superficial reconciliation, but the differences between them – essentially ideological – continued to simmer. Now, as Moscow kept an eye on this potential fissure, a new, personality-driven split opened up rapidly between President Taraki and Vice-President Hafizullah Amin.

Severe opposition to the communist takeover had been growing in many parts of Afghanistan, and President Taraki began taking increasingly rash action to quell it. Amin, a more sober and thoughtful man, gradually gained more influence within the system. By early 1979, he had completely sidelined Taraki and had assumed control of the defence forces.

To Moscow, it was no trifling matter that Amin had not been on the KGB payroll and in fact had studied in the United States. The KGB, unnerved by the turn of events, denounced Amin as an undercover CIA operative: he was fluent in English and held a Master's degree from Columbia University in New York – what more evidence was needed? What also discredited Amin in Soviet eyes was his lack of interest in learning Russian.

Regionally, things were not looking rosy for the Soviet Union: in July 1977, there had been a military coup in Pakistan, led by a religiously conservative general, and then came the Islamic revolution in

Iran in 1979. So to 'save' Afghanistan, the Soviets decided to invade it on the eve of Christmas in 1979.

Whatever the strategic aims of the Soviet Union at this time, the global security dynamics changed dramatically. The invasion of Afghanistan became a hot international issue, which in years to come mobilized a variety of radical forces and altered the balance of power both regionally and globally.

Whether it was a consequence of the Soviet Union's desire to access warm waters and expand its trade and influence in Asia and Africa, or a trap successfully laid by the Americans to induce Soviet intervention, for Afghanistan the invasion was disastrous. More likely, the Soviets simply wanted to install a friendly government and root out any American influence in Kabul. But it proves one thing at least: the Soviets' understanding of Afghan history and South Asian regional dynamics was rudimentary. They grossly underestimated Pashtun motivations and the frontier linkages across the Durand Line, and they had to pay for this blunder in blood.

CHAPTER TWO

Enter at your own risk

Tribes and troubles on Pakistan's unruly Pashtun frontier (1947–2001)

A midnight telephone call at the home of a police officer in Pakistan is not at all unusual. But when I picked up the phone on a cold night in late 1997 in the small town of Swabi, I had no idea what to expect. I rushed to the office.

Apparently Laila (not her real name), a beautiful young girl of Pakistani heritage who lived in Norway, had fallen in love with Zubair, a Pashtun boy from Swabi. When Laila's parents refused to countenance the marriage, the couple had eloped. I was asked to register a case of kidnapping against Zubair, find the girl and hand her over to her parents. When he saw my stunned face, the senior police officer quickly added that Laila's family was very influential and was related to a senior military intelligence officer. In Pakistan, a comment such as that means 'get it done or you are in trouble'.

All my sympathies were with the couple, but I had to confirm that the marriage had been by mutual consent and not under duress. By the time we raided Zubair's house, he had escaped; we were told that he had gone to his cousin's place in *ilaqa ghair* – literally 'the alien land', otherwise known as Pakistan's Federally Administered Tribal Areas (FATA). This was something of a bombshell, given FATA's well-deserved and popular reputation as 'the land of the lawless'. Pakistani laws are not applicable and the Pakistani police cannot operate in the area. The only way forward was to seek intervention through a *jirga* – an assembly of tribal leaders known as *maliks*. A police team had to go to FATA without any weapons and in civilian clothes to ask a *jirga* to hand over Zubair. This was refused, as Zubair was deemed not to have committed any wrongdoing. Instead I was allowed to interview Laila – guarded by tribesmen to ensure that I could not return her to Islamabad against her wishes.

It had become a matter of Pashtun honour, so any failure to understand the sensitivity of the case could have been fatal for me. I had given my word to the tribe that the police case in Swabi would be quashed and that there would be no consequent police harassment if I was convinced that she had married of her own free will. I found Laila to be a smart girl. She assured me that she had taken the decision freely. The case was closed – on one condition: she would have the right to divorce her husband if she wished at any point in her life. This is an Islamic provision, available to every woman, that Zubair and his family promised to uphold. To cut a long story short, the marriage did not work out: the couple realized after a few months that they were incompatible. Restrictions on her movement and the cultural environment created serious adjustment issues for Laila, and finally she returned to her parents in Europe.

Laila was very lucky, as her in-laws lived in the relatively advanced Pashtun areas – also known as the 'settled areas' – and she had friends and family who could help her. But for most women living around the tribal belt of FATA, patriarchy and *purdah* are chains that restrict their freedoms enormously. Even the men of the area are victims of decadent tribalism. This mode of social life instils oppression and obstructs the development of modern state institutions. The semi-autonomous status of FATA and its reputation as a lawless region have led to the maintenance of tribal traditions. A logical consequence of this is that the area has emerged as a place of sanctuary for miscreants and criminals of all sorts. This reality is intertwined with the history of Pakistan and its shameful neglect of the area. For Pashtuns, FATA was born the day the division of their land was enforced by the Durand Line – named after Mortimer Durand, the then foreign secretary of British India.

The Durand Line and the foundation of Pakistan

Ever since its demarcation, the Durand Line, which runs from the spur of the Sarikol range in the north to the Iranian border in the southwest, has been viewed with contempt and resentment by Pashtun on both sides of the divide. Technically, for many of them the line separated their kith and kin. In practice, of course, they continued to cross the so-called 'boundary' at will: though visible on maps, on the ground it remained vague. Given that for most of its route, the 'line' runs through a rough, rugged and sometime inaccessible mountainous area, it was also hugely difficult to police.

The North West Frontier Province (NWFP), today's Khyber Pakhtunkhwa Province (KPK), was created in 1901 by the British colonists as a new administrative unit, by carving out parts of the then Punjab Province and adding certain tribal principalities to it. The province, as it was constituted at the time, included five 'settled' districts (Bannu, Dera Ismail Khan, Hazara, Kohat and Peshawar). Meanwhile the five tribal agencies of Dir-Swat-Chitral, Khyber, Kurram, North Waziristan and South Waziristan (the last four part of FATA today) were placed under the separate administrative authority of a chief commissioner, who reported direct to the governor-general of India. These agencies grouped together areas under tribal influence and control. Pakistan inherited this structure at the time of the partition of British India, in August 1947. The difference in the level of British control over the 'settled areas' and the semi-autonomous FATA region remained significant, and persisted even after the area became part of Pakistan. Given its higher literacy rate and its well-developed institutions, NWFP was far easier to manage than FATA.

Even if it is on the periphery and has an unmarked frontier, FATA has always been part and parcel of Pakistan. The fledgling nation started off as a democratic country, led by a very small but influential group of progressive politicians. For tens of millions of South Asian Muslims, it was the realization of a dream. Millions set out on foot for the 'promised land', leaving behind their property, possessions and childhood memories. And around a million of them perished on the way.

The ill-planned and poorly executed division of British India by Governor-General Mountbatten and his team – described appropriately by Stanley Wolpert as 'shameful flight' – made it extremely difficult for new-born Pakistan to survive.[1] India's refusal to hand over Pakistan's share of the assets and its public taunting of the country only hardened the aspirations of those who had burned their boats while struggling to carve out a new homeland. Frail, old Mohammad Ali Jinnah, the visionary founding father of the country, had in mind a tolerant, secular and pluralist polity; the major religious political parties of India – especially Deobandi-oriented groups and the Jamaat-e-Islami (Party of Islam) of Maulana Abul Ala Maududi – had all been fiercely opposed to the idea of Pakistan.

It is difficult for Pakistanis to understand this, because the very same forces that wanted to block partition back then are today obstructing the peace process between India and Pakistan. The rivalry and animosity with India has been devastating for Pakistan. India, for its part, failed to grow out of its Pakistan phobia, and it needed decades before it could accept that Pakistan was a reality. It threatened the country repeatedly, grabbed a large chunk of disputed land in Jammu and Kashmir (in violation of international law) and left no stone unturned in irritating and goading Pakistan. The kneejerk reaction in Pakistan was to build up its military out of all proportion to its available resources and to plunge itself into two major wars with India – one of which resulted in its dismemberment in 1971, yielding the new country of Bangladesh. To construct a modern army, Pakistan adopted a variety of strategies, the most fruitful of which turned out to be its relationship with the US. As early as 1953, commander-in-chief of the Pakistan Army, General Ayub Khan, made a commitment to US Assistant Secretary of State Henry Byroad: 'Our army can be your army if you want us.'[2] At the time, the US enveloped the Pakistani army in a bear hug; it is unclear whether they regret that today.

Not only did security concerns overwhelm Pakistan financially and psychologically, they also pushed it into repeated cycles of military dictatorship. Besides discouraging the growth of political institutions, this also affected the social fabric of the country. Army generals made a habit of imposing martial law to 'save the country' – they have ruled for 33 of the country's 67 years of independence. Yet Pakistan is lucky, for its people have always disliked authoritarian regimes and have pushed out the military rulers. It has been somewhat less lucky in its ability to produce good politicians, with the exception of the brilliant Zulfikar Ali Bhutto and his courageous daughter Benazir Bhutto. But neither was to live to fulfil their great potential: tragically, General Muhammad Zia ul Haq, who imposed military rule in 1977, hanged the elder Bhutto in 1979, following a dubious and controversial court verdict; while Benazir was assassinated by terrorists in 2007. Both were aware of the approach of death, but faced it bravely in order to nurture democracy in the country. Their graves have today become shrines; but the harsh reality of the situation is that unless feudalism and illiteracy – the two most implacable foes of democracy – are vanquished, their sacrifices will have been in vain.

Only in conditions of democracy could post-1971 Pakistan – a country with four federated units and five major ethnic groups – grow and prosper. Authoritarianism was bound to create ethnic tensions. Economic hardship further eroded a sense of national unity, since each province demanded its 'due share' from a diminishing resource base. International aid was largely directed towards Pakistan's security needs, because the West was keen to pursue its own defence interests, which could only be delivered by Pakistan's armed forces. No one ever reminded Pakistan's leadership that a poor country can never sustain a modern military – especially if it aspires to retain its sovereignty.

The civil–military tussle that gained prominence with the first spell of military rule from 1958 and the persistent India–Pakistan confrontation that started soon after partition in 1947 both created space for religious zealots. Though these elements failed to win any sizeable number of votes in elections, their street power in urban centres increased substantially over the years. Proxy wars in the region and global developments empowered right-wing groups further. Subsequently, religious extremism started gnawing at the vitals of the country, though a majority remained either aloof or in denial. Ironically, the country cherishes the memory of the man who conceived the idea of Pakistan – Dr Mohammad Iqbal, the legendary poet–philosopher (1877–1938) – but ignores his dire warning, given in his famous Urdu verse: *Deen-e-Mullah fi Sabeelillah Fasad* ('the religion of the mullah is anarchy in the name of Allah').

Somewhere along this journey from crisis to crisis, Pakistanis became unsure about their true identity. Their textbook would quote Jinnah saying: 'You may belong to any religion or caste or creed[;] that has nothing to do with the business of the State.'[3] But early on the state apparatus employed Islamic slogans to forge national unity and order – primarily to cover up the failings of the ruling elites. Still, these efforts were not life-threatening for Pakistan, and progressive forces in politics, the arts and the wider cultural domain by and large continued to follow Jinnah's mission. But then, unfortunately, General Zia took Pakistan in an altogether different direction.

His attempts to justify controversial policy decisions by misrepresenting religious ideals destroyed the sectarian harmony that the country had enjoyed for the first 30 years of its existence. From his attempt to impose a contentious version of Islamic criminal law, to the introduction of compulsory *zakat* (charity fund) deductions from everyone's bank accounts, Zia played with the religious emotions of Pakistanis without an iota of shame. The rights of minorities were trampled underfoot, so that they started to feel not only alienated, but harassed.

General Zia redefined the idea of Pakistan. He unequivocally declared: 'Take Islam out of Pakistan and make it a secular state; it will collapse.'[4] Religious political parties were jubilant at this, seeing in Zia a 'messiah' who would transform Pakistan from above. Their own campaigns to 'Islamize' Pakistan from below had accomplished precious little: they had been rejected time and again in elections, though they never gave up. Mainstream Islam in South Asia was soft and egalitarian in essence; but Zia empowered the harbingers of clerical Islam, who favoured a conservative, intrusive and dogmatic interpretation of Islam. This worldview proved to be a recipe for the radicalization of religious identity. At the time, only people of vision in Pakistan could see this coming, and they were vociferous in their condemnation. But the hue and cry barely registered. The media were gagged and pro-democracy activists were thrashed on the streets; but Zia was emerging as a celebrity in Western capitals thanks to his contribution towards the Afghan Jihad and his resistance to the Soviet invasion. Unsurprisingly, those financing Zia's adventures were not interested in hearing any critique of his domestic policies. Democracy promotion was not a buzzword then.

The most damaging innovation of Zia's spymasters, however, was the creation of 'non-state actors' (i.e. religious militants), who were groomed to pursue Pakistan's regional policy (and to relish the prospect of dying for it). This security-driven charade has to be seen through the lens of the entrenched India–Pakistan rivalry. The two countries' competing claims over the Kashmir region had played a critical role in Pakistan's foreign policy calculus since 1947. Pakistan's frustration that India refused to abide by any of the UN Security Council resolutions pertaining to Kashmir in the late 1940s and 1950s pushed it towards a military solution. It nearly succeeded in 1965, thanks to manoeuvres by the brilliant commander Major General Akhtar Hussain Malik, but poor military leadership in Rawalpindi wasted the opportunity.[5]

Finally, in response to major Indian military operations in the Kashmir Valley, unconventional warfare was attempted in the 1990s using proxy militant groups. Islamic warriors, groomed to fight invading 'infidel' Soviets in Afghanistan in the 1980s, had never been decommissioned, and some of them were later dispatched to the conflict zone in Kashmir to fight the Indian army. In recent years, this policy has come back to haunt Pakistan. These armed groups neither won freedom for the Kashmiris nor helped Pakistan become more secure in any major way, and internally the policy backfired for Pakistan: the returning Pakistani militants radicalized others in their hometowns, leading to a rise in sectarianism and misguided religious fervour.

It was only a matter of time before some of this energy was directed towards the West. Ordinary Americans had little idea that their taxes had funded potential Frankenstein's monsters via the CIA's Operation Cyclone in support of Afghan Jihad against the Soviets in the 1980s.[6]

Inside the 'federally mismanaged tribal areas' of Pakistan

At the time of Pakistan's creation, the legal status of FATA was unclear, although it was a foregone conclusion that it would become part of Pakistan. The question was under what terms and conditions. The complicated status of FATA was discussed by Jinnah and the legendary Pashtun leader Abdul Ghaffar Khan (also known as Bacha Khan) during their talks in June 1947. Bacha Khan, a close associate of Gandhi and an ardent supporter of non-violence and a secular India, who has been almost written out of Pakistan's history, presented three conditions for his cooperation: i) the merger of tribal areas with the settled areas in NWFP; ii) full provincial autonomy; and iii) the withdrawal of Pakistan from the British Commonwealth. Jinnah would agree to only one of those – the merger of FATA into mainstream NWFP and Pakistan, and he asked Ghaffar Khan to mould public opinion in the tribal areas, so that it was ready for such a move.[7]

But the deal could not be brokered, and the status of FATA remained in limbo until a *jirga* – in this case a historic one – was convened in the city of Bannu in January 1948. The members of the *jirga* collectively decided to accede to Pakistan, but not before they had negotiated concessions about their status within the new state. They demanded the continuation of British-era subsidies, privileges and allowances – in other words 'don't interfere in our internal matters and never even think of stopping the cash flow'.[8] FATA was to be governed directly by the head of state through the governor of NWFP, so it thus enjoyed a unique status in a federation with five other units. Electricity was to be provided to the FATA area free of charge, and no taxes of any sort could be collected from the region, as per the old arrangement. Nor would FATA be subject to the Pakistani justice system.

Pakistan agreed – it was in no position to do otherwise. About 30 major tribes represented in the *jirga* pledged allegiance to Pakistan.

During a visit to this borderland in April 1948, Jinnah chose his words very carefully. He publicly stated his desire not to interfere with tribal autonomy (which of course was music to the ears of the tribesmen), but he also vowed that Pakistan would aspire to integrate FATA into Pakistan: 'We want to put you on your legs as self-respecting citizens who have the opportunities of fully developing and producing what is best in you and your land.'[9] There was no report of any uproar in the audience; but Jinnah's vision remains a dream.

Pashto-language accounts emphasize that the FATA tribes acceded to Pakistan without any conditions.[10] In all likelihood, this is a rhetorical claim to show the loyalty of tribal Pashtuns to the idea of Pakistan. In reality, the tribal elements wanted to retain their semi-autonomous status at all costs. The *faqir* of Ipi, a legendary Pashtun rebel from Waziristan who had given the British a tough time, had earlier sent shudders down the spines of politicians struggling for Pakistan's creation when, in a letter addressed to various tribes of the borderland in July 1947, he had suggested that 'the "unity of Islam" was perhaps not as important as the unity of tribes of the frontier province'.[11] Simply put, tribal loyalty was deemed to be superior to any other affiliation, and thus defending their relatively independent status was crucial for inhabitants of FATA.

To the tribal agencies of Khyber, Kurram, North Waziristan and South Waziristan were later added Mohmand agency (in 1951) and Bajaur and Orakzai (in 1973). In 1951–52, the government of Pakistan revised some of the original agreements reached with the tribal chiefs, so that it acquired greater control and authority in the areas (though this came only after it committed itself to increasing its financial support). Overall, poor planning and flawed priorities meant that Pakistan always shied away from investing in the area's infrastructure. For their part, FATA tribesmen responded positively whenever their assistance was needed – and especially if that involved fighting. For instance, in 1948, bands of FATA tribesmen offered their services in the disputed Kashmir region, where Pakistan and India were both trying to gain the upper hand militarily. The Pakistani army had very limited resources and equipment (and was also under the command of British officers, who were not very keen on going to war with India), so the tribal help came at a critical juncture. To this day, Pakistanis praise the Pashtun warriors who responded so patriotically to the call.

But some notoriously rebellious tribes of FATA refused to come to heel and were not as cooperative. Resistance to authority was in their blood, and Karachi – the capital of Pakistan at the time – was seen as only marginally better than London. Air bombing was developed as a counterinsurgency tool by Pakistan, even when it had very limited air power. Its air force resorted to bombing certain areas in the borderland in 1949, though it was falsely claimed that this had happened by accident. In the early 1960s, the exercise was repeated in the Bajaur area (at the time under the Khyber agency). Admittedly, part of Pakistan's problem was the treacherous terrain, which made establishing the writ of the state in the area near impossible; but in these instances the purpose was a show of force to discourage rebellion.

Pakistan's contentious and complicated relationship with Afghanistan meant that the area remained critical. Ironically, Afghanistan was the only country to challenge Pakistan's membership of the United Nations in 1947, on the grounds that it claimed parts of FATA and even NWFP. Though it was never defined clearly, the idea of 'Pashtunistan' – an independent country made up of the Pashtun-dominated areas of Pakistan and Afghanistan (or, according to some, the whole of Afghanistan and the Pashtun areas of Pakistan) – emerged in Kabul. It was never a popular idea in the region, but still it was potent enough to create trouble in the minds of Pakistani leaders. The decision of an Afghan *loya jirga* in 1949 to declare the Durand Line invalid must have put more pressure on Pakistan to avoid challenging the status quo in FATA so as to keep the tribes happy.

Tragically for FATA, the Pakistani elite acted contrary to Jinnah's vision and connived to continue with a retrograde set of laws that dated from 1901 known as the Frontier Crimes Regulation (FCR) and with the institution of *maliks*, a class of tribal leaders who acted – often deviously – as middlemen between the federal government of Pakistan and ordinary Pashtuns of the borderland. The purpose of the FCR was primarily to control and suppress crimes, rather than to provide or promote justice. The consequence has been that governance in the tribal area has been personal, discretionary and indirect. A federal administrator known as a 'political agent' – in most cases a career bureaucrat – had enormous powers to implement the FCR, with the help of *maliks*. To all intents and purposes, this agent was (and indeed is) prince, chief of police, judge and executioner all rolled into one. This power and authority, though still available, has been more constrained since the gradual rise of militants in the area from around 2004.

An earlier version of the FCR had been gradually introduced by the British between 1871 and 1876 in order to establish their writ in the area. The laws prescribed special procedures for the tribal areas that were quite distinct from the criminal and civil laws that were in force elsewhere in British India. The regulations operated on the idea of collective territorial responsibility (including collective punishment) and provided for dispute resolution to take place through the traditional *jirga*. A few tribes cooperated with the British for a 'reasonable' sum of money, but this led to internal tribal rivalries as well. The 1901 version of the FCR in fact expanded the scope and range of earlier regulations and awarded wider powers, including judicial authority, to administrative officials in the tribal belt.

The toxic combination of unrepresentative *maliks*, a despotic political agent and coercive FCR was hardly likely to bring progress or enlightenment to the FATA area. The British might be blamed for dreaming up this monstrous package with the aim of 'controlling' the area; but that happened in the late nineteenth century. Pakistan was guilty of following it – in both spirit and form – until the system blew up in its face in the early years of the twenty-first century. Of course, tribal leaders were in cahoots with their masters; but ordinary Pashtuns were victims rather than anything else. As surveys conducted in recent years have shown, a significant chunk of the FATA population is critical of the extensive powers of the political agent, around 30 per cent want the FCR abolished and 25 per cent desire fundamental changes to it.[12]

The FCR, the central pillar of the FATA structure, is believed to encapsulate elements of the Pashtun tribal code *Pashtunwali* and *riwaj* (local custom). Ordinary Pashtuns feel offended when asked about this connection. Many educated tribals told me that the FCR in reality exploits some of the *Pashtunwali* provisions and that it would be unfair to consider the FCR a codified version of local customs.[13] In reality, it is both – a reflection of *Pashtunwali* and an institutionalized embodiment of an oppressive and arbitrary regime. Many FCR provisions also violate fundamental rights that are enshrined in Pakistan's constitution and entail harsh penalties, lack of due process and a very restricted right of appeal.

Even a cursory glance at the FCR reveals its despotic nature. A political agent can basically order the confiscation of anyone's property, can block movement into settled Pashtun areas, and can impose a heavy fine on a whole village or tribe if it is found guilty of harbouring an offender. In the event of a homicide – whether committed or attempted – the burden of proof rests with the headman of a community. The FCR even permits the administration to raze whole villages, if that is deemed to be militarily expedient (section 32), and to demolish buildings used by 'robbers' without any compensation (section 34). Moreover, the finality of such proceedings cannot be challenged in any civil or criminal court (section 60).

Trying to control individual excesses and crimes through the threat of collective punishment is never an effective tool, and is likely to push a community toward extremist ways of thinking and acting. That is exactly what happened in the end. Not without reason has the Human Rights Commission of Pakistan called the FCR a 'bad law that nobody could defend'.[14]

Ordinary tribesmen were often vocal in their opposition to the draconian law; but the political agents had strict instructions always to refute any condemnation of it. A classic response from the political agent of the Khyber agency to demands for the repeal of the FCR is typical of the 1990s: 'Would you like to see the corrupt Pakistani police desecrate your homes?'[15] For honourable and highly conservative Pashtuns, that was the clinching argument.

On paper, the primary task of a political agent is 'to keep general peace, to maintain the roads, and to protect government property';[16] but there is no effective check on his authority or accountability. The office has a licence to manipulate the FCR if instructions from the top (i.e. federal government) require it. The traditional institution of *jirga*, for instance, also came to be within the political agent's purview, as the selection of members of a *jirga* was routed through him.[17] This damaged the credibility of an indigenous conflict-resolution mechanism. It indeed seems surprising that tribal Pashtuns would allow the concentration of so much power in the hands of a government administrator. But the answer is simple: the political agent controls the purse strings. He approves allowances and funds for *maliks*, decides the location and focus of any development projects, awards local scholarships, and hands out food rations and timber permits.[18] Importantly, he also issues identification documents: without an 'identity card' and 'domicile certificate' to prove his or her residence in a tribal agency, no inhabitant of the tribal areas can benefit from any student scholarships or the government job quota that is especially allocated to FATA throughout Pakistan.

To meet the security requirements, the political agent of each agency has a security force consisting of *khassadar* (local police) and levies, both drawn from local clans. Lightly armed, inadequately trained and with little discipline, they are hardly up to any law enforcement task. The Frontier Corps, a better trained paramilitary force, provides security when required to do so – which is a daily routine now. Local roots and meagre resources restrict the capacity of this force. For those living outside FATA, this structure has created a false impression of a security apparatus in place. Underfunded and compromised in most cases, the system was always bound to crumble when faced with a serious challenge.

Contrary to the general perception (even in Pakistan), *maliks* are not tribal chiefs but elders. Many of them are appointed by the state and are on the government payroll, with additional privileges. Many have hereditary rights to the title, but others are either nominated by the political agent or selected by the tribes. Importantly, they function as equals in a tribal gathering, where each participant can speak.[19] Some experts even argue that the control exerted by *maliks* and tribal elders over the populace is 'the only stabilizing force the region has ever known'.[20] Iftikhar Hussain, a former NWFP governor (2000–05) and a Pashtun, provides an update about the changing nature of the institution: 'This system of nurturing local elites at the cost of discouraging voices of disagreement did suit the rulers of the past . . . [today] *maliks* jealously cut down to size anyone who tries to break the ranks.'[21] What he is hinting at, albeit diplomatically, is that the *maliks* have had increasingly despotic tendencies in recent decades.

It may come as a surprise to many readers that in Pashtun areas, mullahs or clerics have traditionally had only a secondary (if not tertiary) role to play in society. They were seldom invited to participate in *jirga* gatherings and were only asked at the end to lead prayers for the success of the decision taken. And they were normally paid for the task. They were not regarded as fit for any political leadership role. In time of conflict, however, mullahs were called upon to inspire the fighters with sermons, and a few would rise to the occasion and lead campaigns. British administrators close to the scene dubbed such instances 'mad mullah movements', largely to dispel the notion that a vast number of tribesmen were in active revolt against the British. In effect, mullahs had neither independent financial resources nor much of a political voice. In fact, they would often ask *maliks* to provide security for the mosques against criminals.[22]

Pakistan was comfortable with the practice of strengthening the hand of *maliks* to manage the area, but Soviet and Indian support for Afghanistan's claims on Pashtun areas of Pakistan made it insecure and forced it to consider additional measures. The president of Pakistan, Iskander Mirza, visited Kabul in 1956 to ease the tense relations, and King Zahir Shah reciprocated in 1958. A tentative arrangement governing transit facilities for Afghan imports did break the ice, but mutual suspicions continued to simmer in the background. General Ayub Khan, the military ruler of Pakistan, made another attempt to improve relations with Afghanistan in 1959–60, but a curious historical nugget dropped into a conversation with Sardar Naim, the then foreign minister of Afghanistan, hardly helped matters: 'if the old conquests were to be our guide, then Pakistan should have more interests in the future of Pathans living in Afghanistan.'[23] Unsurprisingly, Naim was not amused. Possibly Ayub had in mind a pithy statement by the renowned historian Olaf Caroe, who, when discussing the possible political amalgamation of the region in 1958, wrote: 'Peshawar would absorb Kabul, not Kabul Peshawar.'[24]

Such interactions did little to improve bilateral relations, and the situation worsened in the early 1960s. However the good offices of the shah of Iran helped both states to reach a better understanding, and Ayub Khan visited Kabul twice in 1964 and then again in 1966. However, Sardar Muhammad Daud's overthrow of the monarchy in Afghanistan and his seizure of power in 1973 reignited Pakistan's concerns – rightly so, since the Daud government started promoting the idea of Pashtunistan in Pakistan's tribal lands in an attempt to spark a crisis and damage Pakistani–Afghan relations. Pakistan responded in kind. Major General Naseerullah Khan Babar, then inspector general of the Frontier Corps in NWFP, played a central role in 1973 in organizing and grooming anti-Daud Afghan resistance forces. Babar (who was later the federal interior minister in 1993–95 and is blamed for supporting the Taliban in the early days) publicly acknowledges that Gulbuddin Hekmatyar and Ahmed Shah Massoud were among the Afghans who were recruited first (and on paper) as Frontier Corps personnel and then trained by the Pakistani military's Special Services Group (SSG).[25]

The political economy of lawlessness

An interesting experience I had in early 1997, during the final stages of my police training in Peshawar, exposed me to some intriguing economic realities of the adjoining Khyber agency in the tribal region. During a leisurely stint as a trainee assistant superintendent of police, I was provided with a 'Jeep' (every SUV in the area is called a 'Jeep') and two guards (more because that was the custom at the time than because of any security concerns) and was encouraged to visit various law enforcement offices in the province to gain an understanding of coordination aspects.

The great temptation among trainee officers was to slip off home during this two-week stage of 'training'. For some it was their first opportunity to show off their official vehicle and police guards to family and friends. I was similarly tempted, but a junior official deputed to take me around put an interesting idea into my head – to visit Darra Adamkhel in Khyber agency and see the now infamous weapon factories and gun shops. We informed a friendly official at headquarters that we would be visiting the thriving illegal market, whose gunsmiths are widely known for producing exact copies of world-famous weapons. He told me that I could not go there with guards holding official weapons and that I had to be in civilian clothes, because the NWFP police had no jurisdiction in the area and were not welcome in uniform. But knowing how much the tribal Pashtuns respect guests – and especially potential customers – I had no security concerns.

Pakistanis on a tight budget but with a burning desire to own a top-of-the-range imported weapon know that the skilled gunsmiths of Darra can work wonders. I, too, saw this at first hand. The weapons looked flawless, and the shopkeepers had Western brochures with pictures of the actual weapons and their detailed descriptions. My escort could see that I was impressed, and he whispered in my ear: 'Sir, these weapons are not that effective and their performance is quite poor.' Most non-Pashtun customers (mainly Punjabi, if the reports are true) are attracted by the 'look' of the weapons; but Pashtuns are generally more interested in their quality and utility.[26] The most popular brand remained, I was told, the Kalashnikov – the Russian AK-47 – that was popularized during the Afghan Jihad years. Pakistan is now awash with these poisonous machines, and the term 'Kalashnikov culture' denotes the rising trend of violence and crime that is now the bane of the country.

The overall economy of the area was historically dependent on the 'four Ts' – *trucking* of smuggled goods, *toll* collection (both legal and illegal), *trafficking* of drugs and weapons, and *trekking* by tourists. These have now been joined by a fifth – *terrorism*. Unlawful tolls, in particular, have always been an important monetary source for the local economy.[27] Pakistan's power centres ignored these tendencies for so long that they became accepted by all and sundry, and even came to be considered a legitimate local right by some, especially the Pashtun tribes that straddle the border between Afghanistan and Pakistan.

After the partition of British India, subsistence agriculture and nomadic pastoralism rapidly gave way to an unregulated cross-border trade in goods. Smugglers took full advantage of the 1965 Afghan Transit Trade Agreement, under which goods are imported duty free into Pakistan for re-export to Afghanistan. As Afghanistan has no seaport, Karachi in Pakistan has always been very important for the Afghan economy and trade. In practice, many of the cheaper duty-free items destined for Afghanistan are illegally smuggled back into Pakistan within a few hours of entering Afghanistan. In 2001, the World Bank estimated the value of such trade at nearly $1 billion per year. It is safe to assume that the value has since doubled.

As has been mentioned already, the Durand Line is poorly demarcated, and there are regular disputes between Pakistan and Afghanistan about its route. Pakistan treats the line as an international border, but the government of Afghanistan continues to challenge its validity. In October 2012, the Afghan government publicly criticized officials of the US State Department for calling the Durand Line an 'internationally recognized boundary'.[28] There are villages in Pakistan that have their farmland in Afghanistan (and vice versa), and for this reason, until early 2002, Pakistani and Afghan immigration officials never used to ask locals for their passports, even at formal border crossings. Another splendid example: a 2007 conference report on the Durand Line claimed that about half the population of the Pakistani border town of Chaman (in Balochistan Province, adjacent to FATA) daily crosses the border into Afghanistan to go to work in Kandahar.[29] Anyone who thinks that the Durand Line can be plugged to eliminate cross-border movement is living in a fool's paradise. And anyone who makes such a commitment is either dishonest or ignorant of the facts on the ground.

The popular Pashtun leader Bacha Khan never ceased to preach defiance of the superficial Durand Line. When he died in 1988 in Pakistan's Peshawar, his will stipulated that he was to be buried in Jalalabad in Afghanistan. Thousands of mourners proceeded with his body through the historic Khyber Pass from Peshawar to Jalalabad. The war with the Soviet Union was raging at the time, but a ceasefire was declared to allow the funeral to take place.

Historically, there were only two official trade routes between Pakistan and Afghanistan – one via the Khyber Pass (Peshawar–Kabul road) and the other via the Bolan Pass (Quetta–Kandahar road). Now there are around two dozen major crossings used by traders, plus over a hundred minor tracks on which trucks and pick-ups operate frequently. Roughly 55,000 people cross the border each day.[30] Five important Pashtun tribes – the Achakzai, Wazir, Turi, Shinwari and Mohmand – are present on both sides of the Durand Line, and that makes conducting business across the imaginary border easy and even convenient. Intermarriages, intertribal feuds and an ingrained ethos of maintaining tribal connections bond the people together. In fairness to Sir Henry Mortimer Durand, he did provide the divided tribes with easement rights. Little could he have imagined that later militants would use fake permits to prove their tribal association and avail themselves of this facility.[31]

While smuggling is still considered a relatively honourable profession among those living in the border areas, the same cannot be said of the notorious car-theft rackets that operate. Pashtun involvement is fairly limited: most car-jacking crimes committed in Pakistan involve other ethnic groups, although the destination of the stolen vehicles is often FATA. There they are disassembled and sent to auto workshops in the Peshawar area and Punjab Province for sale. Middle-class owners of old cars have been getting their engines overhauled cheaply, in the belief that these 'as new' engines are being imported from Afghanistan – legally or otherwise. The beneficiaries never stop to ponder why

Japan should be exporting second-hand engines in excellent condition to Afghanistan!

This activity has generated hefty revenue for various criminal gangs in the tribal belt. Many tribesmen involved in such activities have moved their families to Peshawar or Karachi – or even to Gulf countries – but their 'business operations' are managed and run from within FATA. For them it offers a tax-free zone, a safe haven for employees with a criminal record and access to Swiss banks, where they can hide their illegal earnings, no questions asked.

But it was not destined to be like this: the political economy of crime was nurtured by acts of both omission and commission. Economic investment and a flow of development funds could easily have altered the dynamics. But for an estimated 6–7 million people living in FATA – around 4 per cent of Pakistan's 180 million people – on average barely 1 per cent of the national budget was allocated to FATA. No discernible change has been visible in recent budgets; foreign aid (mostly from the US and UK) for development work in the area has increased, but this is not reflected in government statistics.

With 60 per cent of its residents living below the poverty line,[32] a mortality rate that is estimated to be as high as 600 per 100,000 live births,[33] and a literacy rate somewhere in the region of 15 per cent,[34] social implosion was a fairly predictable outcome. The per capita development allocation is roughly a third of the national average, and per capita income in FATA is half the national average for Pakistan. The depressingly low literacy rate has closed the doors to any economic opportunities for FATA Pashtuns, even in other regions of the country. Nature, too, has been tough on FATA: a lack of arable land and a shortage of rainfall affects agricultural output.

Political empowerment could have brought change, and indeed some attempts at this were made. For instance, the residents of FATA were granted universal adult suffrage in 1997, though oddly Pakistan's political parties were not allowed to function there until 2013. Under the earlier arrangement, the limited franchise routinely led to 'widespread sale and purchase of votes'.[35] Even more ironically, FATA's twelve members of the National Assembly and eight senators were legally eligible to participate in making laws for the whole of Pakistan, but the federal bodies that they were part of were not entitled to legislate for FATA! For the state, their presence in the legislative chambers was just tokenism – meaningless and downright deceitful on the part of Islamabad.

Even at the best of times, Pakistan's sovereignty over FATA was only partial. It would, however, be inaccurate to conclude that the headstrong and arrogant tribesmen were the sole 'movers and shakers' in FATA: Pakistan's intelligence apparatus, the bosses of organized crime and bureaucrats could always get things done. The wooliness of the Durand Line suited the interests of all parties: for Pashtuns, it kept alive their links with their kith and kin on the other side of it; it allowed Kabul to keep alive its hopes for Pashtunistan; and as far as Islamabad was concerned, it legitimized its treatment of Afghanistan as Pakistan's backyard. None of this was the intended purpose of the line.

But the biggest beneficiaries of this fluid situation were the militants who converged on FATA from around the world in the 1980s. The tradition of offering resistance to invaders had its own unintended consequences; but the international nature of a project that exploited religious passions sowed the seeds of radicalization and turmoil.

CHAPTER THREE

Holy warriors of an unholy war
The Afghan Jihad and the chaotic rise of the Taliban
(1979–2001)

Growing up in Peshawar during the early years of Afghan Jihad against the former Soviet Union was an interesting experience. But it was not until I went into academia that I realized just how useful an experience it was in terms of the background information it offered.

In the 1980s, Peshawar was fast becoming a transit hub for a new warrior class – comprising Pashtuns as well as other ethnicities and nationalities. On the streets of Peshawar, one could buy military camouflage jackets and special blankets (intended as aid for the warriors) very cheaply. All sorts of foodstuffs with the flags of different countries printed on the packaging were widely available at the roadside. The vendors were mostly Afghan refugees, but many Pakistanis responsible for aid distribution were also involved in the pilferage.

Afghanistan emerged into the international limelight in 1979 when the Soviet Union invaded it, only to be faced with a ferocious Afghan 'freedom struggle'. The resistance was initially organized along tribal lines, but it soon mutated into an 'Afghan Jihad', which was planned, organized and launched from Pakistan, whose Pashtun areas became a vibrant base camp. Pakistan was under military rule at the time, and the predominant view in the country's corridors of power was that the Soviets were eyeing its warm waters and contemplating invasion.

Having previously formed an alliance with the US in the 1950s and 1960s against communist expansionism, Pakistan again approached the West for help and money. It volunteered to become a frontline state against Soviet aggression, and there was no shortage of international funds available to help it with its project. The United States and Saudi Arabia were fully on board at an early stage, and that was good enough for Pakistan.

True to their DNA, the kneejerk reaction of Afghans was to shift into resistance mode. The reason why Afghan defiance acquired a religious tinge had as much to do with the political ideology of the invading army and its local collaborators in Kabul as with the interests of the financial sponsors of the insurgency. The Saudis clearly had a purpose – to pursue a religious agenda – while the US and the other Western allies were not too concerned, just so long as the Soviet objectives were being disrupted. Quite soon the Afghan fighters adopted – or, according to some, had foisted upon them – the name *Mujahideen*, which is related to the word *jihad*, literally 'making an effort'. In Islamic tradition, the word 'jihad' refers primarily to a spiritual struggle within oneself, against sin; but its secondary meaning revolves around the idea of religious armed struggle. In daily usage, Muslims often refer to their work or intellectual efforts as 'jihad', especially if those efforts are service oriented. Thanks to Muslim extremists (but somewhat tragically for Islam), the term 'jihad' has assumed negative connotations in the Western world, where it is seen as a synonym for Islamic terrorism. Like many Muslims, I grew up hearing my parents say that education was *my* jihad. I think of my role as an educationalist in the same way – but because of the widespread misuse of the word, I think twice before saying it out loud.

In the 1980s, however, the Mujahideen were largely seen in the West in a positive light, since their interests overlapped. By framing the war as anti-Soviet, its sponsors – both Muslim states and the US – were able to invite religious radicals from Muslim countries around the globe to fight the 'infidels'. FATA, as well as parts of NWFP, hosted these radicals, offered them training facilities, and became a convenient launch pad for attacks. The idea of Jihad was employed as a strategy, and the land of the Pashtuns became a platform from which to wage a global battle between communism and capitalism.

FATA's geography provided good cover for Mujahideen training camps, and the Pashtun warrior traditions came in handy. Many NWFP districts, including those bordering FATA (especially Dir, Dera Ismail Khan, Charsadda, Kohat and Bannu), became part of the supply line supporting Afghan and Arab fighters. Many Arabs, such as Abdullah Azzam and Osama bin Laden, established their offices in Peshawar to make the necessary arrangements for the training of the Mujahideen. Pakistan's military and intelligence agencies spearheaded this effort on the ground, and the US and some European states arranged for the weapons. Soon many Gulf countries joined the impressive list of financial sponsors. All this is well known and well recorded[1] – but is often ignored when the present-day challenges facing Afghanistan are analysed.

Interestingly, the historical narratives in South Asia and the West are slightly different. Within Pakistan, the conflict is portrayed as having been a war of survival, to hold back communist expansion, while the 'Jihad' slogan was a tool to recruit committed and motivated warriors. In the process, Pakistan channelled funds and weapons to many Afghan groups of its own choice – especially to those who were deemed friendlier. For the West, by contrast, the consequent religious radicalization of the area was an unintended consequence of a necessary military campaign. That, however, cannot exonerate it for what happened.

A *madrasa* (seminary) network also popped up quite quickly to cater for the education and religious needs of the 3 million or so Afghan refugees who poured into Pakistan between 1979 and 1989. The conservative Islamic elements in the region benefited hugely from this windfall, which had a variety of by-products – for instance, a well-resourced publishing industry emerged for religious materials. After the Soviet withdrawal from Afghanistan in 1989, the linkages and networks established during the 'Afghan Jihad' strengthened further, and many students of Islamic madrasas moved from FATA and NWFP (especially from Deobandi madrasas run by the Jamiat Ulema-e-Islam party) to Afghanistan in order to participate in the civil war being fought for control of the country. Thousands of Arab and Central Asian fighters who had moved to FATA in the 1980s now started shuttling between Kabul, Kandahar, Jalalabad, Waziristan and Peshawar.

The most important of the Mujahideen leaders was probably Gulbuddin Hekmatyar of Hizb-e-Islami (Islamic Party). An engineer by profession, he was a charismatic man imbued with religious fervour. Even more importantly, he was well connected with the top layers of Pakistan's military and intelligence leaders. This made him eligible to receive disproportionate funds for his group, which boosted his stature, as well as the fighting capability of his forces in Afghanistan. He also owed a lot to Saudi Arabia and certain Gulf sponsors. Hekmatyar learnt his strategy lessons while being groomed in Kabul in the 1960s as an active member of the anti-communist Muslim Youth organization, founded by students and teachers at Kabul University. His base was the detribalized Pashtun groups; but his real strength, according to analysts, lay in his organizational abilities.[2] He was also younger than the other leaders and was fluent in English and French, making it easy for him to connect with Westerners.

One of Hekmatyar's most important team mates was Younas Khalis, a Pashtun tribal leader from Paktia Province. He held radical religious views and had a strong Pashtun power base around Nangarhar and the suburbs of Kabul. Certain differences were later to develop between him and Hekmatyar, so that Khalis created his own faction of Hizb-e-Islami; but he remained a major player, supported by an important field commander in Paktia Province, Jalaluddin Haqqani. Haqqani, the head of the Jadran tribe, which straddled the Durand Line, came to prominence after leading many successful anti-Soviet campaigns. Incidentally, Khalis has a couple of unusual claims to fame. First, a 1987 Getty Images photo shows him speaking at the White House with President Ronald Reagan standing next to him.[3] Second, he was Osama bin Laden's host when the latter returned to Afghanistan in 1996.

Another powerful Pashtun leader of the Afghan Jihad years was Abdul Rab Rasul Sayyaf, who led another group of fighters named

Ittihad-e-Islami Bara-ye Azad-e Afghanistan (Islamic Union for the Liberation of Afghanistan). A staunch fundamentalist, financially supported by Saudi Arabia, he was known for his close links with many Arab fighters, including bin Laden.

Among the non-Pashtun Mujahideen leaders who made life difficult for the Soviets in Afghanistan, we should probably mention Sibghatullah Mujaddidi of Jabha-ye-Milli (Afghanistan National Liberation Front), Burhanuddin Rabbani of Jamiat-i-Islami (Islamic Society) and, of course, the legendary Ahmed Shah Massoud, known for leading courageous resistance to Taliban expansion in the North. Both Mujaddidi and Rabbani were graduates of Al Azhar University in Egypt, had strong academic credentials and were regarded as relatively moderate in their religious views. Rabbani was quite influential, as fighters such as Ahmed Shah Massoud in the Panjshir Valley and Ismail Khan in Herat Province were aligned with him. In his formative years, Rabbani had translated various works of the radical Islamic thinker Sayyid Qutb into Persian.[4]

Many other smaller factions with different sectarian orientations also contributed to the effort, with the result that the anti-Soviet campaign was quite diverse in its outlook. For instance, Sayed Ahmed Gailani leading Mahaz-e-Milli-yi-Islami (National Islamic Front of Afghanistan) with support from some Sufi groups, and the Iranian-supported Shia leader Sheikh Asef Mohseni leading Harakat-e-Islami (Islamic Movement) also made important contributions.[5] Most of these prominent leaders had a political history in Afghanistan and had collaborated before. The names of their parties sounded similar – and even had similar meanings – but their funding sources and operational areas varied.

Allied in pursuit of their common goal, the top players in the Afghan Jihad of the 1980s were quite successful in resisting the Soviet forces and their leftist proxies in Kabul, despite their lack of any central leadership or clear chain of command.[6] Some of their campaigns were quite brutal and led to the death of innocent civilians, but there was barely a murmur in the international press. Their alliance proved quite superficial, however, when the Soviets withdrew, humiliated, in 1989. The collaborative mode vanished and the structures in place for combined planning and strategy crumbled almost instantaneously. Mujahideen groups remained active in Afghanistan, but each had its own ends in view. An all-out civil war for territory, money and political power ensued, and in 1992 the Soviet-backed Afghan President Najibullah was finally pushed out of power. Remarkably, he had survived the Soviet collapse, but could not sustain his rule when Russian funding ceased.

On the Pakistani side, a number of religious groups were now busy developing new formations to pursue their local agendas. These goals were all related to proselytizing, but were no longer limited to the traditional mode of teaching and preaching. Even more remarkable was the role now assumed by Pakistan's premier intelligence service – Inter-Services Intelligence (ISI) – which had expanded massively during the Afghan war years. Its spymasters believed that they had mastered the art of political manoeuvring in the process, and that made it a force to be reckoned with on the domestic political scene. On the Afghan front, it was left with limited options in terms of the future of the Mujahideen: either it could try to disband the cadres or it could give them fresh targets to pursue. While the West was busy celebrating the collapse of the former Soviet Union and managing its aftermath, Pakistan chose the easier option. A new doctrine was crafted – 'Pakistan's strategic depth is in Afghanistan' – which could be achieved with a Pashtun-dominated government in Kabul. That would provide Pakistan with leverage, courtesy of its own Pashtun population. Success in this endeavour would give Islamabad a chance to face any Indian aggression with more confidence.

In Afghanistan in 1992–95 a brutal civil war raged between the heroes of the 1980s Afghan Jihad. Around a dozen prominent leaders – all with their own battle-hardened forces – vied for the top political position in Kabul. Failure to develop amicably a power-sharing formula led to a bizarre crisis, which only grew more serious over time. In some ways it was a replay of the Great Game, though on a more limited scale: the regional players were only concerned with their own interests, and their partners in Afghanistan were treated as mere pawns. Pakistan aggressively promoted the political interests of its favourite players, especially Hekmatyar, whereas Saudi Arabia was consumed with fear of growing Iranian influence in the region. American attention waned, and the diminished flow of US dollars frustrated the newly emerged warrior class, which had become used to the money. A war-ravaged country with a divided leadership, a ruined infrastructure and degraded agricultural fields presented too dismal a picture for ordinary Afghans to dream of a better future. They felt justifiably betrayed at the lack of Western (especially American) interest in rebuilding the country.

Millions of Afghans languished in refugee camps in Pakistan and Iran, as rampant insecurity hampered their return home. For these Afghans, the social fabric of society, with its kinship patterns, was replaced by the cold and impersonal reality of a refugee camp. Even more tragically, the international community also quickly forgot that over a million and a half Afghans had died at the front line of the successful Western campaign against communism. A handful of conscientious international organizations tried to rebuild Afghanistan, but their limited efforts proved inadequate.

The loyalty of individuals and groups to their political parties was a complex affair. These were not unified entities and the struggle for power among the various groups was a constant factor. Ethnic, sectarian and historical dynamics were at play in these shifting alliances, but monetary considerations played the most central role. The financial pipeline constantly refilled by Western and Arab funding was tightly controlled by Pakistan's military and intelligence, which had almost single-handedly established the rules of business for most of the warrior groups. Every Afghan local commander in Afghanistan had to join one of the seven major religious political parties with offices in Peshawar to qualify for weapons and funds. These were considered smart tactics at the time.

Local rivalries and each group's main area of operations were also important considerations. For instance, the Karzais, who were leaders of the Popalzai clan, joined the Mujaddidi-led party because their traditional rivals had joined a competing party. Mullah Nasim Akhunzada, who controlled the opium trade in Helmand, joined Nabi Muhammadi's Harakat-e Inqilab-e Islami (Movement for Islamic Revolution) because of its influence in Helmand.[7] Changing parties to get a better deal was a routine matter and quite acceptable.

The ISI was naturally more inclined towards those who would obediently listen to its directives. Besides Hekmatyar, Haqqani was a favourite with the agency, and a large base was built for him at Zhawar. But relations were not always cordial and congenial: the ISI fell out with Hekmatyar when he refused to meet US President Ronald Reagan in 1985 on the (insightful) pretext that it 'would be playing into the hands of the KGB and Soviet propaganda, which claimed the war was not a Jehad, but rather an extension of US foreign policy.'[8] According to ISI Brigadier Mohammad Yousaf, who claims (with some reason) to have been the real commander-in-chief of the Mujahideen, Hekmatyar wanted US aid to be covert and deniable. Yousaf is critical of the lack of understanding on the part of the US in its dealings with Afghans: 'Aid donations are publicized so much that the receiver loses face and becomes resentful rather than grateful.'[9] Being in intelligence, he is, of course, more accustomed to secretive undertakings; he does not realize that in the international arena states want to take credit for their support.

Without US support, Afghans could never have been in a position to humiliate the Soviets. But the US was in too much of a hurry to forge ahead and analyse future threats, and failed to make sure the Afghan file was properly closed.

For Pakistanis, the war in Afghanistan never ended. From the late 1980s onwards, they had to struggle with its terrible consequences in the shape of a newly emerging 'Kalashnikov and drug culture' in the country. The general feeling among Pakistanis was that 'the Americans ditched us after their interests were served in Afghanistan' and had now imposed sanctions on Pakistan because they did not want to see a Muslim country with a nuclear bomb prosper. Pakistanis needed more time to come to terms with the fact that in the 1980s General Zia ul Haq had set the country on a pseudo-Islamic pathway – via the introduction of many controversial laws – on the pretext of saving it from the approaching communists. Zia was a master of deception, and in the process of securing Pakistan he redefined the raison d'être of the state. A version of Islam, duly modified to suit Zia's political interests, was now to be the overriding force behind the law of the land.

Still, the rise of the Taliban in Afghanistan came as a total shock not only to Westerners, but also to many South Asians, who could not immediately grasp the causes behind their meteoric rise. Part of the problem lay in a failure to comprehend the religious ruptures engendered by the politically crafted 'Jihad doctrine' and in a poor understanding of modern geopolitical realities. Zia's policies in Pakistan had also created a new model – a problematic model – for the region.

Genesis of the Taliban

The rise of non-Pashtuns in Kabul after the overthrow of Dr Najibullah had made the Pashtuns rather uncomfortable. For them it amounted to a gathering storm of northerners. In the midst of intrigue, treachery and violence, this created further uncertainty. In the absence of any state infrastructure and cohesive national personality, Afghanistan started fragmenting. Virtually every city and town came under the control of a local warlord, and this in turn impelled people to gravitate towards their particular ethnic and religious identities. Insecurity grew as sources of livelihood became scarcer; but modern weapons were in abundance, thanks to the regional and global supporters of Afghan Jihad, who had now turned their backs on this unfortunate country.

The second-tier leadership of the Mujahideen, meanwhile, was itching to take over, as they could clearly see the failure of the top leadership to bring about any meaningful change for Afghans. Perhaps senior leaders were only good at fighting off the Soviet invaders? Perhaps governance was not their cup of tea? However, in the transition process, moderate religious forces that preferred to build consensus – such as those represented by the Sufi-oriented Sibghatullah Mujaddidi and Sayed Ahmed Gailani – were almost discarded. Instead, Hekmatyar's authoritarian model of managing parties was now in vogue.[10] Before the Afghan war of the 1980s, to borrow Robert Kaplan's words, 'religion was indistinguishable from the other rituals of rural existence, and thus there was nothing especially political about it'.[11] This was about to change in a momentous way.

Pashtun frustrations and lawlessness had created a void that had to be filled by someone. Seeing Mujahideen leaders at each other's throats was demoralizing as well as disgusting to Afghans. Greater Kandahar (*loy Kandahar*), especially, had turned into a hotbed of corruption and harassment. Checkpoints emerged on every corner and crime rates skyrocketed. A variety of gangs started collecting tolls from all and sundry.

In an attempt to provide the residents of the area with a sense of security, a group of youngsters with rudimentary Islamic credentials – 'Talibs' (literally 'seekers of knowledge') in local madrasas – set up a checkpoint of their own in the village of Hawz-i-Mudat, near Kandahar. The public responded positively, encouraging the 'Taliban' (as they became known) to expand their zone of surveillance to the two nearby districts of Maiwand and Panjwayi. Mullah Abdul Salam Zaeef, a close associate of Mullah Mohammad Omar and later the Taliban's ambassador to Islamabad, maintains that the decision to launch a movement was made at a meeting in a mosque in 1994 attended by 33 colleagues and presided over by Mullah Abdul Rauf Akhund, a prominent Taliban commander in the early days who was killed in 1995.

The meeting decided on a very specific, limited goal: to 'seek the support of other *mujahideen* and *Taliban* and together with them we would clear the streets of the rogue commanders and checkpoints'.[12] Only when the search for a leader began did Mullah Omar feature in the discussion. The criteria were spelt out clearly: 'find a leader who is not a prominent figure, who doesn't have any standing as a commander and thus does not have any political relations from the past with any of the known commanders'.[13]

Mullah Omar was perfect for the job. Unlike the well-networked Mujahideen leaders of the 1980s Afghan Jihad, he was an unknown figure who came to prominence in a very short span of time. He was neither charismatic nor eloquent. The timing of his selection, however, was impeccable. He also took initiatives at a time when chaos, disillusionment and violence had overtaken Afghanistan and when hopelessness was the order of the day. He was then working as a teacher in a small madrasa in the Kandahar area. His battleground experience (in which he had lost an eye) was familiar to the Mujahideen, but he was not known for any great heroics. His great claim to fame was the important role he had played in Kandahar in cleaning up the mess created by the local warlords, but he was not the 'Robin Hood' of some Taliban narratives.

Public support, which initially came in the shape of free food for Taliban members doing volunteer security work, encouraged Mullah Omar to pursue bigger tasks. In October 1994, he led a small group of Talibs that seized Spin Boldak, a trucking stopover on the border with Pakistan, then controlled by Hekmatyar's forces, which used to pocket the customs revenue generated by the border post. This now gave the Taliban a steady stream of income. Even more significantly, Spin Boldak was also home to an arms and ammunition depot, previously at the service of Hekmatyar, the keys to which were now handed over to the Taliban by Pakistani intelligence. With abundant ammunition at their disposal, the Taliban established control over the broader Kandahar area in a matter of weeks.

Criminals and thugs operating freely were taken by surprise at the dramatic success of the Taliban, and they 'voluntarily' opted to rest for a while (which brought immediate relief to people). Many of these criminals were in fact foot soldiers from the anti-Soviet campaign whose salaries had dried up after the Soviet withdrawal. The improvement in the security situation enhanced support for the Taliban. Cashing in on their ethnic identity, the Taliban also artfully co-opted various Pashtun tribes in the south and east of Afghanistan, thereby creating a sense of an 'artificial unity among Pushtuns'.[14] The war-weary public embraced the Taliban in the hope of a fresh start; but they never signed up to a dogmatic version of Islam.

Various anecdotes about the initial days of the Taliban campaign provide some insight into the world of a Talib. One tells of a member of a Taliban force who, in the course of a raid on a suspect's house, spotted a poster of Hollywood tough-guy Rambo. Having had no exposure to the world of cinema, he assumed that Rambo was a family member: 'Tell your cousin that he must hand his machine gun over to us.' The protestations of the homeowner fell on deaf ears, and the Taliban subsequently imprisoned him.[15]

With its profound interest in the fate of Afghanistan, it did not take Pakistan long to place a bet on this new and emerging contender. After all, it had made a heavy investment in Afghan Jihad for a purpose. While for the disenchanted and rudderless Afghans, the rise of the Taliban provided hope of an improvement in security, for Pakistan various economic and geopolitical factors were also involved. Pakistan's democratic regime at the time, under Benazir Bhutto, was seeking to expand its trade links with the newly independent Central Asian states. For this it needed the road link through Afghanistan. Thus stability in that country was very much in Pakistan's economic interests. Secondly, despite many attempts by Pakistan and Saudi Arabia, the Mujahideen leaders had repeatedly failed to come together, and Pakistan was losing heart. All sorts of accords had been signed by the leading Afghan Mujahideen leaders in Peshawar, accompanied by a lot of fanfare and media glare. But they had all come to nothing. Support for Hekmatyar had also failed to resolve anything. Now Pakistan could see that the Taliban were dominated by Pashtuns, with whom it could readily connect. So in many ways it was a natural alliance. The sympathizers and backers of the Taliban in Pakistan and Saudi Arabia were amazingly quick to deploy their public relations skills in order to render the new entity acceptable, but the Taliban's gradual assumption of control in Afghanistan was only possible through the traditional Afghan method – negotiating, cajoling and bribing rivals where feasible, and fighting when necessary.[16]

The Taliban's success came in various shapes. They were quite pragmatic when it came to building alliances and collaborating with powerful groups in certain areas. When his forces evicted Iranian-backed groups from some areas of Kabul in 1995, Massoud made a temporary alliance with the Taliban, who were waiting on the outskirts of Kabul for their turn to move in. In defending Herat in 1995, the Taliban found allies in the notorious warlord Abdul Rashid Dostum and Karim Khalili of the Shia Hizb-e-Wahdat. Ustad Mohammad Akbari, the powerful Shia Hazara leader, also joined the Taliban in 1998 (though not before his forces had been overwhelmed in a ferocious campaign).[17]

Opposition to the Taliban also came in a variety of guises. For instance, in February 1997, when the Taliban tried to clamp down on two timber smugglers from Kunar – Malik Zarin from Mujaddidi's group and Haji Kashmir Khan from Hekmatyar's group – both responded by galvanizing their followers on tribal lines so that the Taliban had to pay through the nose.[18] Among the old Mujahideen groups, who were as surprised at the turn of events as anyone outside the country, Rabbani and Hekmatyar leaned towards Tehran, whereas Saudi favourite Sayyaf joined the Massoud-led Northern Alliance rather than develop any ties with the Taliban. Such moves were ideologically totally unexpected.

Leaving aside the alliances that were needed to achieve military objectives, it is doubtful whether the Taliban ever really transcended tribal and cultural norms in their attempts to establish an Islamic government. The truth is that the Taliban predominantly represented Ghilzai Pashtuns, who were on the lowest socio-economic rung of society.[19] The notion of a Durrani–Ghilzai contest was much less of a factor than the economic realities. Most Taliban belonged to areas that were chronically underdeveloped and that had historically been neglected by the state, so most families would send at least one boy to a local madrasa to benefit from free board and lodging. Arguably, the Taliban's Pashtun identity allowed them to sweep through the Pashtun areas relatively easily – in many cases without a shot being fired. The fighting became intense only when the Taliban moved into non-Pashtun districts, where they faced stiff resistance and even military reversals. Only a handful of Taliban leaders were from other ethnic groups.[20]

Another common denominator among the Taliban recruits was their direct or indirect association with the Deobandi school of thought. A South Asian sub-sect of Sunni Islam, Deobandis are often seen as the architects of the Taliban worldview. This is only partly true, however. Historically, the Deobandis emerged as a religious revivalist movement, designed to arrest the deterioration in the socio-political position of Muslims in mid-nineteenth-century British India. Its two central ideologues were Mohammed Qasim Nanautawi (1833–77) and Rashid Ahmed Gangohi (1829–1905). In 1866, together they founded a madrasa called Dar-ul-Ulum (House of Knowledge) in the town of Deoband (near New Delhi), which provided the movement with its name. The original Deobandi agenda was to train a new generation of learned Muslims who could spearhead a Muslim awakening in South Asia. They eschewed political ambitions at first, and presented themselves as 'inward looking and primarily concerned with the Islamic quality of individual lives'.[21]

There was nothing unique in this line of thinking: all religious traditions routinely experience such trends. However, the group soon developed a retrogressive outlook, with an emphasis on a restrictive view of the role of women in society. It became normal for its members to refer to other sects of Islam in derogatory terms, and in particular they were bitterly critical of Sufi practices. This was to become their hallmark and further distanced them from other Sunni groups. Deobandis were also fierce opponents of British colonial rule before the issue caught the imagination of most South Asians. They claim credit for the creation of a grassroots political effort – known as the Khilafat Movement – which staunchly opposed the dismantling of the Ottoman Empire after the First World War. The movement certainly trained as well as empowered the ordinary Muslims of South Asia to participate actively in the political arena. Barelvi, another sub-sect of Sunni Islam in South Asia that is intellectually aligned with Sufi traditions, is considered to be the major rival of the Deobandi school of thought. Their theological tussle turned uncivil with the passage of time, and lately has become violent, with Barelvis often on the receiving end.

By 1919, a group of politically active Deobandis had already formed the Jamiat Ulema-e-Hind (JUH – Assembly of Indian Clerics) in British India, and this played an important role in the peaceful Khilafat

Movement. This mission and the non-violent approach of the JUH resonated with the ideals of Mahatma Gandhi and the Indian National Congress and led to a Hindu–Muslim alliance against British imperialism.

Interestingly, the JUH was against the creation of a separate Muslim state, since it shared an Indian nationalist perspective. After the 1947 partition of the subcontinent, however, it wasted no time in establishing a Pakistani branch of the party, known as the Jamiat Ulema-e-Islam (JUI – Assembly of Islamic Clerics). By the time the Taliban emerged, the party had split into two factions – the JUI-F, led by Maulana Fazlur Rahman, and the JUI-S, led by Maulana Sami ul Haq (who runs the Madrasa Haqqania in Akora Khattak).[22] Both factions have their primary political base in Pashtun-dominated areas.

A network of thousands of madrasas spread throughout South Asia during the Afghan Jihad years (1980s) – keeping the Deobandi Dar-ul-Ulum as their model. Abundant global funds were now available for the purpose. A new chain of madrasas was built exclusively for Afghan refugees in the 1980s in the Pakistan–Afghanistan border area, on the special instructions of General Zia ul Haq.[23] Most Taliban were educated in these Deobandi madrasas, either in Pakistan or in Afghanistan. It was this history that likely inspired a Taliban spokesman, Rahmatullah Hashemi, to declare (with some hyperbole): 'Every Afghan is a Deobandi.'[24]

The Taliban took many liberties with Deobandi doctrine, even building on some of the excesses introduced by Pakistani clerics associated with certain extremist madrasas. According to Muslim theologians trained at Egypt's Al Azhar University, one of the most respected centres of Islamic learning, the Taliban's 'Knowledge of religion and jurisprudence is lacking because they have no knowledge of the Arabic language, linguistics and literature and hence they did not learn the true Islam.'[25]

What then helped the Taliban emerge as a power to be reckoned with is a critical question. Pakistan's intelligence operators certainly helped the Taliban build alliances that were vital for its survival and growth. According to credible estimates, around 30,000 students from various JUI-controlled madrasas in Pakistan joined the Taliban movement in Afghanistan.[26] That was sufficient for a Taliban 'surge' in its formative phase. The ISI even went a step further and instructed the provincial governments of Balochistan and NWFP during their years of initial ascendance to ensure that no anti-Taliban political activities were allowed in their areas.[27] Progressive Pashtuns in Pakistan who spoke out and denounced this dangerous game and its potential long-term impacts were categorically told to shut up.[28] The chief of Saudi intelligence, Prince Turki al Faisal, also took a keen interest in the planning of Taliban offensives in 1996. Obviously, it had the smell of money.

The real extent of Pakistani support for the Taliban can be gauged from a declassified US confidential document dated 16 January 1997. It states: 'Pakistani aid to the Taliban is more significant and probably less malign than most imagine.' It goes on to say that military advice 'may be there, but is probably not all that significant since the Taliban do quite well on their own'. On the other hand, 'Pakistani political and diplomatic support is certainly significant', as Islamabad plays an 'overbearing role in planning and even executing Taliban political and diplomatic initiatives'.[29]

Put simply, without Pakistan's help and Saudi funding, the Taliban could not have survived. Mullah Mohammad Omar had little political experience before he claimed the lofty-sounding title of *Amir ul Momineen* (Commander of the Faithful). He attended a madrasa in Kandahar, but there is no evidence that he ever graduated. His involvement in the Jihad against the Soviets, too, was as a foot soldier and later as a junior commander. The only indication of his involvement with political parties of the time was his association with that of Younas Khalis.[30]

The number two in the Taliban government, Mullah Mohammad Rabbani, had likewise been a member of Khalis's party. The Taliban's relationship with Osama bin Laden also seems to have been facilitated by Khalis. When bin Laden returned to Afghanistan in 1996, he initially settled in Nangarhar, Khalis's home province. Another of Khalis's protégés, Jalaluddin Haqqani, who was not part of the core Taliban group during its genesis, was 'franchised' into the Taliban in 1996. Haqqani was quick to pledge his allegiance to Mullah Omar, later becoming minister of tribal and border affairs – a position that he practically held onto for a long time, irrespective of who was in control of Kabul!

The new administrative structure of the 'Islamic Emirate of Afghanistan' was entirely dominated by mullahs. Whenever a province was taken over, a mullah was appointed governor, who also acted as the military commander of the area. And it was not just any mullah: it was invariably a Pashtun mullah. In Herat, for example, a Pashtun governor was appointed who did not even speak Dari, the language of the majority there.

A substantial number of fighters from the groups of Khalis, Hekmatyar and Nabi Muhammadi joined the Taliban movement in 1995–96, strengthening its military capacity. Meanwhile, however, the unemployment rate rocketed and the industrial and agricultural sectors were paralysed.[31] Blind to these realities, the Taliban focused on only two things – the military campaign against the armed opposition in the north and the imposition of an obscurantist version of sharia law that was a mixture of tribalism, male chauvinism and illiteracy. Forcing women into seclusion became their favourite pastime. They also fostered a particular dislike of music, entertainment – and trimmed beards. Initially they banned all sports, but in 1998 they relented and mercifully allowed football. A couple of years later, in 2000, a visiting Pakistani men's soccer team was arrested on the pitch in Kandahar for the crime of wearing shorts. The players were punished by having their heads shaved and were then unceremoniously deported back to Pakistan.[32]

In reality, the Taliban were more of a vigilante militia than a political group capable of governing a state. The Pakistani leadership was aware of this problem, but could do little about it. A Pakistani Foreign Ministry delegation visited Mullah Omar in December 1996 in his Kandahar office, in an effort to help broker a deal between the Taliban and various groups in the north, and with the aim of helping them establish a broad-based government. The United Nations Special Mission to Afghanistan (UNSMA) was also involved. Iftikhar Murshid, a scholarly and diligent Pakistani diplomat who participated in the meeting, provides some important insights into how Mullah Omar ran the show. He calls him a reclusive man with a 'lean and hungry look', operating from a very modest office. All visitors were seated on the floor:

> Omar came across as an extremely shy person who was never at ease with outsiders . . . The UNSMA initiative was then explained to him with all its nuances. Although I doubt whether Mullah Omar, a semi-educated cleric, understood most of what was conveyed to him, leave alone the finer points, he said that the proposal would be examined by the Taliban Shura.[33]

Modesty and humility is certainly in accordance with core Islamic principles, and referring the issue to his advisers was also a smart move on Omar's part. But it is not known if he genuinely wanted advice from his colleagues or was just trying to buy time while his fighters attempted to vanquish the non-Pashtun north. As it turned out later, he did continue with the military option, but he failed repeatedly, losing over 10,000 of his soldiers in the process.

An arguably worthy early move by the Taliban regime (on health grounds at least) was a countrywide ban on smoking cigarettes. It is quite another matter that the grounds for this were that smoking was 'a symbol of moral decay'.[34] It is worth pointing out here that many of Mullah Omar's policy decisions contradicted the declarations of Taliban officials in Kabul.[35] If this was a communication problem, then it likely stemmed from the fact that Mullah Omar continued to work out of his home town of Kandahar, while the seat of government was in Kabul.

The Taliban regime's clamp-down on opium production is often depicted as another laudable step, but in fact it is debatable whether it ever did ban the opium trade. Gretchen Peters' important work on the subject shows that, right from the start, the Taliban 'movement appeared to rely on the financial backing of an unholy alliance of drug smugglers, traders, and trucking groups'. In any case, the relationship continued, as is evident from a declassified 1998 CIA report, which states that the Taliban were paid $230 for each kilo of heroin flown out of Jalalabad and Kandahar airports.[36] A more clearly defined and comprehensive ban on opium came into effect only in 2000. On that occasion it was enforced more effectively and was also monitored by the United Nations.[37] Nevertheless, some experts maintain that enough opium stocks were still available within Afghanistan to cater to the international demands for another four years.[38] In fact, the ban at that point caused a massive rise in the market price of heroin, yielding huge profits for the drug traders and smugglers who probably manipulated this – with or without Taliban knowledge.

For the international community, the wholesale massacre of Hazaras in 1998 and 2000 and the destruction of the Buddha statues at Bamian in 2001 damaged Taliban credentials beyond repair. In clear violation of the Islamic laws of war, in 1997 the Taliban had also poisoned wells in the Shomali Plain, a farming region north of Kabul, forcing thousands of civilians to flee the area.[39] Across the world, educated Muslims, traditionalists and modernists alike, were appalled by such practices. Thomas Barfield explains the reason quite succinctly:

Taliban religious ideology was a crude mixture of Salafi Islam and Pashtunwali ... Their religious interpretations were often idiosyncratic and tended to dress local custom in the guise of religion ... The movement was hostile to Sufism as well as veneration of saints and shrines – elements that were deeply embedded in the popular Islam of Afghanistan.[40]

It is a pity that, in spite of all this, no Muslim state mustered the courage to warn and challenge the Taliban. Pakistanis were the best informed because they started feeling the consequences earlier than anyone else. However, Pakistan's military establishment, which could have influenced the Taliban, bit its tongue, since Taliban-led Afghanistan provided 'strategic depth' in case of confrontation with Pakistan's arch-rival India. It also benefited from the militant camps in Afghanistan that trained fighters for Kashmir.

In the early days of the Taliban, the American silence was also deafening: it was eyeing the construction of an oil pipeline from Turkmenistan to Pakistan via Afghanistan, and Taliban support could make it happen. Washington also viewed the Taliban as anti-Iranian and as a 'cleansing', transitional force that would unite Pashtuns and create a new basis for peace'.[41] America corrected its policy course as soon as it realized the futility of such dreams, though the two sides remained in touch off and on.

The last reported meeting between the US and Taliban representatives took place in August 2001, when US Assistant Secretary of State for Central Asian Affairs Christina Rocca met Abdul Salam Zaeef, the Taliban's ambassador in Islamabad. Rocca's mission was to convince him that unless the Taliban gave up bin Laden, the United Nations was unlikely to relax its sanctions against Afghanistan. After the meeting, Zaeef told the media: 'We do not consider the US as our enemy and the US should reciprocate this feeling and not follow a hostile policy'.[42] Behind the scenes, the Taliban government was already paying an American public relations expert for an image-making campaign in the US.

Osama bin Laden, who had left Afghanistan in 1990 disheartened by the civil war, returned to the country in May 1996, empowering the hardliners and extremists within the Taliban ranks. His two years in Saudi Arabia and four years in Sudan only added value to his profile and connections. Bin Laden had global ambitions, supported by the transnational network that he had carefully nurtured during the Afghan Jihad years. The Taliban, by comparison, were parochial in their perspective and their political worldview was much narrower. They were in awe of bin Laden and held him in respect for his services to Afghan Jihad. For his part, bin Laden used and abused this opportunity to the utmost. The moment he stepped off his chartered jet at Jalalabad airport, along with dozens of his friends, guards and family, he focused on re-establishing his base in the country. Jalalabad was not under Taliban control at the time. Bin Laden had bags full of dollars to smooth the process of settling down. It worked well: the Taliban desperately needed money to pay its soldiers and to buy off some local tribal chieftains. Bin Laden's $3 million 'gift' to the Taliban cause was very timely.[43]

Of course, the Taliban and bin Laden shared many ideological aspects, but bin Laden's Salafi orientation was more dogmatic than the Taliban's religious standpoint. Bin Laden initially only made a case for pushing the US forces out of Saudi Arabia and Somalia. His 23 August 1996 'Declaration of War against the Americans Occupying the Land of the Two Holy Places' was not taken very seriously, however, as he was not then thought to have the support base and the means to implement his agenda.

But he was crystal clear about his goals at the time he officially launched Al-Qaeda in Afghanistan, on 23 February 1998 categorically stating 'the ruling to kill the Americans and their allies – civilians and military – is an individual duty for every Muslim who can do it in any country in which it is possible to do it'.[44] Contrary to some recent accounts explaining the Taliban–Al-Qaeda rupture of the late 1990s, the reality was that, despite the rifts, the Taliban never distanced themselves from this statement and continued to host bin Laden.[45] In fact, Taliban support for him apparently solidified after the US cruise missile attack on six locations in Afghanistan in August 1998, coming in response to Al-Qaeda's involvement in attacks on the US embassies in Kenya and Tanzania a couple of weeks previously.

After the 11 September attacks in the United States, the US came down hard on Afghanistan in order to punish the Taliban and eliminate Osama bin Laden and his Al-Qaeda network. Whether or not the Taliban leaders had any advance knowledge of the 9/11 attacks, they refused to cooperate with the US. The Taliban clearly had no qualms about extending their hospitality to bin Laden – and indeed to many other militants from around the world. They cannot claim now that they were naïve at the time. Brutality in the name of religion perhaps makes the crimes appear less gruesome to those committing them; but for those on the receiving end and for those witnessing the unholy drama, it created disgust about the professed belief system of the perpetrator and the enabler. In this sense the Taliban's disservice to Islam was huge.

CHAPTER FOUR

Goodbye Taliban?
The 'gift of democracy' for a new Afghanistan
(2002–05)

The consequences of Mullah Omar's decision not to hand over bin Laden to the Americans after the 9/11 terrorist attacks were predictable. Unmoved by the extent of the looming danger, the Taliban leadership dragged its feet and insisted on seeing evidence of bin Laden's involvement in the attacks. They even disregarded advice from Saudi Arabia to cooperate with the US. Some evidence was indeed provided to them via Pakistani channels, but the Taliban leadership was not convinced. Realizing that the Taliban were under imminent threat, and hoping to save his allies from American wrath, Pakistani President Pervez Musharraf instructed the ISI to arrange for Robert Grenier, the CIA chief in Islamabad, and Mullah Akhtar Mohammed Osmani, an influential deputy of Mullah Omar, to meet and find a way around the problem. Osmani was offered full American support if he was prepared to push out Mullah Omar and assume leadership of the Taliban.[1] There was just one condition: he had to hand over bin Laden soon afterwards. Mullah Zaeef, the Afghan ambassador to Pakistan, was offered a similar deal by Pakistani intelligence. But both Osmani and Zaeef refused to ditch Mullah Omar.

Musharraf stepped up his efforts and tasked the ISI chief, Lieutenant General Mahmood Ahmed (later a devout proselytizer associated with Tableeghi Jamaat),[2] with travelling to Afghanistan, along with various

Pakistani religious figures who shared the Taliban worldview, to knock some sense into the Taliban leadership. But with his soft spot for the Taliban, Ahmed attempted this only half-heartedly, and it didn't work out.

Musharraf, a liberal and pragmatic general, could see which way the wind was blowing, but the ISI was not about to change its views overnight. After all, it had made a huge investment in the Taliban over the years. The ISI leadership had little, if any, sympathy for Al-Qaeda, but in those early days after the attack very few Pakistani security officials were prepared to accept that bin Laden had the capability to conduct such a sophisticated attack on US soil. Conspiracy theories abounded, but time was running out and the Bush administration was in no mood to hear any 'ifs' or 'buts'.

The American decision to punish the Taliban regime under Mullah Omar was swift, and Pakistan's decision to jump on the bandwagon was even swifter. If Musharraf had any lingering doubts in his mind, the American threat to bomb Pakistan back into the stone age brought him some clarity about the stakes involved.[3]

Musharraf had no sympathy for Al-Qaeda whatsoever, but he felt the Taliban could be useful to Pakistan in pursuing its interests in Afghanistan, as well as in its dealings with India. This perhaps clouded his judgement and forced him to commit many mistakes. Nevertheless, he thought he had negotiated a good deal at the time: he was allowed to rescue his military and intelligence officers deployed in Afghanistan; this he achieved via Brigadier Sultan Amir Tarrar (codename 'Colonel Imam'). This legendary special services officer, known by the Pakistani media as 'the father of the Taliban', had trained with the US army's special forces in the 1970s and had himself trained many leaders of the Mujahideen (including Gulbuddin Hekmatyar) and the Taliban during the 1980s and 1990s. The rescue operation was made possible only after Musharraf personally talked to President Bush. To this day no one knows the identities of all the passengers on the Pakistani Air Force C-130 that brought them home; but certainly Brigadier Tarrar lived up to his reputation as a daredevil soldier. Little could he have suspected that, a decade later, he would die at the hands of a new strain of Taliban – the Pakistani Taliban. Unlike Mullah Omar, they had no respect for his past contributions.[4]

Thousands of Americans, meanwhile, came out on the streets to caution their government against a kneejerk reaction; but America was hurt and it was deemed politically untenable for the government not to act. The international community was also sympathetic to America's loss: even Karachi and Tehran held spontaneous vigils and processions to show support for the victims.[5] The writing was on the wall and the days of the Taliban in Kabul were numbered. But it was unclear how matters would develop. In a critical White House meeting on 12 October 2001, President George W. Bush categorically maintained: 'I oppose using the military for nation building. Once the job is done, our forces are not peacekeepers.'[6] Talking points from his presidential political campaign were obviously still fresh in his memory!

And the job was done pretty quickly when the massive US military machine swung into action. The initial inroads made by a few dozen CIA operatives, backed by a small contingent of US special forces personnel, ensured that the Taliban government fell like a house of cards in a matter of days. Afghanistan did not have any extensive military infrastructure and the Taliban did not have the wherewithal to resist the onslaught.

The quick rout of the Taliban surprised many – but not those who were well versed in Afghan history and especially in the genesis of the Taliban. A small core of committed warriors remained loyal to Mullah Omar, but the general cadres simply switched sides or went into the mountains to wait out the impending crisis. According to one of the first Western journalists to enter Kabul after the fall of the Taliban, the US Air Force bombed the villa that had housed the Taliban's head of security in the city, only to find that he had fled two days before.[7] A Taliban fighter from Pakistan who made it back home after the fall of the Taliban paints the picture quite accurately: 'The only people who fought were the non-Afghans. Mullah Omar and his regime would not have fallen if his lieutenants were men of character.'[8]

For tribal warriors, it was in their DNA to retreat to the mountains when faced with a superior power. They simply believed in surviving to fight another day. Other Pashtuns who had been either coerced into joining the Taliban or lured into the fold by the promise of money simply packed up and moved back to the rural areas of the south and east, where they were indistinguishable from other villagers. There was no public outrage against the overthrow of the Taliban. An era had ended. There was no mourning, but there was a widespread feeling of hopelessness and confusion among the Taliban cadres: the regime had crumpled in days before their very eyes. They just couldn't believe it.

The transition was not bloodless, however. Out of an estimated 60,000 Taliban forces, around 12,000 were killed, 20,000 wounded and 7,000 captured.[9] Local opponents of the Taliban, especially those aligned with the Northern Alliance, were especially brutal. The Afghan warlord Abdul Rashid Dostum, who had old scores to settle with the Taliban, mercilessly killed thousands of Taliban foot soldiers, many of whom had surrendered to him. He was known for such tendencies, but on this occasion he did it on the payroll of the CIA.[10]

There was a particularly gruesome episode at Qala-i-Jangi, a vast fortress near the northern city of Mazar-i-Sharif, where hundreds of Afghan and Al-Qaeda prisoners were held. While CIA-led interrogations were going on, some of the prisoners got it into their heads that arrangements were being made to execute them. Some of them had small arms on them, and weapons were seized from the guards. The ensuing riot left around 300 prisoners dead, plus dozens of Dostum's soldiers who were guarding the fort. Dostum packed the surviving inmates, plus thousands of other Taliban prisoners, into shipping containers and transported them to his base at Shibarghan. They were given no food or water, and hundreds suffocated in the containers. More were killed when Dostum's guards shot into the containers. The bodies were buried in a mass grave at Dasht-i-Leili. According to a declassified US State Department intelligence report, about 1,500 Taliban prisoners died.[11] The news of such excesses was unlikely to go down well with the Pashtun population in the south.

As for the Al-Qaeda strategists, a few weeks sufficed for them to disperse and vanish from the scene to a new sanctuary (which incidentally was readily available in Pakistan's Pashtun tribal belt). Bin Laden relied mainly on his financial strength, his extensive communication network and a team of core strategists from across the world to act as the organization's backbone. CIA officials in Islamabad estimated that Al-Qaeda had fewer than 500 members operating in Afghanistan. For routine administrative and security tasks he hired locals. So eliminating Al-Qaeda from Afghanistan in physical terms was not a very difficult project. The real challenge was how to combat the ideological manipulation and rationalization of terror that bin Laden and his associates so deviously disseminated globally. South Asia had been Al-Qaeda's first laboratory for testing its ideas after it emerged in 1989, and alliances with local militant groups were made for the purpose in the early 1990s. The rise of sectarian killings in Pakistan and the heating up of regional conflict theatres in the mid-1990s were ominous signs, but the West remained aloof until the fire reached its shores.

Despite the loss of Kabul and the panic that ensued, the Taliban–Al-Qaeda linkage remained cosy and solid.[12] Some researchers argue that serious differences existed, and even that tensions had grown between the two entities before the 9/11 attacks; but the evidence overwhelmingly suggests that, for all practical purposes, the Taliban–Al-Qaeda operational nexus was a hard reality.[13]

Among the *Pashtunwali* norms that the Taliban followed religiously was *nanawatay* – provision of sanctuary; and the Taliban remained committed to standing by bin Laden and Al-Qaeda. Obviously, there was no possibility of the two merging, because they each had different roots and motivations, and consequently different targets. The Taliban were focused locally, whereas Al-Qaeda had global ambitions. Nor was there complete congruity in their ideological leanings: both believed in imposing their Islamic vision on people, but the Taliban were ready to operate within the confines of a modern state, while Al-Qaeda dreamt of establishing a caliphate and an empire to confront the Western world.

The Taliban appreciated the cash they received from Al-Qaeda; and Al-Qaeda appreciated Afghanistan's open spaces, where its adherents could confer, train and 'hang out'. But with international forces operating inside Afghanistan after October 2001, coordination between the Taliban and Al-Qaeda became difficult. Everyone was looking to take cover, and this upset the applecart.

Pakistan's support for the US at this time was critical. Musharraf had made the requisite commitments to the Americans, but his support was linked to an understanding that the non-Pashtun-dominated Northern Alliance would not be allowed a free run at Kabul. The Northern Alliance was supported by India and Iran, and both of those were jubilant at the sight of the Taliban in trouble. The rise of non-Pashtuns in Afghanistan's corridors of power was certain now. Pakistan realized with horror that its friends in Afghanistan were in deep trouble and that it was no longer in a position to ensure that its likes and dislikes in the country were taken into consideration.

To Pakistan's dismay, the Northern Alliance marched into Kabul around mid-November 2001. Islamabad interpreted this as American duplicity – and it could hardly be blamed for doing so. As Musharraf told his corps commanders soon afterwards, Pakistan would henceforth have to look after its interests more 'carefully' and not trust anyone.[14]

In late 2001, the US special forces mounted an operation in Afghanistan's Tora Bora mountains, bordering Pakistan, with the aim of capturing or killing Osama bin Laden. The effort failed because of the limited resources that were deployed for the task. Apparently, those sitting in Washington were not fully briefed about the terrain and nature of the porous border (and unfortunately Google Earth was not then available for them to see for themselves the reality on the ground). Two senior Pakistan Army commanders, including Lieutenant General Ali Jan Aurakzai, a Pashtun general who was corps commander in Peshawar at the time of the said US campaign, told me: 'Pakistan was not taken into confidence about the Tora Bora operation.'[15] Later the general was even to claim that Pakistan's military leadership got to know about that operation, as well as about the US-led Operation

Anaconda in Afghan areas adjacent to North and South Waziristan in March 2002, through the media![16] Poor communication was not merely incidental; lack of trust was also instrumental here.

Interestingly, American journalist Ron Suskind maintains that the US had cut a deal with Musharraf sometime that November by which Pakistan would seal off the passages to Pakistan from the Tora Bora region of Afghanistan, in return for which the US would give Pakistan nearly a billion dollars in new economic aid.[17] Either Musharraf over-estimated the capacity of his forces to curtail cross-border movement or else this was his way of telling Americans that, in order to get his support, they needed to keep their promises. One way or another, bin Laden had ample time to slip through, and his trusted friends in the Pashtun tribal belt quickly moved him to a safer location inside Pakistan. How he mysteriously survived in Pakistan for almost a decade is discussed in later chapters.

Mullah Omar also remained elusive. The CIA provided Hamid Karzai with all the resources he needed to move on the Taliban base in Kandahar, but Omar had vanished by the time the cautious Karzai entered the city. Legend has it that the mullah escaped on a motorbike at night. He is supposed to have remained inside Afghanistan for a while – in and around Helmand and Uruzgan – before crossing the border into Pakistan, where his location remains unknown (though rumour has it that he operates from somewhere around Quetta).

American forces did succeed in capturing six of Mullah Omar's high-profile associates, who were duly dispatched to Guantanamo Bay. They included Mullah Mohammad Fazl and Mullah Norullah Nori (both military commanders in northern Afghanistan), Abdul-Haq Wasiq (deputy head of Taliban intelligence), Khairullah Khairkhwa (the former governor of Herat Province), Mohammed Nabi (a senior Taliban official) and Ambassador Mullah Zaeef (who is counted as one of the founders of the Taliban).[18] Another dozen alleged members of the Afghan Taliban were also transferred to join this group in Guantanamo.

A few others became official guests in Pakistan, where they promised to keep a low profile. Those who decided to stay on in Afghanistan managed to send their families to safety in Pakistan. A few surprisingly decided to reach out to Hamid Karzai and mend fences: they offered their withdrawal from political life in return for immunity from prosecution.[19] This group included Mullah Obaidullah (former Taliban defence minister), Mullah Baradar (former Taliban deputy defence minister) and Mullah Abdul Razzak (former Taliban interior minister). Unsurprisingly, however, Karzai could not get the approval of the leaders of the Northern Alliance for any such deal. The members of this group all later played a crucial part in reviving the Taliban in Afghanistan, and critics now argue (with the benefit of hindsight) that Karzai should have been allowed to reconcile with them. However, at that moment in Afghan history, such a step would have been very controversial.

Pakistan did much better when it came to Al-Qaeda: Guantanamo Bay records show that around a hundred fighters from Afghanistan who were associated with Al-Qaeda and the Uighur movement and who were holed up in a mosque in the FATA area were arrested on 18 December 2001 and handed over to the US authorities in the first week of January 2002.[20] Interestingly, this information was not publicly shared either by Pakistan or by the US at the time. The arrest in March 2002 of Abu Zubaydah, Al-Qaeda's chief of operations, and in March 2003 of Khalid Sheikh Muhammad, the mastermind behind the 9/11 attacks, in Pakistan also indicates close collaboration between the ISI and the CIA.[21]

* * *

Meanwhile, in Afghanistan a new state structure had to be created virtually from scratch. Realities on the ground soon started directing the course of history, as those who had been on the receiving end during the Taliban's oppressive reign were now free to take control of their lives. The political forces that had fought and resisted the Taliban began descending upon Kabul in November 2001. The Northern Alliance, a conglomeration of all anti-Taliban political and militant groups, hardly needed any encouragement from American intelligence officials on the scene to do what it was all set to do anyway.

Things happened so rapidly that even as US State Department officials were drafting a brief for Colin Powell about the US options vis-à-vis
Kabul, they heard the news that Northern Alliance forces were entering
the city.[22] Earlier, Powell, to his credit, had even asked the Northern
Alliance to slow down and temper its enthusiasm, because he wanted the
planned conference in Bonn to precede the *de facto* formation of a
government in Afghanistan.[23] The State Department was clearly not as
up to date as the CIA and the Defense Department.

The Northern Alliance's leader Ahmed Shah Massoud had been
head and shoulders above his peers in both calibre and character. But
he had been assassinated by Al-Qaeda the day before the 9/11 attacks,
so organizational planning on the part of anti-Taliban Afghans was also
missing. The search was on for someone who could fill his shoes and
lead Afghanistan out of the dark ages.

The United Nations took the first step in this direction (though
American influence was clearly guiding it). Lakhdar Brahimi, an experienced and talented Algerian diplomat, was the UN secretary general's
special representative tasked with leading this effort. Various leaders
from the international community and representatives of different
Afghan factions met for nine days in November–December 2001 in
Bonn, Germany, to deliberate the future of Afghanistan. The varied back-
grounds of the Afghan participants, including some from the diaspora,
and the presence of such important regional actors as Pakistan and Iran
created a positive atmosphere. At the conference, the world's major
powers promised economic support, and that offered further hope to a
distressed and war-torn society.

It was a timely and constructive conference, but laborious negotiations were required before consensus was reached on some sensitive
aspects. Though largely shaped by the interests of the US and its allies,
the effort was seen as credible and productive. Many Pashtuns, however,
grumbled that their interests were not adequately represented. Even
more significant was the absence of anyone representing the Taliban.
No one was expecting Mullah Omar to be at the table, but it might have
been worth trying to engage some moderate Taliban officials (or those

aligned with them) in the process. But the opportunity was missed. Lakhdar Brahimi acknowledged this in an interview in 2009: 'We are now paying the price for what we did wrong from day one . . . the people who were in Bonn were not fully representative of the rich variety of the Afghan people.'[24]

It was a useful exercise nonetheless and resulted in the appropriately titled 'Agreement on Provisional Arrangements in Afghanistan Pending the Re-establishment of Permanent Government Institutions'. Ordinary Afghans, especially those living in the urban centres, were full of hope for a new beginning. The conference's deliberations duly focused on the political, administrative and security steps needed to chart a new path for Afghanistan. It carefully laid the groundwork for establishing political processes and institutions of governance and then leaving it to Afghans to 'freely determine their own political future in accordance with the principles of Islam, democracy, pluralism and social justice'.[25] This all-embracing approach made a lot of sense in Afghanistan, where religion and politics could not easily be separated – as in many Muslim states; but at the same time, America had its favourites. Some of them had terrible reputations, but their human rights records were simply ignored.

It was agreed that an interim council should be formed, to be led for an initial period of six months by Hamid Karzai, who besides other things was a Pashtun from Kandahar. The choice of a Pashtun was intended to blunt the Taliban's appeal to Pashtun nationalism. It is unclear whether the American power brokers behind the arrangement fully understood that, without any significant positive change in the lives of ordinary people, the intended impact of this choice could only be short lived.

More problematically, the Bonn conference micromanaged the configuration of the first cabinet – even to the extent of its ethnic composition. A balance was indeed necessary, but now non-Pashtuns received most of the important ministries. The agreement also stipulated that a provisional government appointed by a *loya jirga* would take over for two years, during which time a new constitution would be written. This was a clever strategy, as Afghanistan needed time to emerge from the trauma of recent years and start settling down.

During a conversation in 2013 with a thoughtful mid-ranking American official with field experience in Afghanistan, I asked what he thought was the most important American contribution to the country. He replied that it was 'the gift of democracy, which Afghans really couldn't benefit from'. Further probing as to whether he thought Afghans were really incapable of adapting to democracy, or if a better strategy was needed to make it work, elicited an even more insightful response: 'It is like we presented an Afghan with a new car but he ran towards us whenever he wanted gas or maintenance expenses. It was an unrealistic expectation.'[26]

To take up this metaphor, in an area with no roads or easy access to petrol the choice of a car as a gift was anyway a poor one. This is not to suggest at all that Afghan culture is anti-democratic in spirit. The legitimacy of any idea is in question if it is seen as a gift from foreigners, but especially so if those foreigners are regarded as invaders or occupiers. For a project to have a reasonable chance of success, it has to be Afghan led and Afghan owned. Any hint that outsiders are calling the shots can jeopardize the whole effort from the word go. For the minority ethnic groups, as well as for many educated Pashtuns based in the urban centres, though, the road to democracy promised a route to empowerment. And that was a sufficient incentive to pursue this path.

* * *

Hamid Karzai was not a bad choice to spearhead the effort. Besides local political experience in the 1990s, he also had sufficient international exposure, having studied in India, survived in Pakistan and conducted business in the US. He had also led the anti-Taliban military campaign in Kandahar in November 2001. Though accompanied by 1,300 US marines, arguably the best soldiers in the US armed forces, it still needed courage to walk the streets of the Taliban's heartland. Despite having to contend with the dominance in his government of the bigwigs of yesteryear, Karzai was able to establish his leadership credentials fairly quickly, and in June 2002 he was picked by the *loya jirga* to lead the country for another two years, during which the new constitution of Afghanistan would be framed.

Whatever his reputation today, it should be recognized that he took over the reins of power at a time when much of Afghanistan's infrastructure was in ruins and when the country was literally littered with landmines. Hopelessness and despair were the order of the day. When he took the oath of office for the first time, Kabul was still enduring shelling and shooting. Under these trying circumstances, his government started out well, but five major issues were to undermine its potential to usher in meaningful and sustainable change.

Survival of the warlords

First, Karzai's hand was forced when it came to accommodating certain notorious warlords who were an integral part of the Northern Alliance. Mohammad Qasim Fahim, successor to Ahmed Shah Massoud, was known for his links to criminal gangs and was widely believed to have brutally murdered hundreds of his opponents during the Mujahideen government in the early 1990s. This group also included Abdul Rashid Dostum, the infamous Uzbek military commander and new deputy defence minister; Daoud Khan, a Tajik commander in the northeast; Ismail Khan, the governor of Herat; Gul Agha Sherzai, the governor of Kandahar; and Karim Khalili, a vice-president in the new political set-up. Most of them had an appalling record. Their private militias, recruited on ethnic and tribal lines, fought each other for resources and control over territory. During the civil war years (1992–94), these commanders had seized as much territory as they could by terrorizing the population. The 2005 Human Rights Watch report *Blood-Stained Hands: Past atrocities in Kabul and Afghanistan's legacy of impunity* documents war crimes during a single year (1992–93) and exposes the involvement of leading members of the Karzai camp in torture, rape and massacres. They all continued to control local armies whose primary loyalty was to them at a personal level and not to the government in Kabul. Many of them unilaterally assumed the title 'general'. Some of these warlords appeared somewhat reformed, having learnt their lesson at the hands of the Taliban; but public opinion was unlikely to change overnight.[27]

For Karzai, those warlords who controlled terrain, and especially customs revenues, were useful allies.[28] In some cases, these warlords were given prominent positions in the government in exchange for compliance with US goals.[29] President Bush's deputy secretary of defence, Paul Wolfowitz, told the US Senate in 2002 that he had sanctioned this approach on a somewhat unique pretext: 'I think the basic strategy here is first of all to work with those warlords or regional leaders, whatever you prefer to call them, to encourage good behavior.'[30]

The confession of Zalmay Khalilzad, the Afghan-American diplomat who was serving as the US ambassador to Afghanistan at the time, rings truer: 'the coalition did not seek a long-term occupation and was unwilling to expend the effort necessary to challenge and remove these figures.'[31] Whatever caused this policy choice, its result encouraged several smaller warlords in the southeast and central areas to maintain their local forces. The fact cannot be overlooked, of course, that many of them were anti-Taliban.

The strategy of cosying up to the warlords served short-term US and Afghan security interests well, but it had a downside. The oppressive mindset of these warlords was documented by a 2002 Human Rights Watch report, which revealed that warlords had intimidated delegates to *loya jirgas* with threats and the heavy presence of their militias.[32] Worst hit was Zabul Province, where local warlords – including the governor, who was aligned with Hekmatyar's Hizb-e-Islami – manipulated the process by only allowing their favourites to represent the province and by harassing independent candidates. The core problem was that these warlords were anti-democratic.

Local commanders associated with warlords were, in some cases, given security contracts and provided with US communications gear. They created the false impression that this equipment was directly linked to the fearsome B-52 bombers. The US's apparent reliance on these warlords to overpower Taliban supporters also led to anti-US feeling.

Besides engendering lawlessness and fear, this trend was especially counterproductive on two levels. First, the regional players (especially

Pakistan and Iran) interpreted this as giving them the green light to support or revive their own favourite warlords in Afghanistan. Ismail Khan, who regained control of Herat after 2001, was a regular recipient of direct aid from Iran, including weapons for his forces.[33] This pattern provoked the gradual resurgence of the Haqqani group, which had its support base in the Afghan provinces of Paktika, Paktia and Khost, though its leadership was stationed in the Waziristan area of Pakistan.

Secondly, for ordinary Afghans this was seen as a rerun of the chaotic pre-Taliban days. The Karzai government derived some political and monetary benefit from engaging warlords, but it was a bad deal for the future of the country. Karzai's closeness to these rivals of the Taliban served to inspire the Taliban afresh in years to come, besides blocking the rise of a new generation of leaders open to democratic culture.

Centralization – a failure to learn from history

The second issue was largely of Karzai's own making. Encouraged by his close political associates,[34] he choreographed the establishment of a centralized state, ignoring Afghan history and geography. The last thing a mountainous country with a tradition of tribal autonomy and strong ethnic rivalry needed was a unitary form of government.[35]

The organizers of the 2001 Bonn Conference had hoped to avert civil war by suggesting the establishment of a strong central government that would share power among the various ethnic groups. This notion was codified in the 2004 Afghan constitution, by which virtually all executive, legislative and judicial authority was vested in the national government. By extension, this made Kabul responsible for policy, budget and revenue generation. The concentration of power in Kabul was a logical outcome, and the disgruntled periphery was further cut off from the centre. The lessons of history were thrown in the dustbin.

Centralization undermined Afghan potential in a variety of ways. The system was simply incapable of addressing the country's diversity. An

overburdened management sitting in Kabul, responsible for adminis-
tering 34 provinces and 398 districts, could hardly be efficient.[36] In a
cultural context, it was seen as intrusive. Districts, which were established as the basic administrative unit, had no direct budgeting provision,
making them powerless and ineffectual. A committed but disillusioned
International Security Assistance Force (ISAF) official explained to me
that 'one of the costs of not resourcing the district centres includes
leaving vacant the position that records land and deeds. This is a prime
driver of conflict among tribes who have property disputes.'[37]

Kabul never recovered from this flawed arrangement, as is evident
from a 2010 assessment of the International Crisis Group: 'With governors appointed by the centre and money controlled by ministries in
Kabul, what little local government that does exist at best provides next
to nothing to people and at worst is predatory.'[38]

The abandoned space at the local level was seen by the Taliban as an
opportunity to reappear in the public square.

Security policy contradictions

Aside from the 8,000 US troops tasked with tracking and tackling the
Taliban and Al-Qaeda leadership in the south and east of Afghanistan,
the separate UN-mandated International Security Assistance Force
(ISAF) was constituted in early 2002 to secure Kabul. Nineteen nations
contributed to this 5,000-strong force to begin with. With this number,
the force could barely police Kabul; monitoring anything beyond the
suburbs stretched it far too thin.

The approach was dubbed a 'light footprint' one, and the idea was
borrowed from a UN report (known in academic circles as the Brahimi
Report) that was released in 2000. The report set the parameters of
'light footprint' and rationalized it as an approach designed to 'avoid the
creation of parallel institutions and dual systems which undermine
local authority, hinder coordination and precipitate competition.'[39]

Ironically, not only was ISAF unaccountable to the Afghan government, but it even shied away from any meaningful coordination with it.

Despite constant demands from the Afghans, it was only after NATO took over the reins of ISAF in August 2003 that the UN extended the force's mandate to cover the whole of Afghanistan. Even then, the expansion happened in fits and starts, and the process was only finally completed in October 2006, when ISAF took over command of the US-led coalition forces operating in the east.[40] In the meanwhile, synchronization between different military commands and various country contingents was poor, to say the least. The absence of any grand strategy to stabilize Afghanistan was obvious, but it took a while before the cause of this failure in planning became clear.

The Iraq campaign proved a fatal distraction for American policy makers and military commanders at a time when the Afghanistan project needed their undivided attention. Saddam Hussain's coterie in Iraq was undoubtedly involved in crimes against humanity, but the Bush administration over-reached itself in trying to fix the world.[41] It altered the power balance in the Middle East – not necessarily a bad thing, but it made the United States much less popular around the world. The prolonged American stay in Iraq especially complicated the situation, and empowered Al-Qaeda and the like. The Afghan campaign became a mere sideshow during the US engagement in Iraq. The demoralized Taliban in and around Afghanistan, on the other hand, drew fresh inspiration from the brutal insurgency in Iraq.

Critical time was also lost as Western strategists struggled with whether counterterrorism techniques were suited to Afghanistan, or whether the situation was ripe for devising a new counterinsurgency (COIN) model. International security consultants minted money while the confusion lasted. Afghanistan needed an effective civilian law enforcement infrastructure to be built with the aid of police professionals, rather than rely solely on 'stabilization operations' conceived and implemented by defence officials.[42] Interagency disconnect in the US was at least partially responsible for missing this point.

Even intelligence resources, a vital element in such a campaign, were not utilized appropriately. In the early months of the military campaign, only a handful of US State Department or other civilian officials were physically available in Afghanistan to conceive and plan any state-building efforts. To make up the shortfall, 13 teams of CIA operatives, whose primary job was to hunt terrorists, were asked to stay in remote corners of Afghanistan to coordinate the political efforts.[43] The task they were given was beyond the capabilities of an organization that was well on the way to becoming a militarized intelligence outfit.

Reform of the security sector in Afghanistan fell to four states, each of which was assigned a specific field: the US was given responsibility for the military; Italy, the judiciary; Germany, the police; and Britain, counter-narcotics. These roles were interconnected, but apparently that was not enough to bring planners from those countries to a single table to think things through, and there was no effort made to develop any management structure that would oversee the four pillars. More specifically, as leading world expert on the subject Robert Perito laments, 'none of the donors focused on the need to strengthen the one Afghan institution – the Interior Ministry – that would be responsible for overseeing and supporting the Afghan police'.[44]

An Afghan National Police (ANP) force was belatedly sanctioned in April 2003 by presidential decree. Recruited in haste and rushed through training, the ANP only exacerbated the local capacity-building challenge.[45] An International Crisis Group report of August 2007 substantiates this claim:

> The state of the Afghan National Police (ANP) nearly six years after the fall of the Taliban reflects the international community's failure to grasp early on the centrality of comprehensive reform of the law enforcement and justice sectors.[46]

In the absence of a dependable local police force, criminals had a field day. The Taliban couldn't be far behind, but no one realized it until the Taliban revival became public knowledge.

Ignoring education – lack of vision

Sadly, the education sector – the most potent instrument of change in any society – failed to receive the donor priority that it deserved. It was understandable that security objectives should drive policy choices in the beginning, but a continuing clash between development goals and security compulsions was unsustainable for nation-building purposes. Education was especially critical in a society where a radicalized minority had dominated society through coercion and oppression. That the Taliban were able to get away with that in the name of Islam was something that was worth bearing in mind while a development agenda was crafted. Even from a purely counterterrorism perspective, a counter-narrative to misdirected and misplaced Taliban ideology was sorely needed. The creation of a vibrant education system was hence a common-sense solution. But, as they say, 'common sense is uncommon' – a truism that is particularly true in war zones.

In 2004, three years after the occupation began, primary school enrolment had risen from 0.9 million to nearly 4 million, and the proportion of girls receiving education from virtually zero to 35 per cent.[47] However, these figures were distorted by the high rate of enrolment in major cities such as Herat and Kabul, where girls made up 35–58 per cent of the total; in the former Taliban strongholds of south Afghanistan, girls' enrolment was pitifully low – 3 per cent in Zabul, 5 per cent in Helmand and 7 per cent in Khost.[48]

Between 2003 and 2011, almost 5,000 new schools were built and enrolment reached around 7 million. This was an important achievement; but it is estimated that throughout this time around 40 per cent on average of the school population was not in school. Even more instructive is the fact that in the period between October 2005 and March 2007, 6 per cent of schools were burned down or closed down by insurgents, and by 2008 the number of attacks on schools, teachers and students had almost tripled to 670 – almost two attacks every day.[49] The Taliban knew exactly how dangerous public education was to their cause and agenda. However, once the pattern of attacks became clear, some steps to safeguard schools should have been taken involving the local population.

To give credit to ordinary Afghans, they wanted their children in school; but, as one astute reporter – Barry Bearak of the *New York Times* – reported in 2007, 'the accelerating demand for education is mocked by the limited supply'.[50] Interestingly, from 2001 onwards, the US Agency for International Development (USAID) invested only 5 per cent of its Afghanistan budget in education.[51] The disconnect between supply and demand was glaring.

Overlooking economic needs

The overwhelmingly security-driven focus of the international forces in Afghanistan left few resources for development projects or to stimulate economic growth. Over 70 per cent of Afghans live in rural areas and depend almost entirely on agriculture-related activities. The fact that this sector generates about 40 per cent of GDP and employs about 70 per cent of the workforce explains its importance in the national economy.[52] Any investment in improving irrigation systems, modernizing equipment, increasing crop productivity and facilitating farm-to-market access would have done wonders for the rural economy.

In parallel, the restoration of the road and communications infrastructure would have stimulated job opportunities and would have connected up different parts of the country, while encouraging local trade. Similarly, large-scale projects could also have signalled progress and the international community's long-term commitment to Afghanistan. None of this was rocket science, but strangely none of it appeared on Kabul's priority list.[53] Some $10 billion were pledged for Afghanistan's reconstruction by international donors from 2001 to 2003, but very little of the money trickled down to the ground level, and some of the funding promises remain unfulfilled. For instance, a $300 million project for small businesses that was authorized early on by the US Congress was never financed.[54]

A 2003 RAND study revealed that:

Among the recent operations, the United States and its allies have put 25 times more money and 50 times more troops on a per capita basis into post-conflict Kosovo than into post-conflict Afghanistan.[55]

In real per capita terms, the aid in the initial two years (2002–03) hovered around $50 per capita. This falls far short of other comparable post-conflict situations: in Kosovo the figure was $814 in 2000–01; in Haiti, $152 in 1995–96; and in Bosnia, $1,390 in 1996–97.[56]

The RAND study, compiled by Ambassador James Dobbins, also focused on the important lessons learnt by the United States in its nation-building efforts since the Second World War. Two of its most salient points were especially relevant for the ongoing project in Afghanistan: 1) It is nearly impossible to put together a fragmented nation if its neighbours try to tear it apart, so every effort should be made to secure their support; and 2) Accountability for past injustices can be a powerful component of democratization, but it should be attempted only if there is a deep and long-term commitment to the overall operation.

The international effort in Afghanistan in its early years was unimpressive on both counts. However, of more significance were the missed opportunities in the socio-political and economic arenas of the nation-building project, which in turn opened up a chance for the Taliban to stage a comeback in the coming years. Afghans themselves were to be blamed, too, for failing to get their priorities right and to engage with donors more proactively. Regional factors were bound to play an increasingly influential role in this debilitating scenario.

CHAPTER FIVE

Setting the stage for the Taliban revival in Afghanistan
The role of sanctuaries in Pakistan's FATA (2002-05)

While Pakistan was experimenting with democracy in the 1990s, its top military brass remained influential and intrusive. They considered it their exclusive and God-given right to define Pakistan's regional and security interests, and Pakistani politicians and the civilian bureaucracy offered them every opportunity to do so through incompetence and poor governance.

But one major change was discernible in this pattern. Some senior military officers now realized that the policies introduced by the former military dictator General Zia ul Haq were proving a disaster for the country. General Pervez Musharraf was one of them. He was an ambitious, liberal and daredevil type of soldier. His education in Turkey and his family's progressive orientation had a lasting impact on his ideas. Though nationalist to the core, he was broadminded and tolerant when it came to religion.

Musharraf had risen to the position of army chief in late 1998, thanks to Prime Minister Nawaz Sharif, who preferred him over Ali Kuli Khan Khattak – a Pashtun general who was not only senior to Musharraf, but was at least as capable and qualified. In making his choice, Sharif was swayed by the chequered history of civil–military relations in the country. Though a product of the Zia era, this was Sharif's second tenure as prime minister and he wanted to be his own man. Khattak came from a renowned military family and was politically well connected; Sharif considered the urban middle-class Musharraf, who belonged to the Urdu-speaking minority community, a safer bet.

The top military were uncomfortable with the signs of 'civilian supremacy' and with the democratic government's friendly overtures towards India. They wanted to retain independence in the security policy arena. Eventually, after some serious differences with the military (especially over the Kargil operation in Kashmir, which is discussed below), Sharif decided to 'retire' Musharraf on 12 October 1999, in a surprise move timed to coincide with Musharraf's absence from the country. A new army chief was appointed. But the drama unravelled with disastrous consequences for Sharif, as Musharraf's loyal deputies defied Sharif. Among them were a handful of generals who were very sympathetic towards the Afghan Taliban, including corps commander Lieutenant General Mahmood Ahmed (later appointed as head of ISI).

Musharraf was on a plane home when all of this unfolded. Sharif unsuccessfully tried to divert the flight and even to arrest the general on arrival. But the army was too strong to take such 'humiliation' lying down: the top generals in Rawalpindi had practically taken over the reins of government by the time Musharraf's plane landed at Karachi and he was presented with a *fait accompli*. Sharif and his cabinet were now enjoying military hospitality in handcuffs! Musharraf wore the crown happily and lost no time in allowing those surrounding him to convince him that he was a man of destiny for his nation. In this respect, all dictators think alike.

General Pervez Musharraf's arrival on the Pakistani political scene was initially a damper for religious extremist groups operating in Pakistan, and the 9/11 attacks allowed him to go after militant organizations inside Pakistan with more vigour. In a major speech to the nation on 12 January 2002, he was quite categorical that 'no party in future will be allowed to be identified with words like Jaish [armed groups], Lashkars [militias] or Sipah [army]' and he emphasized that 'We should stop interfering in the affairs of others and stop using violence as a means to thrust our point of view on others.'[1] He had banned some domestic sectarian terrorist groups in August 2001, but now he added

to that list groups such as the Kashmir-focused Lashkar-e-Taiba.[2] This
was no small step – at least in theory – as this was the same Musharraf
who, in April 1999, had confided to a group of retired military officers
that the 'Taliban are my strategic reserve and I can unleash them in tens
of thousands against India when I want.'[3]

Meanwhile, the country's religious political parties were galvanized
to condemn Pakistan's 'U-turn' on support for the Taliban in Afghanistan
and the country's new status as an ally of the US in the newly launched
'war on terror'. Some religious figures went overboard, with one Mufti
Nizamuddin Shamzai, a well-known cleric and head of the Binori
Madrasa complex in Karachi, issuing a *fatwa* (religious edict) declaring
Jihad in response to the US military campaign in Afghanistan.[4] Very
few responded to the call, as it amounted to an obvious invitation to
commit suicide and no suicide bombers were yet in the pipeline: the
situation would have to turn far more ugly before such fanatics could be
produced.

Still, the organizations that were banned in Pakistan in 2002
continued to operate under different names. Those who were particularly notorious in these outfits and who feared retribution conveniently
moved to FATA. For the Arab fighters coming in from Afghanistan, this
provided a unique opportunity to network with their like-minded
extremist brethren from various parts of Pakistan, especially Punjab. In
FATA they started mingling and planning for future operations.

Many of the home-grown Pakistani militants had been trained and
groomed by the security apparatus to 'bleed India' in the Kashmir
area during the 1990s; but after President General Musharraf joined
the US-led 'war on terror', most of them became virtually 'homeless'.
A couple of groups adopted a lower profile and sent their warriors
on long leave, to avoid any confrontation with the military. Those
groups that were more independent just changed their names and
hoped that the cheques from donors in the Gulf and Arab world
would continue rolling in. This strategy bore fruit, as is evident from a
December 2009 leaked US memo signed by Secretary of State Hillary
Clinton, in which she referred to private donors from Kuwait, Qatar,

UAE and Saudi Arabia as major sources of funding for militants in Pakistan and Afghanistan.[5]

Like the Afghan Taliban and Al-Qaeda, the Pakistani militants were confused and rudderless for a while, but they soon regrouped, benefiting from turmoil in the tribal areas of the country, where they could organize, strategize and train. The Pakistani security services misinterpreted the intervening silence as proof that their strategy had been successful. A series of terrorist campaigns across the country was still some time away.

* * *

In my travels through FATA, I had the opportunity to admire its mesmerizing terrain and beauty. A road journey to the Khyber agency's border town of Landi Kotal in the early 1980s was one of the biggest adventures of my childhood. My father had some official business in the area, and for the family it was vacation time! Those were the 'Afghan Jihad' years, but the route – which since 2001 has been used to transport NATO supplies – was considered quite safe at the time. There were no visible signs of conflict, except for a few Afghan refugee camps dotted around here and there.

On the way, about 10 miles short of our destination, we stopped at the famous Ali Masjid (mosque), located at the narrowest point of the Khyber Pass. The locals firmly believe that Ali ibne Abi Talib, the Prophet Mohammad's cousin and son-in-law, and the 'patron saint' of Sufis the world over, visited this place and built the charming little mosque with his own hands. As evidence, they point to a huge rock perched precariously in the middle of a steep incline that carries what is believed to be the handprint of Ali.[6]

Ali's travels to the area are not recorded in mainstream Arab history, but it is entirely possible that he was here, since the Khyber Pass is named after the fort of Khyber, which is situated near the city of Medina, where Ali led Muslims to a historic victory over a group of Jews after a pitched battle.[7] As referred to earlier, the Afridi tribe, known for its bravery and courage, is the proud guardian of the Khyber Pass.

Intriguingly, Afghans believe that Ali is buried in the city of Mazar-i-Sharif, the most important city in the north of Afghanistan, which is in fact named after Ali's *Mazar* (meaning 'exalted tomb'). Everyone else in the Muslim world believes that Ali is buried in the Iraqi city of Najaf.

The Khyber Pass area is also sacred in the Buddhist tradition, and some Hindu and Sikh families still reside there, too. A nearby nineteenth-century British fort overlooks this strategic point and adds to the historic value of the area for tourists. Unfortunately, hardly any public funds have ever been invested in developing tourism in this historic and enchanting part of the world. Pashtuns – who are very hospitable by nature – would have won the hearts of tourists. The list of missed opportunities is long.

* * *

Pakistan's policy choices have ensured that the only 'tourists' who have travelled to the area in modern times have been Mujahideen, extremist ideologues and criminals. The local inhabitants of FATA, labouring under a tyrannical model of governance but hopeful of change, have naturally been attracted to new ideas presented to them. Tribal identity and ethos held the society in thrall to begin with, but the emergence of a new class of leaders – belonging to militant groups of various stripes – started to transform and tarnish the social order.

The influx of Arab, Central Asian and Punjabi militants that started in 1980s gained real momentum in the aftermath of 9/11. The rising violence confused ordinary Pakistanis and made public policy choices much more complicated. Meanwhile a host of other factors were also at play – from the ill-timed India–Pakistan border tensions of 2002–03 and explosive revelations in 2004 of nuclear proliferation (see below), to the creeping impact of the controversial US campaign in Iraq on the Muslim world in general and South Asia in particular. Only in hindsight can we gain a clear picture of the complex situation. Policy makers and strategists in the US and Europe were perhaps too tied up with trying to manage the erupting disaster in Iraq to see what was happening in Pakistan. General Pervez Musharraf, the darling of America at the time, made all the right noises when he met Western leaders, but his decisions on the ground shattered the country. But to give credit where credit is due – Musharraf did take some bold policy initiatives. The trouble is, those decisions were seldom implemented.

By 2002, Musharraf had assumed the title 'president' after a flawed referendum. National elections were also held in response to public demands for a return to democracy. Musharraf realized that Pakistan was not short of politicians who, given their feudal background and vested interests, would be ready to join hands with a military ruler in the 'national interest'. And his assessment was spot on, though the political wing of Pakistan's ISI also played its traditional role in inspiring the creation of a new political force – basically old wine in new bottles – to form a pro-Musharraf government in Islamabad and the four provinces. But what happened in the Khyber Pakhtunkhwa Province (then known as NWFP) was both mysterious and unprecedented.

The political rise of Muttihada Majlis-e-Amal (MMA) was meteoric. Formed in 2002, this coalition of five religious political parties won the provincial elections in NWFP (and even emerged as the leading opposition party in the National Assembly of Pakistan). This created a propitious environment for radicalization to flourish in the province.

It was an amazing achievement for this assortment of religious parties, associated with various Muslim sects and with divergent political agendas, to come together in government. The alliance comprised the Deobandi-dominated Jamiat Ulema-e-Islam (JUI), the Barelvi-oriented Jamiat Ulema-e-Pakistan, the traditionally Islamist Jamaat-e-Islami (JI), the Shia Tehrik-e-Jafria Pakistan, and the Wahhabi-inspired Jamiat Ahle Hadith.

The alliance made full use of prevailing political opinion, which was highly exercised by the foreign presence in Afghanistan and by Pakistan's involvement in the 'war on terror', both of which were seen in the country as very controversial campaigns. Most interesting was the manipulation of the election symbol – a 'book'. The MMA conveniently claimed that the 'book' was in fact the Holy Koran.[8] Faced with the daunting challenge of competing with two strong, progressive political forces – the Pakistan People's Party (PPP) and the Awami National Party (ANP) – it offered people a simple choice: either vote for the Koran or for American-backed secular parties. Ill-equipped to detect the manipulation, the people voted for the Koran.

For the MMA, constructing a political alliance was relatively easy; reaching consensus on contentious religious issues was much harder. Intolerance and rigidity were serious obstacles to effective policy making. If the alliance ever had a chance of making a positive mark, its association with Maulana Fazlur Rahman robbed it of that hope. Rahman was in charge of the JUI faction that dominated the MMA and was widely known in Pakistan for his greed for power, his financial excesses and especially his proclivity to compromise on principle at the first opportunity. That said, he was not the only one in the MMA with such a reputation.

The outcome was predictable: corruption, nepotism and incompetence were rampant during the MMA's five years in power. Unsurprisingly, its policies curtailed civil liberties, slowed progressive legal reforms and undermined religious tolerance. Women's rights received a setback. So did the reform of madrasas – federal government wanted them to include science on the curriculum and to register foreign students.[9] The energies of the MMA government in the province were channelled elsewhere, though, as they banned music on public transport.

The most significant development, however, was the passage by the provincial assembly in July 2005 of the 'Hisba Bill', which amounted to the strict imposition of Islamic law, as interpreted by the MMA's leaders.[10] Despite major objections by opposition parties – and even by the federal government in Islamabad – the MMA went ahead with the controversial project. Besides opening up more job opportunities for supporters of the MMA alliance, it created a new position of *mohtisib* (ombudsman), tasked with investigating public corruption and monitoring individuals' moral behaviour. Vigilante action, such as the blackening of billboards in Peshawar that featured female models, was the predictable outcome. The MMA was not a militant outfit, but its policies offered extremists a golden opportunity to expand their space and to gain time to organize and pursue their dangerous agenda.

Though the Supreme Court of Pakistan declared various aspects of the 'Hisba Bill' unconstitutional, the MMA government was still able to defy the ruling by renaming provisions of the law and by changing procedural rules. President General Pervez Musharraf turned a blind eye to many of the MMA's excesses because he needed its votes in the national legislature for a major constitutional amendment that would allow him to serve as both army chief and president. This behind-the-scenes alliance with Musharraf inspired critics to call the MMA government a 'Mullah–Military Alliance'.[11]

Afrasiyab Khattak, a respected Pashtun politician and former chairman of Pakistan's Human Rights Commission, went a step further, alleging that:

> [The MMA's] phenomenal rise in the October 2002 elections was not just coincidental, but a part of the political plans of the military. Without the threat of religious extremism, the military would have lost its utility for Western powers.[12]

The fact that the madrasa degrees of MMA leaders were declared the equivalent of a standard BA degree (the minimum qualification required for candidates in the 2002 elections), also indicates government support. A senior military officer I interviewed on the subject, however, claimed that the army's policies only inadvertently helped the MMA in 2002, as Musharraf was reportedly furious when he heard of the MMA's electoral success. If the arrangement was choreographed, it is likely that it was managed at the lower levels of the intelligence agencies (though sheer incompetence on the part of the agencies cannot be ruled out either).

More obvious, however, was the MMA's unwillingness to support the counterterrorism efforts of President Musharraf, allowing the Taliban to establish and expand their networks in the NWFP.[13] As the Taliban groups grew stronger, they started attacking military and government infrastructure in FATA; but in NWFP, the Taliban did not, at least initially, confront the government directly. Instead they focused on ideological targets, such as girls' schools, ancient Buddhist shrines, women's rights activists, video and music shops, and barbershops (for shaving beards, which was deemed anti-Islamic).[14] The failure of the MMA government to monitor and prevent the movement of militants from FATA to NWFP was to prove devastating for the security situation in the province.

Musharraf had instructed the Pakistan Army to move into the FATA area, but very few Pakistani military officers knew the terrain and culture well enough to operate there. The rifts between the FATA agencies and the perennial tribal rivalries within the agencies were a complicating factor for any non-Pashtun. Out of the seven FATA agencies, only Orakzai agency does not share a border with Afghanistan, and each has a dominant tribe or tribal group, as well as physical features that distinguish it from all the others.[15] Across from FATA lie five Afghan provinces – Kunar, Nangarhar, Paktia, Khost and Paktika – all dominated by Pashtuns.

When the US started trying to persuade Pakistan to have a more vibrant military presence in the area, there were not even any proper roads in FATA to connect the seven tribal agencies. The type of terrain in the area can be gauged from the fact that the Khyber railway, built at enormous cost by the British in 1920, threads its way through 34 tunnels and crosses 92 bridges and culverts on its 42-kilometre journey from Peshawar to Landi Kotal.

Though geography has both defined and influenced the role and status of many Pashtun tribes, the 'relationships between them dating back hundreds of years are complex and complicated by feuds, disputes, ancient alliances, and political marriages'.[16] Most tribes in FATA have blood relations in Afghanistan: only Afridi and Mehsud do not (which is why most of their business, political and other networking interests lie inside Pakistan).

It is generally acknowledged that during the post 9/11 US campaign in Afghanistan, 'Pakistan provided extensive land, air, and seaport accessibility, as well as a host of other logistical and security-related provisions'.[17] Counterterrorism operations inside Pakistan were a different story. In response to a US request in late 2001, Pakistan first deployed its forces in Khyber and Kurram agencies in December 2001, primarily to capture Al-Qaeda operators fleeing Afghanistan in the aftermath of the US military campaign.[18] When the US further insisted that it monitor and pursue militants in the area, in 2002 Pakistan launched its first proper military campaign in FATA, carefully named Operation Meezan (implying an effort to estimate the worth of its opponents). Thus the military entered FATA for the first time since the country's independence in 1947.[19] The declared purpose of the operation was to support the US military action across the border and check the flow of militants. A Pakistani military officer who participated in the operation as a major (later rising to the rank of brigadier while serving in the ISI) referred to the experience as a model for US–Pakistan collaboration, as both sides regularly shared intelligence at the time. He complained, however, that the US side seldom acknowledges Pakistani goodwill in the earlier phase of the war on terror.[20] Roughly 25,000 military and paramilitary troops were deployed in this action – an inadequate number, given the long border and the difficult terrain. The figure increased gradually to around 70,000 within a year, as US funds started flowing in to support the operations.[21] Militants responded strongly to this presence, which led to many casualties in the Pakistani camp.

The Pakistani forces involved in Operation Meezan – army units, Special Services Group (commandos) and paramilitary Frontier Corps – were all learning on the job and had received little in the way of specific information about the location and profiles of the militants. Aside from the Frontier Corps, which had some limited experience of counterinsurgency, all the other components of Pakistan's armed forces were trained for conventional warfare with India, so this was a new experience for them. A Pakistani officer who was part of the operation explained to me that all he was tasked with was looking for 'foreigners', a term roughly translated as Arabs and Central Asians. Afghans lay outside the definition. Consequently, many 'cordon and search' operations were conducted in Wana, the biggest town in South Waziristan agency, and targeted tribal leaders who were hiding some 'foreigners' in their midst. Dozens of Al-Qaeda fighters were apprehended and turned over to the ISI, which, after brief interrogation, handed them over to the US. Pakistan kept hold of any Afghan Taliban that it captured in these operations. The US intelligence officials monitoring developments from the US embassy in Pakistan were aware of this 'selection bias',[22] but remained silent because the collaboration between the US and Pakistan in the 'war on terror' did not refer to Afghan Taliban at all. Some CIA and US defence sources later claimed that this was because the Taliban were seen as a 'spent force'.[23] Obviously, both the CIA and the US military grossly miscalculated the potential of a Taliban revival.

At this point, Pakistan's campaign against the militants was derailed by a regional development that overshadows every major issue in South Asia: the continuing India–Pakistan tussle. In the aftermath of two terrorist attacks in India in 2002, a large detachment of that country's troops moved towards the border with Pakistan, with the aim of browbeating Pakistan into taking action against Kashmir-focused militant groups operating from its soil. For Musharraf, this was simply unacceptable. Also the cause of Kashmir was far more important to Pakistan than was Afghanistan – and Pakistan's military seemed ever ready to take on India, despite its size and resources. It was a matter of honour.

India's concern about Pakistani support for militancy in Kashmir – which for Pakistan was a 'freedom fight' – was legitimate, but it was mistaken in the belief that any military projection would deter Pakistan. In a kneejerk reaction, Pakistan moved a significant number of its troops to the border with India, and FATA was neglected just when it needed special attention. In Pakistani policy circles, the view was that the Indian move was fully backed by the US and its purpose was to paint Pakistan further into a corner. This only made Pakistan feel more insecure, diluting its energy to go after groups that were regarded as terrorist organizations by India.

Pakistan's security dilemma was further reinforced by revelations of nuclear proliferation. An internal Pakistani investigation into the matter eventually led to the appearance on national television, on 4 February 2004, of Dr Abdul Qadeer Khan, a national hero for his role in Pakistan's nuclear programme: 'The investigation has established that many of the reported activities did occur, and that these were invariably initiated at my behest.' The decisions, he said, 'were based in good faith but on errors of judgment related to unauthorized proliferation activities'.[24]

Dr Khan was referring to allegations that he, along with a handful of his colleagues, had sold nuclear technology secrets – especially about uranium enrichment – to Libya, Iran and North Korea. Benazir Bhutto, who twice served as prime minister of Pakistan (1988–90; 1993–96), voiced the suspicion of many Pakistanis and Westerners: 'Dr Khan was asked to fall on the sword in the name of the national interest, which means a cover-up for Musharraf.'[25]

US Deputy Secretary of State Richard Armitage had by now become a true diplomat. He was also certainly aware of the CIA briefing given to Musharraf to alert him to the proliferation racket operating from Pakistan. Armitage quickly declared that only individual Pakistanis were being investigated for nuclear proliferation and that the government of Pakistan was not involved.[26] This reassured Musharraf, but Pakistan's security establishment – senior army and intelligence officers – were not that sanguine about the direction of developments. They became more reclusive and inward looking.

Dr Khan was not popular in the country's top military circles, which knew of his financial corruption; but he remained very popular among the ordinary people, who continued to see him as the 'father of the bomb'. He was known to have given up a comfortable life abroad to struggle with meagre resources to build Pakistan's nuclear infrastructure. Under General Zia, Pakistan had carefully choreographed that image of him and now there was no going back. In reality, hundreds of Pakistani scientists were involved in the process, and some had contributed at least as significantly as Khan. Meanwhile a consensus was emerging between Western experts and Pakistani investigators that Khan was probably motivated by a desire to defy the West, make himself a hero to the Islamic world, and gain wealth.[27]

Pakistani public opinion about Khan did not alter, but the overall mood of the country turned more conspiratorial. For ordinary Pakistanis, the country was in the eye of the storm, and this episode was seen as a

Western effort to humiliate it and discredit its successes. In the public imagination, it was only a matter of time before there was a US assault on Pakistan with the aim of removing its nuclear weapons. The US did little to allay such misconceptions and fears. It is difficult to judge whether this was a 'strategic silence' or merely a failure of the US State Department to understand the dynamics on the ground in Pakistan and to respond with a smart PR strategy. This led to an environment in Pakistan where denial of the worsening situation in FATA became more entrenched. Every problem was attributed to outside factors. Only wrong policy choices could emerge from such trends.

Pakistan's 'peace deals' with militants in Waziristan

Around 2004, US intelligence assessments started indicating heightened militant activity inside Pakistan's FATA. At the same time, the Afghan government's complaints of support for the Taliban coming from Pakistan also became more vigorous. News of the presence of terrorist training camps in the area started to appear in the media. This led to an increase in US pressure on Musharraf to deliver.

The second phase of deployment and military action began in March 2004, when Pakistan's army launched the Kalusha operation near Wana in South Waziristan.[28] All attempts to convince tribal leaders to help flush out terrorists from the area fell on deaf ears.[29] The hurriedly organized campaign was meant to be a surgical operation targeting militant hideouts, but it turned out to be an utter failure, as the militants responded swiftly and decisively. An estimated 500 foreign terrorists and around 2,500 local militants were now at war with the Pakistani army.[30] This was an unexpected blow to the security forces, which had not been expecting much resistance. Pakistan's army responded with indiscriminate bombing, unintentionally aiding the militant cause with the resultant high civilian casualties.

Contrary to standard principles of warfare, it was at this juncture in 2004 that a peace deal was struck with the militants. Known as the Shakai Agreement, it was conceived and implemented by the military leadership based in Peshawar. Pakistan's army was in a weak situation on the ground, and this was an inappropriate time to opt for a negotiated deal – but Musharraf was convinced by Lieutenant General Safdar Hussain, the then corps commander in Peshawar, to move in this direction. The general had little sympathy for the militants, but he had realized that his forces were neither trained nor mentally ready to operate in the area. Even within military circles, there was widespread confusion about the purpose of the whole military effort.

The 'peace deal' was a devastating blow to the tribal system in place. For the first time in modern Pashtun history, a deal was cut directly between the military and militants in a public ceremony held at a madrasa. For ordinary Pashtuns, it was a sign that it was now militants, not *maliks*, who held real power. It was only a matter of time before the *maliks* would be sidelined – a consequence that was not anticipated by the military leadership (likely because of poor homework).

* * *

It is pertinent here to introduce the two most important tribes of Waziristan – tribes whose mutual rivalry defines the politics of the area. The Wazirs (divided into two main sub-tribes – Ahmadzai and Uthmanzai) control the border regions between South Waziristan and Afghanistan. Their ancestral home is believed to have been in the Birmal Valley of Afghanistan, but now two-thirds of them live in the Bannu district of the KPK, while the remainder live in South Waziristan agency near Wana and the Shakai Valley. Known for their tribal unity and the harmony between their sub-tribes, the Wazirs have engaged in frequent blood feuds with the Mehsud tribe, which shares their home agency. Both Mehsuds and Wazirs are proud of their formidable reputation as warriors, and they take pride in their independence. For instance, Wazirs often mention in discussions that they have never paid taxes.[31]

The Mehsud tribe inhabits the northern regions of South Waziristan, near Razmak (North Waziristan). Most of the areas where Mehsuds live are mountainous, and they control critical road networks connecting Wazir land with the rest of Pakistan. According to historian and a former British governor of NWFP, Sir Olaf Caroe, Mehsuds would never consider submitting to a foreign power that has entered their land. They are also known for their trustworthiness. Over the decades, many Mehsud families have migrated to KPK and Karachi, and they have extensive links within mainstream Pakistan.

* * *

The Shakai Agreement was the first of several 'peace deals' that Pakistan negotiated with militants in FATA under President Musharraf during 2004–07. Within military circles, the officially stated purpose of the deals was to prevent the conflict zone from expanding and to avoid a head-on collision with the militants. The reality fell far short of this objective, and the approach proved counterproductive. The Shakai Agreement was signed by the government of Pakistan, through the FATA Secretariat in Peshawar, and the charismatic 27-year-old militant leader Nek Muhammad and his militant commanders at Shakai, South Waziristan, on 24 April 2004. Nek Muhammad, a Wazir tribesman, was known in the region for his courage and fighting skills. He was close to Afghan Taliban commander Saif Rahman Mansour and had provided sanctuary to Uzbek militant leader Tahir Yuldashev during the confrontation with Pakistan's army.[32] He also provided space for Arab militants to run their training facilities. The Zalikhel clan of the Ahmadzai sub-tribe were the main hosts to the Arabs, while its Yargulkhel sub-clan mainly hosted Uzbeks on the Wana side of South Waziristan.[33]

The presence of these foreign fighters in South Waziristan is abundantly clear from the fact that on 2 October 2003, the Pakistani army killed an Al-Qaeda leader, Ahmad Said Khadr (alias Abdur Rehman al-Canadi, also known as Abdur Rehman al-Masri) and Hassan Makhsum, chief of the China-focused East Turkestan Islamic Movement (ETIM), in a helicopter gunship attack in the Shakai area.[34] China considers ETIM to be a separatist movement involved in many violent attacks in its Muslim-dominated Xinjiang Province. This was a major Pakistani military success, but Chinese pressure to target Hassan Makhsum played a critical role in this decision.

The Shakai Agreement's ten signatories from the militants' side included two important names, besides that of Nek Muhammad – those of Noor Islam and Baitullah Mehsud, both of whom later emerged as prominent leaders of the Pakistani militant Taliban movement. Interestingly, two representatives of the area in the National Assembly of Pakistan who were known for their pro-Taliban leanings acted as mediators in the deal: Merajuddin Qureshi and Maulana Abdul Malik Wazir. This explains the problematic role in state policy of the religious parties' political alliance, the MMA (see above).

The 'confidential' agreement notably included a clause stipulating the release of prisoners taken before and during the recent operations in the area. Accordingly, around 160 dangerous militants were released, which served to empower the militants rather than clip their wings. The government of Pakistan also agreed to pay compensation for those militants referred to as *shuhada* (martyrs) and for the collateral damage caused during the military operation. All this amounted to a surrender to the militants and acknowledgement of their rise to power.

The government also promised not to take action against Nek Muhammad and other wanted individuals and (most importantly) to allow 'foreign Mujahideen' to live peacefully in Waziristan – a totally unrealistic expectation, even at that time. The government expected all these foreign militants to be registered with the government and to hand over their weapons. In response, the representatives of the self-proclaimed Mujahideen e Waziristan (Fighters from Waziristan) undertook not to resort to any action against the land and government of Pakistan, nor to take any action against Afghanistan.[35] The reference to Afghanistan was vague enough to allow militants to continue their activities in that country, and they could interpret an attack on NATO forces there as beyond the domain of the agreement. The Pakistani military was at best naive not to have thought of this.

The agreement was described by both sides as 'a reconciliation between estranged brothers'.[36] In reality, huge amounts of money were also involved.[37] Nek Muhammad had made a case that he could only cut his links with Al-Qaeda fighters once he had repaid their loan – or returned the gift his group had received from them for providing them with sanctuary.[38] Against the advice of the FATA Secretariat, and especially its head, Brigadier Mahmood Shah, General Safdar Hussain paid the amount. US General Barno, commander of the Combined Forces Command in Afghanistan in 2003–05, wasted no time in calling General Safdar Hussain to congratulate him and thank him for formulating a policy that would isolate Al-Qaeda by draining it of local support in South Waziristan. This shows that he, too, was clueless about the dynamics of the situation in FATA. Pakistani militants had no intention of abiding by this understanding, since they had offered sanctuary to the foreign militants and it was against their custom to violate that.

The arrangement did work for roughly seven weeks – in the sense that there was no flare-up of violence; but soon differences arose as to the interpretation of a clause dealing with the 'registration' of foreign militants. The government believed that such militants were to be handed over to the state authorities, whereas the militants argued that there was no specific agreement on this point. When pushed, the militants asked for more time to deliver on this aspect, but clearly they were just procrastinating. After they missed a couple of deadlines, military operations were resumed on 11 June 2004.[39]

Nek Muhammad was killed by a Hellfire missile launched from a US Predator drone on 19 June 2004,[40] indicating US–Pakistan collaboration. The two countries' militaries, especially their special forces, had also been conducting joint training exercises in the area.[41] A few amendments were then made to the original Shakai Agreement to curb the activities of Al-Qaeda, but to little effect.[42]

The negative consequences of the deal outweighed its utility. Nek Muhammad became a hero in the eyes of the local populace; and although he was killed after he backed out of the deal, he created a new model of defiance for young radicals of the area. The recent history of FATA had witnessed many fighters, but hardly anyone had challenged Pakistan's military: in this sense Nek Muhammad had set a precedent. Secondly, Pakistan's army faced immense obstacles to re-arresting the militants who had been released as part of the arrangement and who had gone back to business as usual. At the end of the day, in the eyes of the local population, the militants achieved greater importance than the traditional tribal leaders, since Pakistan's government had accorded them an elevated status by engaging with them directly in negotiations.

The corps commander in Peshawar, General Safdar Hussain, had also emerged as the man in charge of everything in FATA, sidelining all political offices. He had done what he was trained to do: use force (he declared 'we are going to sort out the Ahmadzai Wazirs') – a strategy that backfired almost immediately.[43] He then jumped to the other extreme – appeasement – and that, too, failed (as it almost always does). In my interviews with Pashtuns from Peshawar and Mardan, they blamed the 'Punjabi' General Safdar Hussain for his ill-advised policy choices that enabled militants to acquire more space for manoeuvre and power projection.

In 2005, the militancy, which now increasingly had the appearance of an insurgency, expanded from the Wazir tribe of South Waziristan to the Mehsud tribe in the agency, an extremely dangerous development, given the British-era historical evidence that when the Wazirs and the Mehsuds pool their efforts they become truly invincible. Regular attacks on Pakistani military convoys and the targeting of military installations and local elements that were cooperating with the military were unnerving for Islamabad. The militants wanted the military out of FATA and desired total freedom to operate across the Durand Line in Afghanistan. The Iraq war had further inspired the militants in the area to take up arms against American forces next door.

Two interesting characters, Abdullah Mehsud and Baitullah Mehsud, emerged as major militant leaders during these times. The pro-Afghan Taliban Abdullah was captured in Afghanistan by the Northern Alliance and handed over to the US forces, which quickly dispatched him to Guantanamo Bay. There he stayed for a couple of years, lied to American interrogators about his nationality and posed as an innocent Afghan, caught in the middle of war.[44] He was duly released and, on his return to Waziristan, resumed his work where he had left off. Baitullah Mehsud, according to a senior Pakistani intelligence officer, was a semi-literate imam in a village mosque, having been a drop-out from a madrasa. He had fought on the side of the Taliban in Afghanistan during the late 1990s.

To bring calm to the Mehsud territories, Pakistan tried to broker yet another peace arrangement. A deal was inked between Baitullah Mehsud and the government of Pakistan on 7 February 2005 at Sararogha, South Waziristan.[45] General Safdar Hussain famously declared that Baitullah was 'not a rebel but a patriotic citizen and a soldier of this country'.[46] A secret agreement was signed, whereby Baitullah Mehsud undertook to neither harbour nor support any foreign fighter in the area. He also vowed not to attack any government functionary and property and agreed to allow development activities in the area. In return, Pakistan promised not to take any action against Baitullah Mehsud and his supporters for their previous activities.

To head off any future problems the government agreed to abide by the prevailing laws in FATA. It completely forgot that the prevailing law in FATA was lawlessness. Baitullah Mehsud also pledged that if any 'culprit' were to be found in his area, the Mehsud tribe would hand him over to the government authorities in FATA.[47] How he could ascribe to himself leadership of the Mehsud tribe was not explained. Reportedly, Maulana Fazlur Rahman, the leader of his own faction of Jamiat Ulema-e-Islam, helped bring the two sides to the negotiating table.[48]

This 'deal' had some major shortcomings. Interestingly, no clause covered cross-border infiltration or attacks in Afghanistan, and there was no demand for the surrender of 'foreign militants'. Pakistan was now increasingly concerned about security in its own area, and for that the authorities were ready to meet the militants halfway. This was bad news for the US, but it was not fully cognizant of the changing scene in FATA. So this loophole in the agreement meant that the Mehsud tribe could not be faulted by the Pakistan government if it was found to be involved in supporting militants' movement towards Afghanistan. Serious controversies also arose regarding the issue of financial payments to the militants during the peace negotiations. The BBC confirmed such reports, but some sources claimed that the money was meant as compensation for damage to property in South Waziristan that had occurred during the military campaign.[49] In any case, the arrangement clearly strengthened militants' influence and status in the area, as they practically won the freedom to expand their activities.

Two related issues are noteworthy here. First, as mentioned earlier, the Waziri–Mehsud tribal rivalry in the area was well entrenched, and the Pakistani army was attempting to widen that gulf by being soft on one tribe – to pit Mehsuds against Wazirs. This was a dangerous gamble, and it failed. For both Wazir and Mehsud tribesmen, the Pakistani army was an 'outside force', against which both tribes would eventually join hands. Second, Baitullah Mehsud and Haji Omar (a militant commander in Waziristan), principal signatories to the deal, continued to state publicly that they were committed to continuing their Jihad against the US-led coalition in Afghanistan – statements that were reported in the mainstream Pakistani media.[50] Their Jihad was directed at the foreign presence next door, as that was a popular theme in the region and made it easy to recruit the unemployed youngsters of the area. It was also another way of attracting funding from Al-Qaeda sources.

By 2006, the militant revolt had spread to the Uthmanzai Wazirs of North Waziristan, who started regularly attacking security forces and their convoys.[51] To give it its due, the Pakistani army did conduct various operations in the area, but the two 'peace deals' had set a new precedent: whoever challenged the government's writ derived greater leverage during negotiations.

The Musharraf government refused to learn this lesson and proceeded callously to cut another deal – which came to be known as the Miranshah Peace Accord – with the militants of North Waziristan on 5 September 2006. For the Pakistan government, there were some improvements in the way the arrangement was negotiated and signed. For instance, this time civilian administrators were involved in the process, and a detailed agreement was drafted before the 'signing ceremony'. The group of Uthmanzai Wazirs, which included local Taliban, religious leaders and tribal elders, undertook not to attack law enforcement agencies and government property, nor to establish parallel administrative structures. Importantly, they promised to halt cross-border movement in support of militancy in Afghanistan, provided no restrictions were imposed by the government on border crossings for the purposes of trade or to meet relatives. They agreed to reach out to all foreigners residing in North Waziristan and ask them either to leave Pakistan or to remain peaceful and abide by the agreement.

In return, the government promised to release all militants and civilians from the area who had been arrested during the recent military operation; to resume funding to local *maliks*; to remove all newly established checkpoints on roads; and to return all vehicles and weapons captured during the operation. As a bonus, it accepted the other side's demand for compensation to be paid to affected families for collateral damage. It also agreed to allow the tribesmen to carry small arms.[52]

Among the signatories, Hafiz Gul Bahadur and Sadiq Noor were known for having good relations with the Pakistani ISI. Some analysts believe that Mullah Omar endorsed the accord and persuaded the local militants to sign.[53] As under the Sararogha arrangement, some financial compensation was included in the deal, indirectly strengthening the militants' influence. Though the agreement was stricter over the issue of 'foreigners', around a hundred mid-level Taliban and Arab fighters were released from Pakistani custody, according to a 2006 International Crisis Group report.[54] This was a self-defeating proposition under any circumstances. Despite the agreement's clear mention of the supremacy of government authority in the area, the militants' flag (al-Rayah) was hoisted at the stadium where the deal was signed. *The News*, an important English-language newspaper in Pakistan, aptly said in its 7 September 2006 editorial: '[T]he government has all but caved in to the demands of the militants. More ominously, the agreement seems to be a tacit acknowledgment by the government of the growing power and authority of the local Taliban.'[55]

The militants upheld their end of the bargain for a few months after the deal was signed, but then returned to their old policies regarding collaboration with foreign militants and directly supporting cross-border movement. These deals in reality provided 'much-needed respite to the militants, enabling them to re-group and re-organise themselves'.[56] The militants expanded their support networks during the months of 'peace', and even during the relative calm in North Waziristan, militants continued to support some Taliban factions in South Waziristan and parts of Afghanistan. Brigadier Asad Munir, an ace officer in Pakistan's ISI who served in the area, acknowledges this: 'A focused strategy to deal with terrorists was never followed ... Because of this deal, foreign militants started operating openly. The only option for the locals was to accept Taliban rule.'[57] No further proof of the disastrous nature of Pakistani policy is needed.

Pakistan intended to reduce the losses its military was suffering, unaccustomed as it was to the terrain and lacking the weapons it needed in the area. It was also insufficiently motivated to take on the militants. A fact often ignored in Western discourse on the subject is that the US presence in Afghanistan was highly unpopular in the Pashtun areas of both Pakistan and Afghanistan, and it was an uphill struggle for the Pakistani army to go against the flow of public opinion in the country. Parallel to this, Pakistan all along wanted to remain friendly with elements of the Afghan Taliban, so that in time of need they could help Pakistan confront the spectre of rising Indian influence in Afghanistan. The 'peace deals' were, in part, a product of such factors and fears. In this process, Pakistan's policy makers and top security officials failed to understand the true nature of emerging radicalization trends in FATA. The Taliban were bound to move into KPK and beyond if unchecked, as many Pakistani writers and journalists warned – warnings that went unheeded by the state.[58]

Learning lessons from mistakes is a process, and thus Pakistan's limitations with regard to the initial 2004 peace deal are understandable. However, once the consequences of that faulty arrangement were exposed (in the shape of heightened militancy and expansionist Taliban tendencies), Musharraf should have employed smarter tactics in FATA. Arguably, his personal political ambitions and his dependence on his approval ratings within the military stood in the way. Just as the first of these deals was being finalized, he was pushing for major amendments to the constitution of Pakistan, drawing on help from religious parties in the country. Within military circles, he was also careful not to be seen to be too friendly with the US: he knew he was lucky to have survived two assassination attempts in 2003–04 involving junior officials from the armed forces, including a special forces soldier.

In a lighter vein, the lawlessness of the Pashtun tribal belt brought some unexpected dividends for Pakistan also. A Pakistan Air Force officer shared with me an interesting episode. In late 2006, the air force was trying hard to convince its US counterparts that it needed Falcon View, US software used in aircrafts for advanced mapping and referencing. At the time, it was a restricted item under US law and Pakistan could not gain access to it. As luck would have it, a Pakistani army officer visiting Bara market in the Khyber agency of FATA – known as a hub of smuggled items – found the software going cheap in a shop. It was duly presented to the Pakistan Air Force. Apparently someone had stolen it in Afghanistan from a US military base and it ended up in the open market across the frontier. The Bara market shopkeeper had believed it to be a computer game for kids![59]

The return of the Afghan Taliban and the role of 'Quetta Shura'

The terrorist sanctuary in Pakistan's tribal belt was a critical enabling factor for the Taliban insurgency in Afghanistan; but other equally important factors cannot be ignored. Local and national issues in Afghanistan were the primary driving force behind public disenchantment and confusion. This assertion is supported by estimates from US military analysts that three-quarters of the Afghan insurgents were fighting within five kilometres of their homes.[60] The restrictive nature of the political dispensation in Afghanistan pushed many to join the insurgency, as that was the only way they could register protest. The feeling of alienation set in early on in Pashtun areas, as non-Pashtuns were seen to be favoured for jobs in the new security sector expansion. More than anything else, the energizing power behind the Taliban resurgence remained the presence of international forces. Given the historical legacy, Pashtuns could not get over the fact that they were living under occupation. Any expectation to the contrary was unrealistic.

By early 2005, there were strong indications of a Taliban revival in Afghanistan. This was as much a function of the Taliban's survival skills as of the international failure to rebuild Afghanistan and usher in peace.

As was briefly mentioned above, some high-ranking Taliban leaders did try to reach out to Kabul in the early years, but in vain. Even Jalaluddin Haqqani tried to patch things up with the new government in Afghanistan, to this end sending his brother Ibrahim to Kabul in 2002. But Ibrahim was beaten up and sent back to Waziristan.[61] The US also actively discouraged Karzai from offering any amnesty guarantees to the Taliban leaders who approached him.[62] When the situation became tough, a more flexible approach was considered; but by then the initiative was no longer with the Afghan government.

Former leading Mujahideen commanders Burhanuddin Rabbani and Abdul Rab Rasul Sayyaf, who were now key supporters of the new political system under Karzai, contacted the Taliban through mediators to elicit their support in the September 2005 parliamentary elections in Afghanistan. But now it was the Taliban's turn to refuse any cooperation.[63] The tide was turning. The frequency of attacks on government officials and installations during the 2005 election campaign was an important indicator of that.

The toxic influence of conflict in Iraq also started to impact on Afghanistan around that time. A group of Iraqi insurgent leaders even met the Afghan Taliban in FATA in late 2005 and taught them lessons from the Iraq theatre.[64] The flow of ideas and information from Iraq about the use of improvised explosive device (IED) technology and suicide bombing was also gaining momentum, leading to a significant rise in suicide bombings – a particularly disturbing sign.[65] Kabul became a major target for such attacks, and this pattern continued despite a fatwa by 30 *ulema* (religious scholars) in Khost, proclaiming that 'suicide is strongly prohibited by Islam.'[66] The figures speak for themselves: in 2005 there were 25 recorded suicide attacks; by 2006 that figure had soared to 139; and by 2007 to 160.[67] The tactic was indeed imported from the Iraq theatre, but the frustrations and motivations were largely indigenous. In the initial years, a significant number of suicide bombers in Afghanistan came from Pakistan; but from 2007 onwards, the proportion of Afghans carrying out such attacks jumped considerably.[68] The foundations of new Afghanistan, so cautiously constructed, were now crumbling under the feet of a new generation of Taliban.

Civilian casualties caused by NATO airpower were a potent bone of contention for the Afghans. Karzai's constant complaints to the US about the negative impact of the night raids were not unfounded. The number of casualties was low, but their impact was huge – especially in light of the delayed acknowledgement of mistakes made in operations and (in some cases) total denial. Collateral damage and cases of mistaken identity increased in 2005, creating a backlash that forced Karzai to express publicly his despair over his inability to do much about it.[69] To exploit such issues fully, the Taliban made the necessary adjustments to their outreach. In the period 1996–2001, they had banned music, photography and television; but around 2005 they were found by Hamid Mir, a resourceful Pakistani journalist, to be embracing these tools for their propaganda goals.[70] Using modern communication methods, the Taliban successfully played on the suspicions of local people that Western values were being imposed on them, thus creating further distance between the government in Kabul and people on the periphery.

This renewed Taliban activity obviously benefited from some planning, and there were signs that it was all a result of a choreographed strategy. From 2005 onwards, there was talk in Western capitals of the Taliban's 'Quetta Shura'. A *shura* is a consultative body, and Quetta is the capital of Pakistan's Balochistan Province, which shares a long border with Afghanistan. The distance between Quetta and Kandahar is about 125 miles via the well-traversed Chaman border crossing. Since the 1980s, the suburbs of Quetta had hosted hundreds of thousands of Afghan refugees, and there is a sizeable local Pashtun presence there as well. In the Chaman area, Afghans constitute almost half of the population, and many former Taliban bureaucrats reside there with their families, having acquired new identity documents.[71]

Thus Quetta was potentially an ideal location for the Afghan Taliban leaders during their exile. There are reports that from 2003 onwards,

1 Operations by British and Indian troops against the hostile Mahsud and other tribes on the Waziristan section of the Indian North West Frontier, 1937.

2 A hero of the anti-Soviet Afghan Jihad years, and persona non grata of today, Gulbuddin Hekmatyar remains hopeful about his future role.

3 Zia ul Haq, the man who redefined Pakistan, pushing the country away from the vision of Jinnah that was built around democracy, tolerance and pluralism. Behind him stands Chaudry Nisar Ali, interior minister under Prime Minister Nawaz Sharif since 2013. Zia's legacy continues…

4 Rising from the ashes of the Mujahideen, once they were in the saddle the Taliban never looked back.

5 Taliban atrocities during their 1996–2001 reign were publicly condemned, such as at this rally in 2000 where members of the Revolutionary Association of the Women of Afghanistan protested against them and all other fighting forces. Such voices, however, fell on deaf ears in Islamabad.

6 Jalaluddin Haqqani (*right*), leader of the Haqqani network, is Pakistan's asset in tackling Indian influence in Afghanistan – if need be.

7 The hapless and clueless Taliban foot soldiers were ditched by their leaders and Al-Qaeda in the wake of the US military campaign in late 2001.

8 CDs and DVDs are consigned to the flames by a student of the Lal Masjid (Red Mosque) during an 'anti-vice' rally in 2007. The rise of Lal Masjid vigilantes in the capital city Islamabad, and the devastating consequences, still haunts Pakistan.

9 Benazir Bhutto, one of the most courageous Muslim leaders of modern times. She embraced death so that democracy could have a second chance in Pakistan.

10 Militant leader Baitullah Mehsud speaks to journalists from his South Waziristan stronghold, 2008. The media-savvy Pakistani Taliban are masters in the art of deception and propaganda.

11 The destruction of girls' schools – such as this one in the Swat Valley, reduced to rubble in 2009 – is a favourite pastime of Taliban across the Pakistan–Afghanistan frontier.

12 Presidents Barack Obama, Hamid Karzai and Asif Ali Zardari, in 2009. Whether the umpteen trilateral heads of state meetings over the years actually helped build mutual trust between Kabul, Islamabad and Washington, DC, is doubtful.

13 Clearing the Swat Valley of militants in 2009 and bringing it back to life was one of the critical successes of Pakistan's military.

14 The Taliban are increasingly active across social media, using it to aid recruitment and to spread misinformation, as well as to harass those who challenge their worldview.

15 Tangible progress: women in the Afghan police – something inconceivable under the Taliban rule.

16 Ostensibly, Angoor Adda's is the last outpost in South Waziristan. Part of the evolving COIN/ counterterrorism tactics is ensuring that military patrol vehicles have no obvious army markings, sometimes even non-army colours – just the Pakistan flag and what the army calls the 'national slogan', 'God is great', as can be seen on this converted pickup truck used by the Frontier Corps' 2nd Wing.

Mullah Omar tasked his deputy, Mullah Baradar, with organizing and managing the Taliban insurgency from Quetta.[72] Initially, the Quetta Shura focused on Afghan refugees and locals, trying to convince them to support insurgents inside Afghanistan. But gradually, friends and supporters of the Shura started managing neighbourhood security in their new location, and even started supporting local hospitals where militants returning from Afghanistan were treated.[73] This remained a small-scale operation, and the 10–12 members of the Shura started losing touch with developments on the ground, where new leaders were emerging. The support for the old guard continued, but their control of the network waned as insurgency grew in Afghanistan from 2006 onwards.

The question that has naturally taxed many in Washington and Kabul is about the linkage and association between the Afghan Taliban and Pakistani intelligence during these critical years. Mullah Omar was very annoyed with Pakistani leaders for siding with the US in the military campaign in Afghanistan. Pakistan had practically ditched the Taliban in October 2001 and had even handed over the Afghan ambassador in Islamabad to the US, in the process violating all diplomatic norms. It would stretch credulity to believe that Mullah Omar would have listened to everything that Pakistani intelligence was telling him after that. Pakistani intelligence officials, however, were certainly observing the activities of Afghan Taliban leaders in Quetta, Peshawar and Karachi quite closely. It is a logical conjecture that the ISI must have tried to regain the trust of the Afghan Taliban. The former handlers of the Afghan Taliban in the ISI were rehired as contractors after their retirement, and they remained in control of the 'Afghan desk' at the ISI headquarters in Islamabad until around 2008.[74]

On the ground in Afghanistan, the Taliban action started slowly from parts of Zabul Province and eastern Paktika Province in 2003, expanding into Uruzgan and Kandahar by 2004 and then stretching to northern Helmand Province by 2005. In parallel, different insurgent groups were pushing hard in Ghazni, northern Paktika, Khost and southern and central Helmand.[75] This new emerging reality was not a united group operating under a hierarchical structure, and cohesion was certainly lacking.

The high-handed tactics of local strongmen associated with the Karzai government, especially in Kandahar, Helmand and Uruzgan, was also creating public discontent, motivating many Afghans to join the insurgency.

Meanwhile, the establishment of a Taliban shadow government, in which the Quetta Shura played a role, was an impetus towards better organization. The shadow government signified a parallel political structure, separate from the official institutions that the Taliban introduced in 2003. Judging by Taliban publications, I gauge that more Afghans started joining Taliban ranks in the south and east of the country around 2004, and more positions were created to accommodate this influx. By 2005 it had appointed shadow governors in 11 out of 34 provinces. This led to better coordination and communication between various insurgent factions operating at the provincial level. Consequently, the strengthening of the centralized control of field units and a return to guerrilla warfare tactics enhanced the Taliban's capacity significantly.[76] Their success in expanding their following from clerics and madrasa students to ordinary Afghans from 2006 can be attributed largely to their growing popularity among the people, as they were now seen to be spearheading resistance to the foreigners.[77]

The Taliban's ideological outlook during this transitional phase remained the same: they wanted to return to the days of sharia and oppression. But as a matter of strategy, they avoided repeating this too often in public. Apparently, the Taliban leadership on the ground had a good idea that ordinary Afghans were not really looking forward to a return to that era. Many of Mullah Omar's new edicts (for instance, banning music) were not received positively by the new generation of Taliban insurgents, which forced him essentially to retract the ban and leave it to local commanders to decide on its implementation.[78] For public consumption, the Afghan Taliban now harped on the tune of resistance, defiance and revolt – ideas that were more effective in inspiring and mobilizing people.

CHAPTER SIX

Islamabad under siege
Red Mosque vigilantes, protesting lawyers and Musharraf versus Bhutto (2007–08)

The quirky manner in which the global war on terror was fought was not without consequences for Pakistan. It gave a new lease of life to the military dictatorship, disabled the growth of civil society and put a premium on the use of violent means. Internal divisions and regional rivalries were also instrumental in pushing the country towards the abyss. These multiple crises together engendered state dysfunction. At the core were the disproportionate use of force and disregard for a law enforcement model that would entail the collection of evidence by modern policing and the provision of justice through courts. This reckless approach was bound to exacerbate the terrorism problem, rather than resolve the schisms.

Al-Qaeda ideologues and operators indeed poisoned the atmosphere in Pakistan, but a host of local pseudo-clerics did not lag far behind in tarnishing the message of Islam. From 2007 onwards, suicide bombing became a popular tool for terrorists in Pakistan, whose security forces retaliated by shooting in the dark, as they remained largely clueless as to the workings and motivations of the new generation of extremists. A considerable number of ordinary Pakistanis remained blinded by denial and ignorance. This kept them in the dark about the real nature of the threat and stopped them from joining together to arrest the slide.

In the midst of everything, Musharraf was battling for survival by saying one thing to his partners in the West and another to his own people – a trademark of authoritarian rulers lacking legitimacy. He was also hamstrung by his political allies, who were mostly turncoats who shied away from taking any initiative, unless it helped their vested interests. Fighting extremism was certainly not something that interested them. Insightfully, Chaudhry Shujaat Hussain, who led the 'King's party' in parliament, is on record as having said that 'our hearts are with Osama and brains with Musharraf'.[1] These contradictions only deepened the Pakistani predicament.

The Lal Masjid or Red Mosque crisis that erupted in 2007 exposed this paradox as never before. It offered critical insights both into the perverse nature and modus operandi of the new class of extremists in Pakistan, and into how the state thoughtlessly responded to such trends and thereby created more problems than it solved.

I had the chance to pray in the Lal Masjid a couple of times, many years before this disaster, and I do not recall any troubling signs or unusual activity. It was just an ordinary mosque, conveniently located for those dependent on public transport and with some good food places nearby, which added to the attraction. Those who visited the mosque regularly were mostly middle-ranking and junior government officials who lived in the vicinity.

Things started to change when General Zia arrived at the helm in the 1980s. The mosque had existed since 1965, when its foundation stone was laid in the nascent capital city and when the military ruler General Ayub Khan appointed Maulana Abdullah as its imam. This was one of the very few mosques built on government land with state funds, and hence the government could appoint its leader.[2] Most likely the general was unaware that his appointee was a Deobandi, as it hardly mattered then. More importantly, the mosque was called 'Lal' after Lal Shahbaz Qalandar, a revered thirteenth-century Sufi saint buried in the city of Sehwan in the country's Sindh Province. The saint was famed for teaching religious tolerance – a critical lesson that the clerics of Lal Masjid failed to learn.

Maulana Abdullah became politically active at the invitation of General Zia ul Haq's associates, who valued his contribution in the anti-Soviet Afghan Jihad. He served the cause well in collaboration with both the ISI and local religious groups, earning as a reward government land in the prized and posh E-7 sector of Islamabad, where he established the Jamia Faridia seminary (named after a great Sufi master from Punjab, Baba Fariduddin Ganjshakar).[3] It is another matter that the broadminded teachings of the Sufi were not part of this madrasa's curriculum! The new friendships Abdullah developed in Afghanistan, especially with Arabs, helped him expand his network. A new economy of religious activism was taking shape in Pakistan at the time. It had certain noble aspects to it, such as the funding of charities for orphans and the poor. Problems arose when Abdullah and his like started using religion as a tool to pursue political-cum-sectarian agendas and when violent methods started to be employed.

This became obvious in 1989, soon after Benazir Bhutto became the first Muslim woman ever to be elected prime minister of a Muslim state. Abdullah immediately issued a fatwa declaring the participation of women in politics to be un-Islamic. The majority of Pakistanis were unmoved, as Abdullah had neither the religious authority nor the credibility to make any difference to the national political scene. A similar fatwa had been issued in 1965, when military dictator General Ayub Khan was facing Fatima Jinnah, the sister of the country's founding father Mohammad Ali Jinnah, in presidential elections. Ayub Khan had orchestrated that despicable move, but Fatima Jinnah received support from Maulana Abul Ala Maududi, the founder of the religious political party Jamaat-e-Islami, who to his credit declared the anti-woman fatwa null and void and made a case in support of her in line with Islamic tenets.[4] Though Maududi also had political goals, his credentials as a religious scholar were well established. Abdullah was an intellectual pygmy in comparison to Maududi.

Apparently, some sectarian transgressions cost Abdullah his life, as he was assassinated in 1998. It was unfortunate, because violence begets violence, and in this case it also contributed towards the radicalization of his two sons, Abdul Aziz and Abdul Rashid Ghazi, who soon took over control of the mosque. This transpired when the two brothers took a strong pro-Taliban stance and called Musharraf a traitor for his policy of cooperation with the United States in the aftermath of the 11 September attacks. Intriguingly, they continued to draw a government salary.

A second alert came in October 2003, when Lal Masjid students committed serious vandalism in Islamabad in reaction to the assassination of Azam Tariq, leader of a banned sectarian group.[5] The angry miscreants also marched on the ISI office, but special forces were deputed to secure the area. Intriguingly, the Jamiat-e-Ulema-e-Islam-Fazl (JUI-F) had publicly alleged that the country's intelligence agencies were actively involved in the murder in order to spur sectarian violence![6]

The Lal Masjid leaders felt more empowered with this show of force and even dared to issue a fatwa in 2004 against the soldiers of the Pakistani army who were fighting in the tribal areas bordering Afghanistan. The clerics declared that 'any army official killed during the operation should not be given a Muslim burial' and that 'the militants who die while fighting the Pakistan Army are martyrs'.[7] This was too serious not to be registered. Abdul Aziz's official status as the mosque's imam was rescinded and an arrest warrant was issued against him. It was his bad luck that explosives and a rocket launcher were found in his vehicle. All of this brought him to his knees. But then Chaudhry Shujaat Hussain and Ijaz ul Haq, son of the late General Zia, came to his rescue, and a deal was struck with Aziz, who apologized in writing and promised to distance his followers from any armed struggle.[8] In Pakistan, it seems there is always a deal to be made.

During my research into the causes of the crisis, a middle-ranking police officer in Islamabad showed me evidence of the local police force's repeated requests to the government in 2004–06 to authorize it to deal strictly with the excesses committed by Lal Masjid clerics; but the permission never came. Another police officer told me that, according to an intelligence report he had seen, Osama bin Laden had also visited the Lal Masjid after 2001. Abdul Rashid Ghazi not only admitted meeting bin Laden, Mullah Omar and Ayman al-Zawahiri, but also acknowledged that many other wanted people visited the Lal Masjid.[9] Abdullah had met bin Laden in 1998 and promised to continue his work inside Pakistan. Abdullah's sons proudly followed in his foot-steps.[10] The association with security agencies, especially intelligence services, also survived the generational shift.

In an echo of the peace deals in FATA, the Lal Masjid clerics used the 'peace' time to expand their network, hone their strategy and procure more resources. The final episode in the saga began early in 2007, when female students at Jamia Hafsa (part of the Lal Masjid complex) seized control of an adjacent children's library and started vigilante action in the city. Music shops were attacked, police were kidnapped and uncon-stitutional demands were made of the government. The government offered talks to resolve the differences, but to no avail. Haji Omar, the militant commander in Waziristan that we met above, meanwhile asserted that 'if the government tried to attack Lal Masjid, [the mili-tants] would take revenge.'[11] Few realized at the time that the threat was real and that militants in FATA were capable of translating it into action.

When politicians, including those sympathetic to the Lal Masjid crowd, failed to bring any sanity to the situation, the military adopted an aggressive posture. First, they hired the services of some 'reputable' militants to convinced Abdul Rashid Ghazi to give up his arms and avoid confrontation with the military. The mediators even included the leaders of banned militant groups, such as Masood Azhar (from Jaish-e-Mohammad), Malik Ishaq (Lashkar-e-Jhangvi) and Fazlur Rahman Khalil (Harkat ul Mujahideen), the first and last having served as assets of the intelligence agencies in campaigns in Kashmir and Afghanistan.[12] The Saudi ambassador to Pakistan was also involved as a 'peacemaker' and spent over an hour and a half with the clerics.[13] A bit surprisingly, none of these mediation efforts bore fruit, and Musharraf gave the go-ahead for a decisive military action codenamed Operation Silence (later renamed Operation Sunrise). Mindful that some old hands in the ranks of the ISI could be sympathetic to the clerics, Musharraf tasked the director general of Military Intelligence (MI) with spearheading the intelligence aspects of the whole operation, and the relatively liberal Lieutenant General Tariq Majeed, then the corps commander in Rawalpindi, was given overall charge of the ground campaign.[14] The renowned Special Services Group (SSG) was also in action at the site.

Military units moved in early July 2007, and on 9 July Operation Sunrise began with a massive show of force that destroyed a large part of the mosque and madrasa complex, killing Ghazi and dozens of armed individuals.[15] Interestingly, around 70 per cent of the seminary students involved belonged to Khyber Pakhtunkhwa Province and FATA.[16]

The crisis was closely followed around the globe because it was unfolding right in the heart of Islamabad – just a few minutes' walk from Constitution Avenue, home to Pakistan's parliament, presidency, supreme court and federal secretariat. The Foreign Office and ISI head-quarters are even closer. The action was shown on live television locally, with many inexperienced and 'hyper' talk-show hosts causing viewers emotional distress.

The battle, however, was far from over. Ghazi, with an ample supply of mobile phones, had given many last-minute interviews to major news channels, telling millions of people on live television that he had bravely decided to lay down his life for the cause of Islam, rather than bow to the dictates of the state. He called Musharraf a tool in the hands of the United States.[17] This was an utter failure of government media manage-ment and of the military's public relations department, and public opinion quickly turned highly critical of the operation, with its reported human rights violations. Reports of hastily dug graves around Islamabad and of secret burials encouraged rumours of a massacre and a cover-up. Disproportionate use of force is almost always counterproductive.

Operation Sunrise was a success in military terms, but its political consequences were devastating. Not only did it deepen instability in the country, but it also further stimulated militants in the tribal belt to intensify their operations targeting Pakistan's security forces. Faqir Mohammed, a leading militant figure in Bajaur agency of FATA, wasted no time in declaring before thousands of tribesmen: 'We will seek revenge for the atrocities perpetrated on the Lal Masjid.'[18] The 1,300 and more seminary students who had surrendered outside the Lal Masjid before the final clampdown were only briefly interrogated before being released by the local law enforcement and intelligence. This lapse alone proved deadly.[19] Many of them wasted no time in congregating in the Waziristan area, the emerging hub of terrorists.

Since 2002, suicide terrorism had fast been developing as the weapon of choice for militant groups in Pakistan, but there was a significant increase in intensity after the Lal Masjid event. It can be argued that the Iraq theatre popularized the idea among Al-Qaeda affiliates around then, and the signs of Taliban revival in Afghanistan from around 2006 also had an impact. The figures alone demonstrate the trend. In total there were 22 such attacks between 2002 and 2006; but in 2007 alone, Pakistan faced 56 suicide attacks, with 44 taking place after Operation Sunrise in Islamabad.[20] Even more significant was the disclosure that former students of the Lal Masjid, under the banner of the newly formed 'Ghazi Force' (named after the slain Abdul Rashid Ghazi), were involved in many of the suicide bombings and other terrorist activities in the following years.[21]

Pakistan was truly in the eye of the storm as it approached the final, highly turbulent phase of President General Pervez Musharraf's rule around 2007–08. Musharraf, who was admired in Western capitals but increasingly loathed at home, had clearly overstayed the welcome he had received from the hapless Pakistanis in 1999. Recurrent military dictatorships in the country had not only failed to deliver, but had also weakened the state. Musharraf started off reasonably well, but his ill-planned participation in the 'war on terror', the lack of transparency surrounding his security policy, the mysterious disappearance of alleged terrorists, and his ineffectiveness in dealing with some armed groups all damaged him. Few of his close associates had the moral courage to correct him, and those who did soon fell out of favour. The mismanagement of the Red Mosque crisis and his undue reluctance to dismantle terrorist hubs in southern Punjab only complicated the challenges of extremism. Empowering the civilian law enforcement infrastructure and smart investment in the education sector could have strengthened

Musharraf's hand, but these were never his priorities. To his credit, more than once he moved in this direction, including in the realm of madrasa reform; but unfortunately he always retreated at the first hint of resistance.

Musharraf could still have survived in office, since he retained the loyalty of senior military officers, who relished the extra perks, and also had in his pocket a group of political turncoats whose lack of character was legendary. But it was not to be. His poor handling of the erupting Swat Valley crisis and his adoption of authoritarian tactics in dealing with the judicial arm of the state proved his undoing. His heart was in the right place, it appeared; but he was over-ambitious and had a soaring belief in his invincibility. Benazir Bhutto, the brightest star on the horizon of Pakistani politics, now returned to the country from self-imposed exile, as some too-clever-by-half officials in the Bush admin-istration choreographed a conciliation between Musharraf and Benazir. It was destined to be a disaster. Musharraf's ship was already sinking, and forcing Benazir to cut a deal with him at that moment amounted to nudging her into her grave.

Benazir Bhutto, the dashing daughter of indisputably the country's most popular politician since Jinnah, Zulfikar Ali Bhutto, had inherited leadership of the Pakistan People's Party (PPP) from her valiant father, who was hanged by General Zia ul Haq after a fraudulent judicial verdict (see above). Benazir rose as a symbol of resistance at a young age while facing jail and exile, earning the respect of her party colleagues. In 1988, she was elected prime minister, but the military leadership and its cronies who had imposed undemocratic conditions on her (such as non-interference in the country's nuclear programme and Afghan policy) conspired to overthrow her government before it had completed even two years in office. She persisted in politics and staged a comeback in 1993, outsmarting Nawaz Sharif, who had fallen out of favour with the military–bureaucratic establishment that had brought him to power. Benazir's performance in government on both occasions was mixed, but then again it was no ordinary challenge to deal with a dominant military that never trusted her and simultaneously to tackle the right-wing parties that had a right royal dislike of her. After losing power, she left Pakistan in 1998. During the Musharraf era, she ran her party from Dubai, while her husband, Asif Ali Zardari, languished in jail in Pakistan and as the government instituted many corruption cases against both. She refused to be browbeaten – and after all, her party had nationwide support, which was enough to keep her morale high. Zardari also gained some public sympathy, as he remained incarcerated for over eight years (1996–2004) without any court conviction. A controlled democracy could not deliver rule of law.

The West was conveniently looking the other way, as Musharraf – during his one-on-one meetings with Western political leaders, especially US President Bush and British Prime Minister Blair – was seen as being committed to fighting terrorism. Contrary to the view of his critics, he was not faking: some of his initiatives were indeed well-meaning, but the policies bore little fruit, partly because of his poor choice of partners.

Shaukat Aziz, an international banker who was first picked as finance minister and then elevated to the office of prime minister, was one such example. His lack of political credentials, coupled with his meteoric rise, led him to be dubbed 'Shortcut Aziz'. A Musharraf-era corps commander in Karachi told me that generals close to Musharraf were very critical of Aziz, but Musharraf was unwilling to change his mind. His generals were certain that the Americans were backing Aziz.[22] Perceptions of American support (or lack thereof) forms an important public opinion barometer for any political or military leader in the country. In the corridors of power, to be seen as having American support is usually a catalyst for career-building; but in the public eye it can have an adverse effect. This contradiction is now deeply rooted in Pakistani society.

Among the good things that Musharraf did, the most profound was his back-channel diplomacy with India, which aimed at resolving the perennial Kashmir dispute. The process came tantalizingly close to success around 2007, after many years of hard work. This transformed approach was a dramatic departure from the Kargil adventure of 1999, when a secret operation involving active army soldiers dressed as Mujahideen was mounted to occupy certain key areas in Indian-administered Kashmir. It brought the two countries to the brink of war – some Westerners even think it could have been nuclear war. Rather than gain international recognition for the cause of Kashmir – which was the strategic objective – the campaign only tarnished Pakistan's image. India quickly recovered the territory it had initially lost and did much to salvage its military reputation. For Pakistan, retreat was the only option, and the lives of many brave soldiers were sacrificed need-lessly. Besides augmenting the civil–military rift, it also opened the door to military intervention. For the military top brass, the loss of Kargil was compensated for by 'victory' in Islamabad. Some things never change.

It appears that Musharraf did change, however, when it came to his dealings with India. Though he never opted to completely dismantle the militant groups focused on Kashmir – Lashkar-e-Taiba (LET – the 'army of the pure') and Jaish-e-Mohammad (JEM) – he became progressively convinced that peaceful resolution of the Kashmir conflict was necessary for his country's economic progress.[23] In search of a 'paradigm shift', nominees of President Musharraf and Indian Prime Minister Manmohan Singh met secretly in various cities across the globe and developed an understanding, which was unprecedented.

Pakistan's foreign minister at the time, Khurshid Kasuri, later revealed that a final agreement had been 'only a signature away'.[24] It included special visa relaxation for Kashmiris to move across the divide and trade freely, demilitarization on both sides and – even more importantly – increased autonomy for both sides of Kashmir.[25] The ideas were not new, but it was momentous that top leaders on both sides got this far in their negotiations. Prime Minister Nawaz Sharif had made a similar attempt in 1998–99, but Musharraf had thrown a spanner in the works via Kargil. Everything was set in 2007 for the process to succeed, but Musharraf's hold on the country started waning and India got cold feet. Musharraf's enthusiasm on the subject was not matched by any of his top generals in the army, though they would have nodded their heads if their consent had been demanded. Such is the culture within the military. In hindsight, India missed a crucial opportunity, though it is too egotistical to acknowledge it. Unfortunately, it is the Kashmiris who will pay the price for this lapse, in the form of more blood and oppression.

In Islamabad, Musharraf was unwilling to pass up any opportunity to shore up his dwindling fortunes. He decided to clip the wings of the judiciary, which had started showing some signs of 'insubordination'. Musharraf was readying himself to be elected president for another term by a parliament whose mandate was about to expire in November 2007. He had also indicated his intention of remaining chief of the army (in addition to the presidential office) – a job he had promised to relinquish in December 2004! Both of his plans were constitutionally questionable, and it was becoming obvious to Musharraf that the top judiciary was unlikely to bend over backwards this time to oblige him.

Musharraf thought of himself as a 'benign dictator'. Trying to live up to this self-image, he asked the culprit-in-chief (as he saw it), Mr Iftikhar Mohammad Chaudhry, the chief justice of the Supreme Court of Pakistan, to resign 'honourably'. Chaudhry refused point-blank and Musharraf decided instead to suspend him on some serious charges. Even if some of the allegations were true, Musharraf's intentions were *mala fide*.

Historically, judges were known to be pliant, and especially accommodating to military rulers. So Musharraf had history on his side in not expecting a judge to stand up to him. But times had changed, and more people were itching for political change. Thanks to an increasingly free and vibrant electronic journalism, the nation watched the humiliation that Chaudhry had to face at the hands of Islamabad police, when he decided to take a walk to the Supreme Court to challenge Musharraf's action. Viewers saw a policeman grab him by his hair and rudely push him into a vehicle. This touched a nerve across the country and a movement was born. Pakistan has a low literacy rate, but even the uneducated could understand that they have very little hope of ever getting justice if this is the treatment meted out to the chief justice of the country! People were desperate for change, and this dramatic development provided an opportune moment.

While the suspension case was being heard in the Supreme Court, the chief justice decided to address various bar associations across the country – a tactic that prompted huge shows of public support. Pakistani lawyers took to the streets in protest, galvanizing thousands of Pakistanis to struggle for the rule of law, an independent judiciary and the supremacy of the constitution. Defiance was in the air. Though many lawyers, human rights activists and judges joined the movement, it was Aitzaz Ahsan, a brilliant lawyer and politician, who gave direction to the movement through his ideas, speeches and – most importantly – by representing the chief justice in front of the Supreme Court. Chaudhry was the symbol of the movement, but Aitzaz was the brains behind it.

I cherish the memory of having marched in one of those protests in Islamabad. The atmosphere was simply electric. The commitment and dedication of lawyers and civil society actors to build a better Pakistan was truly inspiring, but it was not an easy journey. Athar Minullah, an important leader of the lawyers' movement, told me how he, along with his senior colleagues, worked hard to save the movement from slipping into the hands of religious elements, who were trying to hijack it from within.[26]

Finally, in July 2007, the full bench of the Supreme Court restored Chief Justice Chaudhry and trashed Musharraf's charges against him. Subsequently, the energized judiciary continued to rule against government decisions, embarrassing the executive – and especially its intelligence agencies. Government officials were held accountable for actions that were usually beyond the reach of the law, ranging from brutal beatings of journalists to illegal confinement on grounds of 'national security'.[27] Much later, a Pakistani brigadier who had served for many years in intelligence told me that the ISI simply despised Chief Justice Chaudhry, as he held the intelligence organization accountable for the unlawful arrest of alleged terrorists. Such an accountability check on the intelligence services was unprecedented in the country's history.[28] Like most intelligence agencies, the ISI liked to operate above the law.

When Musharraf realized that things were slipping out of his hands, he imposed a state of emergency in November 2007 in contravention of constitutional provisions. He also 'dismissed' the chief justice and asked the judiciary to take a new oath that called on all judges to undertake to abide by the new emergency law and the changes it had brought. In a major development, around 60 judges from the Supreme Court and four provincial high courts refused to give such an undertaking and were consequently sent home. So by just one stroke of his pen, Musharraf had truncated the state's judicial arm.[29]

He further instructed the state authorities to place several of these judges, including the chief justice, under house arrest. Pakistanis were surprised and dismayed when Western governments remained silent, and they wondered why the American administration kept supporting and praising Musharraf at this traumatic juncture. This truly was the 'Pakistani Spring', but few around the globe recognized it, probably because a vibrant rule of law movement did not sit well with the tarnished media image of Pakistan.

Musharraf was now a weak man trying desperately to cling on to power, by hook or by crook. It was at this point that Benazir Bhutto returned to Pakistan on 17 October 2007, to be welcomed by hundreds of thousands of her supporters in Karachi. Terrorists were also waiting for her, knowing full well that she was committed to challenging them head on. A devastating suicide attack that targeted her procession killed over 170 of her supporters and security personnel, but luckily she was unhurt.

A week or so after the incident, I shared with Benazir Bhutto an article that I had published, entitled 'Who tried to kill Benazir Bhutto?', in which I analysed various possibilities that ranged from militant leader Baitullah Mehsud to rogue intelligence elements – and even to state involvement.[30] Within minutes of my email she responded, asking why Musharraf was reluctant to involve 'foreign investigators if govt has nothing to hide as u rightly say'. Her next comment, however, shook me. While analysing the threats to her life, she maintained that the real 'threat [is] not from US perceived angle but estab[lishment] elements who want Islamic revolution'.[31] She was hinting at the extremist elements within the powerful establishment – generally believed to comprise senior military, intelligence and civilian bureaucrats – who aspire to impose a dogmatic and distorted version of Islam.

Undeterred by the horrific experience on the day of her return, she travelled across Pakistan to lead political processions and address mammoth crowds. The heroic way in which Benazir Bhutto embraced death on 27 December 2007, while challenging extremists publicly and repeatedly – knowing exactly how dangerous that could be – is testament to her gallantry and dedication to Pakistan. A part of the idea of Pakistan died with her that day, it seemed, as the country sank into depression for weeks.

The tragedy struck as she was being driven away in her SUV after addressing a huge election rally at Liaquat Park in Rawalpindi.[32] She was waving to the crowd that was chanting 'Long Live Bhutto!' when a 15-year-old Pashtun boy named Bilal shot her at close range. A few seconds later, Bilal blew himself up on the same spot, killing dozens. Benazir was rushed to hospital but did not survive. The fact that the scene was washed clean shortly after the attack, before the police had enough time to collect all the evidence, raised many eyebrows. Some believe that snipers from a nearby rooftop had targeted her. There have been various investigations – by Britain's Scotland Yard and the United Nations, among others – in an attempt to figure out what really happened and who was behind the assassination. Nothing conclusive came out of the investigations, though, and this has given rise to various conspiracy theories.

Intriguingly, Afghan President Hamid Karzai had met Benazir Bhutto in Islamabad on the morning of her assassination and had shared with her an intelligence tip about an impending assassination attempt against her. Pakistan's own intelligence organizations had conveyed a similar assessment to her the night before, and there had been messages from Saudi and UAE intelligence. After the meeting with Karzai, Benazir stated publicly that Pakistan and Afghanistan could effectively confront the challenges of extremism and terrorism through joint efforts. This was a 'no brainer', but few other Pakistani leaders were prepared to stand up and say such a thing.[33] For the Afghan Taliban, such collaboration could sound their death knell.

Benazir, who was brilliant at dealing with military dictators and their cronies, had outmanoeuvred Musharraf by making her compact with him conditional on his surrendering his military position, thereby ensuring that the military would no longer feel obliged to remain unduly loyal to him. The military's institutional culture is such that defying an incumbent army chief is seen as an unpardonable sin; but retired generals are disposable. By the time Musharraf realized this, it was too late and the Western guarantors of the deal had little left to offer. Musharraf reportedly threatened Benazir at that juncture and reminded her that she was dependent on him for her security needs in Pakistan. Despicable and mean as his approach was, it is doubtful that he really wished her physical harm. Musharraf was indeed responsible for many deaths in the country – especially in the name of the 'war on terror' – but no concrete evidence has yet been produced of his direct involvement in Benazir's assassination.

The murder was most likely the work of Al-Qaeda-inspired operators. They had extensive networks in various parts of the country and saw her as a serious threat to their agenda of religious extremism. A deviously crafted propaganda campaign was launched when she arrived in the country, depicting her as an American puppet who was now tasked with confronting Islamic radicals in Pakistan. Benazir ill-advisedly voiced her willingness even to hand over the Pakistani nuclear scientist A.Q. Khan for questioning by the International Atomic Energy Agency (IAEA) if she returned to power. This sent shockwaves through hardliners in the country's military and intelligence circles, as it was seen as highly damaging to the national interest. In an age of confusion and misguided zealotry, all of this was enough to create an environment in which potential killers would be inspired to do the job, considering it their supreme religious or national duty.

No single actor can be exclusively held responsible for the murder of Benazir Bhutto. Given the prevailing security situation in the country then, the cards were stacked against her from the word go. For the love of Pakistan, she valiantly walked into a death trap. All those who poisoned the atmosphere through conspiracy theories about her return not only did Pakistan a disservice, but also contributed to her tragic end. A couple of people in her own team also share the blame: they suggested that she should make powerful statements about sensitive security issues, which created discomfort in military circles. Musharraf certainly deserves to be held accountable for providing inadequate security arrangements – and for not punishing those who tried to cover up their incompetence by shifting the blame. As far as Benazir was concerned, she left a very clear message on record: if anything happened to her, she said, 'I would hold Musharraf responsible. I have been made to feel insecure by his minions.'[34] Around the same time, when Anne Patterson, the US ambassador to Pakistan, patronizingly advised Benazir to continue cooperating with Musharraf, despite his extra-constitutional measures, she shot back: 'Do you want me to cooperate with someone who wants to kill me?'[35]

Musharraf sealed his political fate when his security officials came up with lame excuses for their total failure to provide her with adequate security. Benazir's secret understanding with Musharraf, reached with the active support of American and British officials, had almost broken down even before the tragedy, due to Musharraf's dictatorial instincts and her refusal to be manipulated any more.[36] The Bush administration had agreed only reluctantly to her return to political life in Pakistan, and only with the aim of strengthening Musharraf's hand. She wanted to carve out a path of her own, independently of anyone else, in order to save Pakistan. But that was not to be.

In September 2009, I had an illuminating meeting with the powerful chief of Pakistan's ISI, Lieutenant General Ahmed Shuja Pasha. I asked him to comment on the view held by many Pakistanis (especially supporters of the PPP) that the ISI was in some way involved in the assassination of Benazir Bhutto. I asked this while the two of us were alone, seated across the dining table. He stopped eating, stared at me and almost roared: 'We can be accused of anything, but we are not stupid . . . We could see the terrible consequences of such a happening and we can never do that to Pakistan.'

The general sounded genuine to me; but he did not similarly harangue me for my follow-up remark criticizing Musharraf for failure to ensure the security of Benazir Bhutto. In our long conversation about security threats, it is striking that he uttered not a single word in defence of Musharraf. To me, that was an indication of how the intelligence service viewed Musharraf's performance.

The unexpected turn of events put Benazir's husband, Asif Ali Zardari, in the spotlight. He managed to take over the reins of the shocked party and lead it into national elections on 18 February 2008. Through elections Pakistanis fought back and the country rebounded politically, bringing to power a coalition of progressive political forces comprising the PPP, the Awami National Party (ANP) and the Muttihada Qaumi Movement (MQM). The religious parties were trounced. It was the beginning of a new era and people had high hopes, believing that mainstream politicians had learnt their lessons during adversity and exile. They were in for a shock – but that was some time in coming.

The Sharif family returned from exile in Saudi Arabia ahead of the 2008 elections and initially joined the PPP government in Islamabad. Their faction of the Muslim League had emerged as the second-largest political party in the federal legislature. This enabled Zardari to wreak his revenge by ensuring that Musharraf had to pack up unceremoniously in August 2008, when all political forces joined together to impeach him. Zardari proved an astute politician, and there was public appreciation for his efforts directed towards political reconciliation. The idea was nurtured by the 'Charter for Democracy' – a laudable initiative that Benazir Bhutto and Nawaz Sharif signed in May 2006 in London, while they were both in exile.[37] To cap it all, Zardari was elected president, despite the fact that for the army this was quite distasteful. But the public's expectation that extremism would automatically diminish with the dawn of democracy turned out to be highly misplaced.

Deepening crisis in Afghanistan

On the Afghanistan front meanwhile, increased violence and instability had provided the Taliban with a sense of empowerment, and they had stepped up their efforts to assume control of the ensuing crisis. Guerrilla warfare tactics were their preferred mode of operation in the phase that began in 2007, according to Mullah Abdul Jalil, a pioneer of the Taliban movement in Kandahar. He also explains the reasoning behind this move: 'We cannot afford any mass uprising or face-to-face war, it would only cause a lot of unnecessary casualties.'[38] Though the Taliban's understanding of international relations and global political dynamics was poor, they were adept at military transformation in an insurgency context. However, an interview I had with a local journalist (who, I believe, is well informed about the Afghan Taliban) cautioned me not to read too much into statements emanating from the Taliban, as these are often geared towards boasting of their accomplishments and drawing more recruits by giving the impression that they are winning. He explained that Taliban leaders at times exaggerate hugely and even claim responsibility for attacks that are conducted by insurgents and gangs that are not under their command.

Poor governance by Karzai and his teammates was also a major factor in giving a new lease of life to the Taliban leaders who were in hiding. On the ground, Afghans had little say in setting the agenda of donors; and when they failed to reap the benefits of the development model in place, frustration grew. The Taliban were ever ready to tap into this disenchantment. They increased the levels of violence to discredit the Karzai government, which was already facing a legitimacy crisis, being seen as hand in glove with foreigners. The phrase 'ten-dollar Taliban' – a reference to the perception that many Taliban fighters were receiving a wage of $10 per day – was also gaining currency in Afghanistan around 2007–08.[39] Money was becoming as powerful a factor in fuelling insurgency as politics and ideology.

By 2008, the Taliban campaign had really gained traction, and the frequency of their attacks was now greater than at any time since 2001.[40]

President Karzai was increasingly critical of Pakistan's role in supporting the Taliban, though this was in part a way of shifting the blame and covering up his own failures. He was no longer even on speaking terms with Musharraf, who thought he was playing into the hands of the Indians. On the ground, Taliban numbers were increasing and a new generation of fighters, equipped with relatively modern tools of communication, was ready to play its part. In a brazen attack in June 2008, 30 Taliban fighters assaulted the central prison in the city of Kandahar in a well-organized operation that freed around 1,200 inmates.[41] Even more dangerous was the alliance between criminals and Taliban that was being coordinated from a secret cell inside Afghanistan's largest prison, Pul-e-Charkhi, located on the outskirts of Kabul. Through smuggling mobile phones and radios, and recruiting inside the prison, these elements expanded their network. Some prison guards were co-opted through bribes, while the less malleable were threatened with dire consequences. In their remaining free time, the inmates ran extortion rackets and organized terrorist attacks in Kabul.[42] The Taliban were alive to the advent of the digital age.

Mullah Dadullah, a prominent Taliban leader known initially for his brutal ways, had played an important role in this transformation. Though he was killed back in May 2007, Dadullah had been involved since 2002 in 'the revival and remodelling of the Taliban as an insurgent group'.[43] He was part of the ten-member *Rahbari* Shura (leadership council) appointed by none other than Mullah Omar himself in 2003. He had led the 2003 military campaign to take over Day Chopan district in Zabul Province – the first major post-2001 Taliban success – and that had brought him fame and status in modern Taliban folklore. His regular media interviews boasted of the global agenda of the Taliban and helped him raise more funds for his forces from Al-Qaeda sources. And his emphasis on the use of IEDs was also instrumental in reinvigorating the Taliban brand: in 2006, there were 2,000 IED attacks, killing 78 foreign soldiers; by 2009 this had jumped to around 7,000 attacks and 275 foreign fatalities.[44]

The Taliban had indeed benefited greatly from the limited presence of NATO forces in rural Afghanistan, especially in the Pashtun-dominated areas before 2007. But equally important for the Taliban was the failure of Kabul to establish its credibility by providing basic services and a functioning government with effective reach across the state. When they were in power, the Taliban's track record on this was much worse, but they claimed that both crime generally and violence had been far lower. For a traumatized people who had witnessed decades of war, this was an important factor.

CHAPTER SEVEN

The battle for the soul of Pakistan
The loss of the Swat Valley and the rise of the Pakistani Taliban (2006–13)

While the goings-on in the major urban centres of Pakistan were watched with concern both within and outside the country, more trouble was brewing up in the north. Though it appeared on the radar of the security forces, it was typically not on the minds of policy makers in Islamabad.

Sitting at the base of the Hindu Kush mountains in the Pashtun region, the magnificent Swat Valley used to be a popular tourist destination, almost until the last decade of the twentieth century. With its generally peaceful population of around 2 million, the area was famed for its rich history, ethnic diversity and effective local governance. Hence, compared to the nearby restless tribal belt, the Swat district was quite progressive both culturally and in terms of religious orientation. This started to change from the mid-1990s, and a decade-long period of neglect led to a gradual expansion of the space available to radical elements. By 2007, Swat was burning and already unrecognizable to those who knew it in its heyday.

The murderers in the Swat Valley didn't arrive from Mars. For the ordinary people of the area, they were familiar faces with local roots. These were the followers of Tehrik-e-Nifaz-e-Shariat-e-Mohammadi (TNSM – Movement for the Enforcement of Sharia Law), an extremist group with an intriguing history. It was founded by Maulana Sufi

Mohammad, who in 2007 was languishing in jail in Peshawar. He had landed up there after a disastrous attempt to lead thousands of 'volunteers' to Afghanistan to fight the American forces in late 2001. After losing most of his young warriors within weeks of his arrival in the Kabul area, Sufi Mohammad retreated quickly. But on his way back to the Swat Valley he was unexpectedly confronted by the parents of his young recruits, who demanded to know what he thought he had achieved by 'sacrificing' their kids. Frightened for his life, he asked the local authorities to take him into protective custody![1] His wish was granted instantly. The officer who arrested him won accolades for gallantry, while Sufi Mohammad lost no time in claiming that he had been arrested on America's behest – a truly win-win situation for everyone!

Sufi Mohammad came from the nearby Dir district in NWFP (now Khyber Pakhtunkhwa Province). He had started his career working for the Jamaat-e-Islami party (JI – Party of Islam), a conservative religious political group formed by the well-known South Asian religious ideologue Abul Ala Maududi. As briefly mentioned above, Maududi had been a staunch opponent of both Jinnah and of the creation of Pakistan. He believed that societies would become Islamic if the elite was educated in proper Islam. In the words of scholar Vali Nasr, Maududi claimed that 'the dominoes would fall once Islam was polished and its cultural accretions removed'; to this end, he built his strategy on educating people, rather than on political action.[2] However, the strategy changed over time, and his party did become actively involved in politics. At the time of General Zia's martial law in 1977, JI jumped on the bandwagon and joined Zia's cabinet. JI saw it as a short-cut to power, but things did not work out, as Zia merely used the religious parties to earn a degree of public legitimacy. These shifts instigated ideological debates within the party, leading to many defections. Sufi was among those who decided to quit JI in 1981, when he issued a decree declaring that religious political parties and 'politics of votes' were unlawful and contrary to Islamic principles.

Soon after, he moved to the Afghan Jihad theatre, which offered him a grand opportunity to mingle with like-minded warriors from around

the world – one of the deadliest contributions of the Afghan war. On his
return to the Swat Valley in 1989, he formed the TNSM, with an agenda
to lead an 'Islamic revolution' from his hometown.[3]

The organization experienced its first glory days in 1994–95, when
Pakistan had its first taste of this indigenous Taliban-style movement.
Benazir Bhutto was at the helm, as the country's prime minister, when
the group took to the streets in large numbers in the Swat Valley and
neighbouring districts (also known as Malakand region) to demand the
enforcement of a highly conservative and rigid version of Islamic law.
The government did not take things seriously and responded in a lack-
lustre way, which only boosted the confidence of the TNSM's members.
It was only when the group used violence to take charge of the area,
especially government buildings and the local airport, that the government was spurred into action to resolve the crisis (though it failed to
take the culprits to task). With peace restored, everyone tried to forget
what had happened, treating it as a bad dream. The implication was that
serious analysis of the causes of the crisis was not necessary. In South
Asia, this is the standard approach to problem solving.

For Pakistani policy makers, the 1994–95 episode should have raised
some disturbing questions, as Swat district historically was both more
developed and better integrated into the regional and national politics
than the isolated tribal belt. Besides its higher literacy rate and economic
activity, the area was politically vibrant. But Swat was faced with a
different challenge. This came in the form of a feudal landholding
structure that over a period of time became more oppressive and unaccountable. This requires a brief historical digression.

In northwest Pakistan, three semi-autonomous states – Dir, Swat
and Chitral – were amalgamated to form the Malakand Division of
NWFP in 1970. Since the British era, Swat had been a princely state
(dynastic and nominally sovereign) with its own laws, local security
set-up and revenue system. The laws of Pakistan were now extended to
the area, sweeping aside old legal and judicial systems that drew inspiration from aspects of Islamic law, as well as traditional codes. The old
judicial system in Swat was especially known for its efficiency: litigation

services were free and courts were required to decide cases quickly – in some categories after a fixed number of hearings (usually only two or three).[4] The new system was in its transitional phase when a legal battle erupted in 1975 between the government and timber merchants over forest royalties. This led to violent street protests, orchestrated by powerful landowners with a monopoly on forestland. The government panicked and agreed to amend the relevant law to accommodate the influential timber mafia. Feudal landowners benefited too. This proved a self-defeating concession in the long run and created an unhealthy precedent.

Back in 1994, the people of Swat could only feel nostalgia for the old administrative system, as the new system brought with it corruption, dysfunction and, most importantly, little relief for the ordinary people against the oppressive landlords. In this context, the TNSM demand for the establishment of an effective justice system based on egalitarian Islamic principles attracted popular support not only for its religious dimension, but also because it held out the hope of social justice in a society, which, though relatively prosperous, was marked by huge inequality. The TNSM itself was pleasantly surprised by the public support it received. However, there's many a slip 'twixt cup and lip.

The TNSM's agenda was catchy and touched a nerve, but the party lacked the capacity and know-how to carry it through. Official instructions were hastily issued to establish religious courts. Meanwhile TNSM supporters started driving on the wrong side of the road, in defiance of the traffic rules introduced by Great Britain a century before! This should have been a wake-up call for Islamabad, but the government was too busy dealing with civil–military tensions and democratic transition.

In time, the people of Swat came to realize that the TNSM's promises were not being fulfilled. Sufi Mohammad could sense public frustration and knew that he had to reprise his earlier performance. In early 2001 he renewed his efforts to see the introduction of Islamic law, now calling for more effective implementation by the government. The governor of NWFP could clearly see that the TNSM had been infiltrated by criminal elements with vested interests, and his public response to TNSM demands was apt: 'The real issue in Malakand is not the implementation of Sharia, but of non-custom paid vehicles, unlawful deforestation and avoidance of taxes.'[5]

Worried about declining support, the TNSM leader needed something to show off to his constituency – hence his abortive 'Jihad' journey to Afghanistan in late 2001. After Sufi's arrest in 2002, the TNSM was banned and rather faded into the background, since it lacked both resources and inspiring second-tier leaders. It still had a support base in Malakand region and even in parts of FATA (especially Bajaur agency), but the government calculated that its support would fizzle out now that Sufi was out of the picture. However this expectation was misplaced, as public disenchantment and growing disturbances in FATA started to have an impact on the Swat Valley.

In the absence of any functional local platform, the movement resurrected itself around 2005. Ironically, in this volatile setting, the deadly earthquake of October 2005 in the northern parts of Pakistan played an important role: the re-energized TNSM effectively preached that the natural disaster had been visited upon the region because its inhabitants were becoming irreligious. The remedy was simple – live by the strict sharia code. This resonated with people because of their shallow understanding of religion and their failure to make sense of their declining socio-economic position.

By early 2006, the stage was set for 33-year-old former chairlift operator Mullah Fazlullah to launch himself on a new career as a radical preacher. It is fascinating to see how Fazlullah gained control of the area. The son-in-law of TNSM founder Sufi Mohammad, he gained notoriety in 2006–07 thanks to his daily FM radio broadcasts, during which he lectured his listeners about the US presence in neighbouring Afghanistan and about the need for young people in the area to cross the border and take up arms against the invaders.[6] Fazlullah calculated that he needed to radicalize the environment before his ideas would be taken seriously, and in that spirit he started issuing some fanatical fatwas to stir up religious zeal among people. One of his earliest instructed parents not to send their daughters to school, which he described as the 'centre of all evil'. He had neither any religious qualifications nor any priestly credentials to issue such directives, but he had what it takes to implement them. His carefully selected terrorist cells were ever ready to execute anyone who dared to defy his commandments. Watching television, listening to music and even shaving beards was deemed un-Islamic. Fazlullah was soon nicknamed 'Mullah Radio' and he was able to expand his network at an amazing speed: neither was his unlawful FM radio blocked, nor was he pursued by the local law enforcement bodies in any serious manner. His strategy was simply to terrorize people into submission.[7]

Fazlullah was able to garner support relatively quickly, as he functioned quite systematically: he established an effective communication system, manipulated the class divisions that existed in the area, and introduced a court system offering quick justice. This reminded people of the old days, when the justice system in the area was known for its fairness and speed. Finally, the fear factor sealed the deal for him. The number of actual courts was low, but the idea of getting a judgment within hours naturally attracted people.

Fazlullah's activities were widely reported in the Pakistani media at the time. Military units were moved into the area, but they were not given the go-ahead to engage with the militants directly. Ordinary Swatis suffered gravely as they waited for the state authorities to act, but a sense of hopelessness made them surrender in the end. They had resisted initially, but Fazlullah's onslaught was massive. For instance, in the town of Mingora – the largest city in the Swat district – people would wake up in the morning to find the executed bodies of those who had challenged the militants slung from electric poles in the town's central square, in full view of the security forces – and with a note warning them not to remove the bodies before midday.[8] Ordinary Swatis interpreted the situation as a conspiracy, where the state's security forces were hand in glove with the militants. Perhaps there was no other rational way to understand the criminal silence of the security forces.

Half of the local police force deserted, many of them joining Fazlullah's brigade – an indication of his success. The Pakistan Army did begin limited operations in 2007 to retake the region, but it encountered stiff resistance and suffered many casualties. For the people of Swat, if the army couldn't retrieve the situation, it was all over.

The MMA (the alliance of religious parties that had formed the government in the province in 2002 – see above) was deservedly swept from office in 2008, but in the process Pakistan nearly lost Swat. Pro-Taliban in its ideological outlook, the MMA exploited the religious card to the hilt and did nothing to check the extremist groups operating in the area. A damning indictment of the MMA came from a politician from Swat, Mohammad Ayub Khan, who, addressing a public rally in Swat, asserted: 'MMA is responsible for terrorism in Swat. It overlooked terrorists' camps and their explosive-laden vehicles in Swat and made huge money by promoting weapons.'[9]

The new progressive Awami National Party government that took office in early 2008 was no fan of Sufi Mohammad, but it opted to release him from jail in 2009 as part of a secret deal to rein in his notorious son-in-law. The ANP explained its decision to negotiate with the TNSM by arguing that if the 'army is not interested in challenging the expanding writ of Taliban, why should we continue to sacrifice our lives?'[10] Asfandyar Wali Khan, president of the ANP, secretly visited Washington in May 2008, apparently in an attempt to convince the US counterterrorism authorities about the proposed deal.[11] Sufi Mohammad's move to the Swat Valley clearly enjoyed official blessing – both from the political and the military power centres. Ameer Haider Khan Hoti, the ANP's chief minister of the provincial government, was clear about his approach: 'Our policy is political dialogue. That will eventually be the way out.'[12] Consequently, a ceasefire was arranged and the provincial government agreed to enforce a moderate and tolerable version of sharia law.[13] Asfandyar Wali, the ANP leader, disclosed in 2013 that he had proceeded with this plan despite being pressed by then US Assistant Secretary of State Richard Boucher and then US Ambassador to Pakistan Anne Patterson not to go for this peace deal.[14]

For their part, Pakistan's security and intelligence services were sending out confused messages. For instance, Baitullah Mehsud and Fazlullah were both even declared 'patriotic' at a special, confidential media briefing conducted by Pakistani intelligence in late 2008. This was around the time when rumours were rife about Indian surgical strikes in Pakistan in the aftermath of the terrorist attacks in Mumbai in November 2008. Leading Pakistani journalists attending the briefing in Islamabad were told: 'We have no big issues with the militants in FATA. We have only some misunderstandings with Baitullah Mehsud and Fazlullah. These misunderstandings could be removed through dialogue.'[15] Most probably the announcement was a ploy, designed to warn India that Pakistan could reconcile with all its militants, who could then join together to fight India. It also highlights the critical nature of India–Pakistan rivalry in the region. The bluff worked for a while, until Mehsud recommended his terror campaign against Pakistani security forces operating in FATA and urban centres, targeting ordinary people.

In the Swat theatre, Sufi Mohammad's sponsors were also in for a rude shock as things didn't go to plan. When Sufi saw the thousands of people welcoming him on his journey back to Swat after his release from prison in Peshawar, he must have been reminded of his dream of leading an Islamic revolution. He intended to deal with Fazlullah, as agreed, but apparently postponed the plan indefinitely. Later Fazlullah would take full advantage of this. Addressing a big gathering in Swat, Sufi came out strongly against democracy, declaring it to be un-Islamic. He also provoked a public backlash over the 'pearls of wisdom' he dropped in an interview with an intelligent journalist, Salim Safi, on GEO TV: 'Islam does not permit women to leave the home except to perform Hajj in Mecca'; 'Women are not permitted to receive education'; and 'The judiciary in Pakistan and the country's constitution are un-Islamic.'[16] He even showed a keen interest in expanding his movement to the rest of Pakistan, not realizing that most Pakistanis would not stand for this kind of extremist agenda. A private news channel's broadcast showing a video clip, recorded on a mobile phone, of the public flogging of a 17-year-old Swati girl, further gave the public a stark sense of what Taliban justice really meant.

Public opinion started turning against Sufi Mohammad. And the developments in the area sent shudders down the corridors of power, forcing the government to seriously consider alternative ways of dealing with him. A major military operation in the area was planned – appropriately named Operation *Rah e Rast* – the 'straight path'. A delay in the military action cost a number of human lives. The massive operation forced the people of Swat Valley, hundreds of thousands of them, to flee their homes in mid-2009.

The transformation of Swat from a tourist destination to a sanctuary for terrorists shocked many in the nation at the time. Swat had trembled as the illegal FM radio had broadcast the names of those people who would be found slaughtered the next morning in the public square. Meanwhile the rest of the country was paralysed with helplessness and fear. And yet this was the valley where tourists used to go ice skating; where painters went to capture the spectacular views (the region used to be known as mini-Switzerland on account of its scenery); where the literacy rate – even among women – was higher than in the rest of the province. The square – now known as *Khooni chowk* (bloody square) – was where locals had formerly gathered to enjoy pashto music while sipping *kahwa* – the local green tea. Truly a 'Paradise Lost'.

Pakistan had waited far too long before directly confronting the TNSM. By the second half of 2009, when the security forces had largely cleared the district, adjacent regions were convulsed by the arrival of 2 million displaced people. The ad hoc response allowed some religious conservative groups to increase their influence among the internally displaced people. For instance, Jamaat-e-Islami's Al-Khidmat organization and Jamaat-ud-Dawa's new incarnation, the Falah-i-Insaniat Foundation (FIF), established various charity camps in the Swat area to build goodwill and potentially attract future recruits.[17] Significant US funding helped Pakistan tackle this gigantic task, but on the ground it was the religious activists who appeared to be doing most.

On the battlefront, several thousand militants were reportedly killed, yet surprisingly Fazlullah escaped unscathed. The overall military campaign was a success, though it was not without controversy. Fazlullah was apparently allowed to escape in 2008, after having been surrounded by police. It is believed that this was done on the instructions of a local military commander, who wanted to avoid a violent confrontation. Fazlullah shifted to Afghanistan in 2009 and has been involved in attacks on the Pakistan Army and on others opposed to him in the FATA and Malakand areas.[18] He only returned to the FATA area in December 2013, after being appointed the new chief of the Pakistani Taliban – a move that was as surprising as it was terrifying for the people of the Swat region.

I had an opportunity to interview three senior Pakistan Army officers involved in the Swat campaign. Their side of the story deserves to be heard. They maintain that the military started operating in the area in or around 2007, and in fact cleared some areas of militancy. But the political representatives failed to move in and regain control of the situation. They believe that the lack of policing capacity in the area also made the military's task more daunting – and there is indeed evidence to support this contention. Commendably, the military later became proactively engaged with training police in the province. Lack of public support at the national level for a major military action is another factor that the military blames for the delay in taking action. This is a more problematic assertion: it is not the military's job to gauge public opinion before mounting counter-terrorism action – is the prerogative of the political leadership to decide when to call on the military for internal security operations.

In parallel with the rise in militancy in the Swat Valley, the situation in FATA was also deteriorating considerably. The Sararogha peace deal (discussed in chapter 5) was scrapped unilaterally by Baitullah Mehsud in August 2007, in reaction to increased movement and patrolling in the area by the Pakistani army. As it later transpired, the deal enabled him to become much more powerful. The ten-month-old 'peace deal' in North Waziristan also collapsed in July 2007, but not before it took a heavy toll in terms of the expansion of militant infrastructure in the area.[19] Breaking deals with the military served an important purpose. There was method to this madness: the formation of a new terrorist platform was in the offing.

The deadly rise of the Pakistani Taliban

The emergence of the Tehrik-i-Taliban Pakistan (TTP) in December 2007 was a deadly new addition to the alphabet soup of terrorist organizations in Pakistan. There was a discernible increase in the number of attacks on military convoys, and an upsurge in the targeting both of government infrastructure and the civilian population. All this violence and coercion compelled adjustment to the new reality – the rise of militants and the downfall of the tribal *maliks*.

It is still hotly debated in Pakistan whether the Pakistani Taliban were a natural corollary of the Afghan Taliban, or whether the 9/11 attacks and the consequent military action in Afghanistan led to their creation. Retired Pakistani Brigadier Asad Munir, who served as ISI chief in Peshawar during 1999–2003, insightfully argues that 'even if there had been no 9/11, the Pakistani Taliban who had been in existence since 1998–99 would have expanded their presence and operations in the FATA area; but it would have been a slow process.'[20] Much had already transpired in the region to stimulate the birth of such groups.

The organizational skills, leadership quality and resourcefulness of the Pakistani militants operating in the tribal territories, however, improved in the years following 9/11, thanks to the influx of Taliban fighters and Al-Qaeda strategists from Afghanistan. Hot conflict zones in FATA and flow of funds from a variety of sources also contributed to this. Still, they were lacking a unifying platform right up until the dying days of 2007.

In the period since 9/11, many small militant groups that operated independently in FATA worked together whenever their political and security interests converged, but intertribal rivalries ensured that they never merged. In the turbulent Waziristan area, the traditional

Waziri–Mehsud rivalry never subsided, but in the face of a growing military presence they decided to pool their resources and band together.

Forty notorious militant leaders, representing both FATA and parts of the NWFP, met around mid-December 2007 to establish the TTP as an umbrella organization. Baitullah Mehsud of South Waziristan became the top commander; Hafiz Gul Bahadur of the Wazir tribe (North Waziristan) was his deputy; and Faqir Mohammed of the Mohmand tribe (Bajaur agency) became the third in command.[21] Mullah Fazlullah (of Swat fame) was also given a largely symbolic position as secretary general, in order to project support for the ongoing Swat militancy. The TTP mission statement was brief, but in scope was both extensive and idealistic:

a) *Enforce Islamic law* – a demand without which they could not claim to be 'Taliban'. They never clearly defined the term – partly in order to attract all religious groups, but also because they lacked the religious credentials even to attempt it. As later events suggest, for the TTP this served as a rhetorical call rather than a declaration about their organizing principle.

b) *Unite against NATO forces in Afghanistan and wage a defensive Jihad against Pakistani forces* – a call that clarified the main purpose of the organization. Fighting an outside force was nothing unusual for them, but any decision to fight the Pakistan Army effectively needed a collective effort – hence this entire exercise.

c) *Abolish checkpoints in FATA and end military operations in Swat and North Waziristan* – a threat that was certain to be popular with ordinary tribesmen and was aimed at regaining the right for them to roam freely and continue with their nefarious activities.

d) *No more negotiations with the government on any future peace deals* – this was more subtle, as they had benefited greatly from past peace deals and must have desired more of them. At best it was a bargaining chip.

e) *Release Lal Masjid cleric Abdul Aziz* – underscoring their efforts to continue to recruit elements associated with the Red Mosque crisis and build further support against security forces.[22]

The TTP was also trying to ride the wave of extremism, visible in a significant spike in the number of terrorist attacks, including suicide bombings, across the country in 2007. Nothing was beyond the reach of the militants – sensitive installations, including an air force base, ISI offices and police infrastructure; leading politicians; the family members of security forces; and ordinary citizens in marketplaces and even mosques.[23] Militants in FATA were at the forefront in creating this mayhem, and the TTP was only expected to coordinate the terror campaign more effectively.

Media reports indicate that the inaugural TTP meeting also discussed cooperation in intelligence collection, identification and elimination of 'spies' and enemies, funding, the outline of a new court system, and even policing of the area – issues on which there were serious differences between the groups. According to a local journalist, Aqeel Yusufzai, Afghan Taliban and Al-Qaeda often helped different groups within the TTP to develop consensus on such divisive issues and to stick to 'basic goals'.[24] This is corroborated by the Pakistani defence attaché to Kabul in 2003–06, Brigadier Saad Mohammad, who believes that the TTP, the Haqqani network and Gul Bahadur were all associated with Al-Qaeda in one way or another; but he also argued that the Afghan Taliban (which he called the Kandahari Taliban) were largely independent of Al-Qaeda influence by mid-2010, when he made his remarks.[25]

The TTP and the Afghan Taliban operated under different command structures, but the Pakistani Taliban looked up to their Afghan counterparts, especially those who were commanding operations inside Afghanistan. They were the role models. Almost all the top leaders of the TTP – Baitullah Mehsud, Hakimullah Mehsud and Waliur Rahman – at one time or another had fought inside Afghanistan side by side with, and under the command of, the Afghan Taliban.

It should be stressed that Mullah Omar is not the commander of the Pakistani Taliban, though communication channels between the Afghan and the Pakistani Taliban have always remained open. Pir Zubair Shah, a very talented and well-informed Pakistani journalist from South

Waziristan, explained to me in an interview that the Haqqani group was the bridge between the two sides.[26] He also referred to an instance where an Afghan Taliban leader played the role of a mediator, resolving an internal dispute in the TTP between Baitullah Mehsud and the notorious suicide-bombing trainer Qari Hussain Mehsud.

One of the most potent factors at play, however, was the representation of all major tribes in the TTP – except perhaps the Turi (residing in Kurram agency) and sections of the Orakzai and Bangash tribes, which, being Shia Muslims, had ideological differences with the Taliban and Al-Qaeda worldview. Importantly, the Wazir tribe was fully on board, as it had a huge stake in the matter, being cultivators of fertile land in Wana, Shakai, Zalai, Spin and Zarmelan and being settled on the Durand Line, which enabled them to manage and benefit from the formal and informal trade.[27] The Mehsuds, though they held a little more than 60 per cent of all South Waziristan, were less fortunate, as they inhabited rugged and inhospitable mountainous terrain, with no direct access to the border with Afghanistan. This made the Mehsuds less ready to compromise and harder to negotiate with. Hence the Wazirs were always more concerned with developments in Afghanistan, whereas the Mehsuds kept a relatively more watchful eye on internal developments in Pakistan.[28] That is why the TTP's choice of a Mehsud leader and a Wazir deputy needed very careful management. In a matter of months, a personality clash alienated Gul Bahadur from the TTP. Whether or not Pakistan's ISI provoked this rift, it was certainly a major beneficiary.

Gul Bahadur, a pragmatist and the only one of the new generation of militants with a religious degree, had cordial relations with another Wazir tribal warrior, Maulvi Nazir Ahmed, who operated in South Waziristan.[29] Bahadur was uncomfortable in the company of a crude bunch of Mehsuds like Baitullah – and especially his crazy driver-cum-spokesman Hakimullah, who took over the TTP after Baitullah's elimination in a US drone strike in 2009. More revealing, however, were the common likes and dislikes of Bahadur and Nazir. They loved the regular 'honorarium' and the occasional armaments they received from the ISI for their services; and they shared a special distaste for Uzbek and other foreign militants who were enjoying sanctuary in North Waziristan.[30] Similarly, they had an interesting and complicated relationship with the infamous Haqqani network, a vital part of the puzzle.

But for all that they had a new religious identity and newfound power, the militants could not give up their old habits. This is evident from a TTP leadership notice to all its members on 23 January 2009:

> All the managers and workers of the organization are instructed that from today onwards mujahideen are banned from looting vehicles, kidnapping and plundering civil and government property . . . All the previously issued licences are cancelled today and any claim that you have special permission from your local leader will not be acceptable.[31]

The impact was negligible, because the criminal activities of the TTP were an important source of funds for the member groups: that would be cutting off their noses to spite their faces. In some cases, purely criminal gangs carried out the abductions, but then they would sell the kidnapped individuals to the Taliban; the Taliban would subsequently get a better price on the market because of their higher profile.[32]

The crimes, of course, damaged their public standing, but the TTP had no plans to contest an election any time soon, and their formula for success was built on the coercion of ordinary people to defeat dissent; beheadings of *maliks* to pack up the old order; and terror attacks across Pakistan. For this last and most critical part of their strategy, they needed a constant stream of suicide bombers – people who were prepared to give up their lives. Motivated by both dogma and tribal ethos, they were unleashed with uncommon ferocity. Sohail Tajik, an outstanding counterterrorism expert in the ranks of Pakistan's police, reveals that 90 per cent of recruits in suicide training centres in South Waziristan were found to be Pashtuns, and around 70 per cent of those belonged to the Mehsud tribe.[33] This alone shows the extent of tribal anger and frustration. The Mehsud tribe was targeted not only by

Pakistani military operations, but also by the US drone campaign. This was a recruitment bonanza for the TTP in the Mehsud territory. The US drones were a new tool of war: unmanned aerial vehicles, armed with weapons and controlled from thousands of miles away by pilots who had live access to ground intelligence. Pakistan was officially, but secretly, fully on board with this.

But the TTP looked further afield, too. Punjabi militants, disgruntled by Musharraf's freezing of the Kashmir campaign, moved to FATA in droves. The TTP needed them because any sustained terror campaign in the heartland of Pakistan – Islamabad area and Punjab Province – needed local support (for logistical reasons, if nothing else). Around 2,000 militants from southern and northern Punjab Province had moved to South Waziristan even before the TTP was launched to help out Maulvi Nazir's campaign against the Uzbeks; and more followed in their footsteps.[34]

This trend had certain consequences. Militants from Punjab had proved during the 1980s and 1990s more prone to mercenary actions and freelance activity. They would hop from organization to organization, depending on which Kashmir-focused group was more popular among Arab, Gulf and local intelligence funders at any given point in time. Put simply, they went about their profession greedily. Asked by the *New York Times* about the financial side of militant operations, Zulfikar Hameed, a decorated senior police officer in Lahore, disclosed: 'The money that's coming in is huge.' He went on: 'When you go back through the chain of the transaction, you invariably find it's been done for money.'[35] Zulfikar is a good friend and we did our police training together in 1996 in Islamabad. He is an avid reader and a thorough professional. I have not an iota of doubt that his assessment must be based on credible and empirical evidence.

But Punjabi militants were also highly experienced at pursuing narrow sectarian goals, especially against pluralistic-minded Sunni and Shia elements that honoured the mystical traditions of Islam. By further adapting to the TTP worldview, they earned the name 'Taliban', becoming known as the 'Punjabi Taliban'. Many of the most deadly attacks – for example, the Islamabad Marriott bombing of September 2008 and the attack on the Sri Lankan cricket team in Lahore in March 2009 – were planned and executed by the Punjabi Taliban.[36] An important district of Punjab, Dera Ghazi Khan was a gateway to both the Taliban-controlled territories in the Pashtun-dominated region and the heart of Punjab, but the government did little even to reinforce the security apparatus in this area. It was not mere incompetence: denial of the reality was also a contributory factor to the government paralysis.

Even if it was deemed to be 'America's war', Pakistan should not have shied away from properly investigating the local actors and analysing the trends. Militants from across Pakistan were joining together and putting aside their ethnic and political differences; but Pakistan as a nation was rudderless and confused as to the real identity of these fanatics. The mixed messages emanating from the corridors of power and from the media hardly helped.

All the same, Gallup polls at the end of 2009 showed that 72 per cent of Pakistanis believed the Taliban were having a negative influence in Pakistan, and only 4 per cent took the opposite view.[37] Pew Global surveys from 2008 to 2012 also showed similar trends: Pakistani support for the Afghan Taliban and Al-Qaeda declined from 27 per cent or so to 13 per cent.[38] The Taliban 'brand' was never hip in Pakistan, but crucial years were taken up in debating conspiracy theories about the Indian and the American role in supporting the TTP. Pakistan's return from the shadow of military rule to democracy in early 2008, and especially a vibrant lawyers' movement, helped many Pakistanis see things more clearly and freely; but it was just the beginning of a major transformation. Things were expected to get worse before they would get better.

During my travels in Pakistan in 2008 and 2009, I was amazed to hear from many interviewees that 'there is evidence that some suicide bombers from South Waziristan were Hindus', which would imply an Indian intelligence connection. When asked what the evidence was, they would refer to news reports that the post-mortem examinations of some of the terrorists killed showed that they had not been circumcised.

There is indeed a religious injunction on Muslims to circumcise a male child soon after birth. What is not well known in Pakistan is that a few Mehsud sub-tribes do not routinely follow this practice![39] For many Pashtuns, especially in remote areas of FATA, if something is not part of the tribal code, it is not mandatory.

The TTP turned out to be a very successful enterprise, and its terror campaign expanded across Pakistan between 2007 and 2014. The facts are staggering: 361 suicide attacks were carried out between January 2007 and December 2013, an average of 51 a year.[40] Tens of thousands of people lost their lives, including scores of military and law enforcement officials, and the TTP showed its lethal capacity by hitting the most secure, as well as the most sacred of places – from the general headquarters of the Pakistani army to the naval base in Karachi; from the shrine of the highly revered Data Ganj Bakhsh in Lahore to the widely celebrated Eid gathering in the tribal areas. Anyone seen to be in collusion with Pakistan's security forces and the United States was a legitimate target. Politicians who dared to condemn the TTP were hounded mercilessly. In consequence, Pakistan was on the edge.

Among the militants, the perception of close collaboration between the US and Pakistan was a powerful mobilizing factor. In reality, things were not as rosy between the two states, though it is a fact that CIA–ISI cooperation improved during the 'war on terror' period. There were ups and downs, but the lines of communication were seldom blocked. Over the years, the ISI 'collected tens of millions of dollars through a classified CIA program that pays for the capture or killing of wanted militants'.[41] Surprising as it may sound, a counterterrorism division at the ISI also benefited significantly from CIA funds and expertise.[42] Some of the money was, in fact, used to construct a new and modern complex of buildings at the ISI headquarters in Islamabad. Many ISI and Military Intelligence officers were awarded US study scholarships in an effort to improve the working relationship between the intelligence organizations of the two countries.

* * *

Political push and favourable public opinion helped the military to launch a major operation in South Waziristan in 2009; but it was not a smooth ride. It could not be. The TTP had strengthened its defences and was ready for battle. Tens of thousands of ordinary tribesmen and their families had moved to Khyber Pakhtunkhwa Province at the first hint that military action was on the cards.[43] Many of the foreign fighters had conveniently shifted to North Waziristan. The TTP knew that this time around they would be faced not with an ill-equipped and tired Frontier Corps, but with a 30,000-strong military contingent, complete with the latest weapons, a logistics supply line and intelligence support. And that was a different ball-game altogether. The force indeed moved in swiftly, but as it turned out it was there for the long haul to 'clear, hold and build', as per the American counterinsurgency manual it was now following. Ambassador Anne Patterson, the US envoy to Pakistan, had pushed for this adaptation on behalf of the US Department of Defense.[44]

At first alarmed by the appropriately named Operation *Rah-e-Nijat* (Path to Salvation), the TTP's fighters even retreated to higher mountains.[45] They continued with sporadic attacks on the military and shifted some of their assets in adjoining areas. I had the opportunity to interview a few senior Pakistani military commanders, including a corps commander and two brigade commanders, who supervised or directly led military operations in FATA and especially in South Waziristan. Their perspectives and observations were both enlightening and surprising.[46]

Major General Shafqat Asghar, an unusually open and courageous army officer who led a brigade in the 2009 South Waziristan operation, recounted that the first batch of TTP militants arrested by his forces were dumbfounded to learn that they were fighting a 'Muslim army': TTP warriors had been told that they were at war with 'infidels'. After a discussion with his team, Asghar decided that they would immediately start broadcasting the call to prayer on loudspeakers five times a day, in order to dispel the impression that they were 'outsiders' or non-Muslims. In the course of my extensive interviews with Asghar, during which I probed the subject of the mindset of the militants he had had a chance to interview, he insisted that he could not find any sign of religiosity among them. He was also convinced that the TTP had some regional backers.[47] From other military officers who served in the conflict zone I heard that rape and sodomy were quite common in the TTP camps.

Another army officer I interviewed during my research trip to Pakistan stunned me when he explained that he had not received any detailed intelligence briefings with profiles of the tribes that his military unit was to confront in FATA in and around 2010. Interestingly, there are no ISI officers attached to the military units operating in FATA. They operate in parallel in certain areas, but normally there is no regular interaction between army units and intelligence operatives.

I was also told that the US drone strikes were regularly coordinated with the Pakistani military authorities until 2010, and during the early phase (2004–07) even 5–7 days' notice was given by either side for the other to monitor the target and mutually decide whether to go for it or not. Within military units operating in the tribal area, drone attacks were generally seen in a positive light. The Pakistan Air Force was also routinely used for air cover and to target militant hubs. Almost every senior army officer I interviewed carped that the Pakistan military's requests to the US for specific military equipment needed for operations were not met. This served to strengthen the grave misgivings among army officers about US intentions and seriousness. When I took this complaint up with a US Department of Defense official, he quipped that the Pakistanis were only keen to get military hardware that is used in 'COIN' (the usual jargon for 'counterinsurgency'). While I was wondering what could be wrong with that, he went on to add that in this case 'COIN' meant 'Counter-India'. Apparently, in Washington defence circles, this is an oft-repeated joke.

Pakistani security forces often complain that their plight goes unappreciated in Western capitals. They expect some recognition of the fact that the Pakistani military's casualties from the fight against the Taliban and Al-Qaeda have outstripped the combined losses of the US and other NATO countries in Afghanistan. The statistics support this contention, but Pakistan underestimates how much damage was done to the country's image and credibility by the presence there of Osama bin Laden.

The second of May 2011 was a particularly bad day for Pakistan. On that day, the US raid on bin Laden's compound in the town of Abbottabad (a city that hosts Pakistan's premier military academy) made headlines across the world. At the end of the stealth operation, bin Laden was dead; but Pakistan has had to do a lot of explaining since then. Whatever trust existed between the US and Pakistan was destroyed.

Though US President Obama said that, 'it's important to note that our counterterrorism cooperation with Pakistan helped lead us to bin Laden and the compound where he was hiding', the question asked in capitals across the world was whether Pakistani intelligence had been complicit in or ignorant about bin Laden's whereabouts.[48] F.B. Ali, a respected former Pakistani brigadier who now lives in Canada, intriguingly maintained that a retired senior ISI officer spilled the beans about bin Laden's location when he walked into a US embassy in a Gulf country; that is how the US came to know of the Abbottabad location.[49] It is nearly impossible to verify this version of events.

At the time, US Defense Secretary Robert Gates forcefully asserted that he had seen no evidence at all that the senior Pakistani leadership had any information about bin Laden, but obviously a support network for him was at work.[50] Disclosures by bin Laden's young wife, who was living with him at the Abbottabad compound, about how she travelled freely across the country later raised further suspicions. Most surprising, though, was the revelation in an official Pakistani commission report that just a couple of years after the 9/11 attacks, bin Laden's car had been pulled over by a traffic police sergeant in Pakistan for speeding, but he had managed to get away scot free.[51] The poor cop never knew that a big reward had slipped through his fingers. (For those who know traffic police in Pakistan, no other interpretation is possible.)

Getting intelligence on bin Laden was a remarkable feat for the US, and thousands of pages of documents and hundreds of CDs acquired from the bin Laden compound at the time of the raid are considered invaluable in understanding how Al-Qaeda functioned all those years. A select few documents from this treasure trove have been declassified by the US government. They show that bin Laden believed in distinguishing between 'good Taliban' and 'bad Taliban'. He was fully supportive of Afghan Jihad, but his top lieutenants, at his direction, wrote to Hakimullah Mehsud of the TTP, expressing displeasure at the group's 'ideology, methods and behavior'.[52] Apparently, he was no longer in control of Al-Qaeda and its affiliates.

During my interviews with security officials in Pakistan, they dispelled the notion that there is any distinction on the ground between 'good Taliban' (who do not attack Pakistan's security forces, e.g. the Haqqani group) and 'bad Taliban' (meaning the TTP and its ilk); but on the US side this dichotomy is believed to be a hard fact. The US naturally wants Pakistan to go all out and reclaim ownership of the tribal area, which is used as a sanctuary for cross-border attacks. The Taliban and other militants who moved into the tribal belt have gradually become more confident in organizing attacks inside Afghanistan. The border is porous and Pakistani border checkpoints – though vastly increased in number – are still inadequate to monitor the movement of militants. Thousands of ordinary Pashtuns cross the border daily from dozens of crossing points, and to figure out who is a militant and who is not is a gigantic task. When pressed on this point, Pakistani security officials typically retort: 'Well if we can't manage it on our side, what stops the newly minted Afghan army and American forces on the other side of the border from obstructing the path of militants on their side?' I have not heard a good answer to this. The American counterargument is more along the lines of: 'So what happens to all the billions of dollars that the Pakistani military has received from us for counterterrorism in the tribal areas and for securing the border with Afghanistan?' Pakistanis get worked up over this and start bandying about the statistics for soldiers lost in the area. They blame Afghan and Indian intelligence, too, for supporting TTP elements. The debate continues in this circular fashion.

Pakistan's apprehensions about linkage between the TTP and Afghan intelligence (and by extension Indian intelligence, according to their view) received some attention when the US special forces in Afghanistan arrested the deputy TTP leader, Latif Mehsud, in late October 2013, while he was inside Afghanistan to meet Afghan intelligence officials. This naturally led to a deterioration in trust between the two countries. South Asia has paid heavily for such proxy campaigns, but is still refusing to learn any lessons.[53]

General Ashfaq Parvez Kayani, the former chief of army staff, wanted to pursue a step-by-step approach, and was of the view that it was important to consolidate the army's hold in South Waziristan and other tribal regions before embarking on another army offensive, especially in North Waziristan.[54] Pakistan certainly has some favourites among the armed groups in FATA – chosen on a case-by-case basis in various agencies – and it overlooks their excesses so long as they are not directly involved in attacking military personnel and infrastructure. In some cases the Pakistan Army is guilty of delayed action caused by its inadequate analytical capacity. Despite a large deployment – around 140,000 in 2011 – some militant groups have assumed so much power that the army is not sufficiently confident to take them on, fearing a backlash it could not cope with.[55] (By 2014, the number has risen to around 175,000.) In other cases, some battles are contracted out to local *lashkars* or militias, and for that policy to succeed certain compromises need to be made. Overall, Pakistan has gained very little from such short-term policy prescriptions, but it is almost as though acknowledging and learning from past mistakes is taboo in the country. Overall policy direction has remained incoherent.

The ISI officers on the ground who make crucial recommendations about available options were seldom the brightest in the army. That began to change when President Musharraf elevated General Kayani, a former head of the ISI, to be the army chief in 2007. Kayani handpicked one of his most trusted officers, Lieutenant General Pasha, to be the ISI chief, and he in turn asked for some of the best army officers to be deputed for ISI duties. Kayani not only obliged him, but also ensured the promotion of many important ISI officers to the ranks of major general and lieutenant general. Thus ISI appointments became more attractive to career officers, who had previously shied away from joining the ISI, as the organization was generally regarded as a dead-end assignment for middle-ranking officers. One can never be certain about trends within an intelligence organization, but there are many examples that reinforce this notion.

* * *

By 2013, the Pakistani Taliban had emerged as a new elite in FATA, after eliminating over 800 *maliks*. Its empowerment of many tribes considered to be less prestigious or influential has also swayed local dynamics. The semi-educated but ambitious class of mullahs of course led this transformation. It started off as a Pashtun phenomenon, but other ethnic groups, especially Punjabis, joined in and helped the network expand. Now Karachi has also emerged as an important base for the TTP fighters, because a large chunk of money flows from there. But it is not about greed and power only. The fact that legitimate grievances, disproportionate use of force and abuse by security forces also fuelled local participation in the Pakistani Taliban movement is often overlooked.[56] Hence, it was a mix of socio-political, economic and religious factors that galvanized young tribesmen over the years.

The TTP has also constantly expanded its objectives, as is evident from a 2010 statement by Azam Tariq, a TTP spokesman: 'Our [TTP] bonding force is our common cause of waging jihad in Afghanistan . . . the ultimate goal is to implement sharia law [in Pakistan].'[57] Before placing the TTP on the Foreign Terrorist Organizations list, US Secretary of State Hillary Clinton aptly declared that 'the Pakistani Taliban [is] a "mortal threat" to the world'.[58] Barely a few months earlier, General David Petraeus had hinted at the other side of the coin, when he argued that 'there are a lot of organizations out there that are wannabe international terrorist organizations . . . the Pakistani Taliban has been much more focused internally'.[59] Both were right.

While funding for operations came through bank robberies, kidnappings for ransom and Al-Qaeda financiers, the TTP leadership cared deeply about both its fallen heroes and those arrested by the security

forces. The families of the deceased were helped financially, and negotiations to get TTP fighters released from jail were always ongoing. The
TTP is constantly on the look-out to kidnap security officials and their
family members for 'exchange of prisoners' deals. The son-in-law of the
chairman of the joint chiefs of staff, General Tariq Majeed (who had
also spearheaded the Red Mosque operation), remained in TTP custody
for years and the family reportedly had to pay close to $3 million in
ransom for his release.[60]

Jailbreaks were yet another tool in the TTP arsenal, and civilian law
enforcement and security forces repeatedly failed to secure even highly
sensitive jails – something that raised a host of suspicions. Three examples will suffice.

Usman Kurd, a known sectarian terrorist convicted of massacring
members of the Shia Hazara community in Quetta in 2003–04, escaped
from a high-security prison in 2008 and revived his sectarian terror
campaign in the city, leading to hundreds more deaths.[61]

A jailbreak in Bannu in May 2012 led to the escape of some key TTP
leaders and hundreds of other dangerous convicted criminals. The TTP
later released a video showing the planning of the operation and its
successful execution.[62]

Even more audacious was a major jailbreak in Dera Ismail Khan in
July 2013, when TTP militants mounted a highly sophisticated and well
coordinated operation to free around 250 inmates, including over a
dozen high-profile terrorists.[63] Ironically, a specific and timely intelligence tip was passed on to the local security forces, as well as the prison
management, but to no avail.[64]

In the wake of such failures, it is impossible to convince international
observers that Pakistan is serious about defeating terrorism in the
country. Security forces often refer to lack of public support for massive
military operations. But that is incorrect: the public approves of and
demands action (though admittedly at the same time it expects little or
no collateral damage). For instance, a significant majority of FATA residents oppose the presence in their midst of the TTP, and around 70 per
cent support military action in the area by the Pakistan Army, according

to a New America Foundation poll in 2010.[65] It forces one to question whether it is just a capacity issue or something more Machiavellian. Concerned citizens of Pakistan have not avoided dealing with this critical issue. In December 2009, a group of civil society organizations and representatives of many progressive political parties issued an insightful statement – known as the Peshawar Declaration – maintaining that 'the main and real factor behind the present chaos and instability in the region is the Strategic Depth policy of Pakistan' and demanding respect for Afghanistan's sovereignty.[66] Pakistan's confused counterterrorism policy, which is reactive in approach and burdened by its regional interests, surely poses a very serious challenge.

Finally, it is true that American drone policy, geared towards keeping the Al-Qaeda operators and TTP on the run, does appear to be succeeding. After all, the top leaders of TTP – Baitullah Mehsud, Waliur Rahman and Hakimullah Mehsud – were eliminated by drone strikes. Still, the issue also has a different dimension that deserves consideration.

It may be hard for security hawks to swallow, but it is nevertheless the case that drone strikes also help the TTP recruit fighters. This, from Baitullah Mehsud, is credible proof of that: 'I spent three months trying to recruit and got only 10–15 persons. One US attack and I got 150 volunteers!'[67] We must not forget that Pakistani-American Faisal Shahzad, who tried unsuccessfully to blow up Times Square in New York in May 2010, cited drone strikes as a key motivation for his action.[68] A video recording of Shahzad hugging Hakimullah and vowing to attack the West also showed that the TTP had no plans to remain confined to South Asia.[69]

In the words of my friend, the accomplished columnist Mosharraf Zaidi, back in 2009: 'The key question is not about the populism of the Taliban, the TNSM, or any violent extremists in Pakistan. It is whether Pakistani Muslims will remain hostage to their sense of religious inferiority to the mullah.'[70] Zaidi continues optimistically: 'Violent extremists can flog the odd alleged straying couple, but they cannot flog 172 million people. They cannot win this war, and that is why they're so angry all the time.'

He is right, but the problem in Pakistan has been that, due to the inadequacies of its law enforcement and intelligence services, there is a pervasive feeling of insecurity, which allows a small group of thugs to take a whole nation hostage. The silence of the majority also further emboldens such miscreants. Subsequently, the number of gangs operating under the TTP umbrella has increased and various newer organizations, with a strong Punjabi Taliban presence, have also popped up in FATA, all competing with each other for resources, as well as recruits. These often warring TTP factions now have separate representatives even in the city of Karachi.[71] These turf wars could potentially open up opportunities for the state to confront the groups more effectively, weaken their resolve and dilute their energy.

The story of Swat and the Taliban would not be complete without a reference to a young Pakistani girl, Malala Yusafzai, who shone a beam of light in Pakistan even on the darkest of days.[72] While girls' schools were being targeted by militants, she challenged the Taliban worldview by writing a diary for the BBC, in which she narrated what terrible things were going on in her hometown. Her demand was simple – the chance of education. She was lionized for her bravery when Swat was rescued, but militants came after her in 2012 and she was shot in head while on her way to school in Swat. Luckily for Pakistan, she survived – and her message got a further boost. She is now an icon for young Pakistanis and is recognized worldwide for her courage and passion. But tragically, Swat is not safe for her.

CHAPTER EIGHT

The political economy of Taliban resurgence in Afghanistan

Opium, crime and development funds (2006-13)

By the time US President Barack Obama came to office in January 2009, the revival of the Taliban was no secret. Taliban ascendance – in terms of its expanding territorial control in the Pashtun-dominated areas and its capacity to mount audacious attacks on US bases across Afghanistan – had been a hard reality since as early as 2007.[1] Unlike Iraq, Afghanistan was a 'legitimate war' for Obama, but he had made up his mind during his campaign that the way forward for the US was to 'help Afghans grow their economy from the bottom up'.[2] His clarity was obvious from his commitment – 'We cannot lose Afghanistan to a future of narco-terrorism.'[3]

Four years later, in July 2012, US Secretary of State Hillary Clinton, while making a case for more international aid support for Afghanistan, was rightly arguing that Afghanistan's future security would have to be judged by jobs and economic opportunities for all Afghans.[4] Slowly but surely, Western power centres could see that economic factors were contributing to the Taliban insurgency. It is rather early to conclude whether this realization has come too late for any remedial measures to have a real impact on Taliban momentum.

When it comes to timely assessments and solid strategic analysis on Afghanistan, something was indeed rotten in the state of Denmark. Stanley McChrystal, the US commanding general in Afghanistan, deserves credit for pointing out in a 2009 assessment that 'ISAF has not sufficiently studied Afghanistan's peoples, whose needs, identities and grievances vary from province to province and from valley to valley'.[5] Thankfully the report came to light, otherwise this awareness – which was almost common knowledge in South Asia – would have remained classified while matters deteriorated even further.

Steve Coll, a respected American journalist, aptly says that 'dearth of reliable, independent-minded, fine-grained, reporting about the Taliban and other local actors' at the time also contributed to a poor understanding of Taliban resurgence.[6] In this scenario McChrystal's belated but accurate assessment led to a transformation of the US counterinsurgency doctrine, which started to build a new model to pacify the Taliban using political and economic tactics, and with less dependence on military force.

It was conceived against the backdrop of conflicting development strategies that had been devised and executed since 2001 by a host of international donors, including non-governmental organizations (NGOs). Unfortunately, these policies were marred by lack of coordination, duplication, and in some cases poor assessment of local needs. For instance (as discussed in earlier chapters), capacity building of vital state institutions, such as law enforcement, was not a priority during the critical early years. Moreover, certain security and development goals clashed, while rampant corruption hampered both sets of goals.

Amidst all this, the space for indigenous Afghan efforts through local NGOs remained limited, while the international presence grew in the initial years. With rents for large houses in central Kabul rising from $100 to $10,000 per month, Afghan NGOs could barely survive.[7] Given the high salaries and the perks, many qualified Afghan individuals preferred to work for international NGOs in Kabul in comparatively insignificant roles, rather than reach out to populations away from urban centres and help build local capacity. Without a new class of trained workers, bureaucrats and technocrats, it was impossible to create hope for a new future. In such circumstances, a return to the old order was only a matter of time.

In a country that ranked 173rd out 178 countries on the basic index of human development in 2004, there was an enormous opportunity for growth – if only financial investments were made in the sectors that could jump-start the economy. In the event of failure (or even delayed action), the whole nation-building project could be jeopardized and advantage could shift to the shadowy and sinister forces with their own economic matrix. And that is exactly what happened on the ground. All the well-intentioned, concerted efforts by the aid donors and all the sacrifices by the international security forces were almost nullified in the process.

A conversation I had in early 2012 with Omar Khan, a mid-ranking Afghan Taliban leader, was both intriguing and insightful.[8] It opened up to me a new perspective on what it was that gave the Afghan Taliban a fresh lease of life. The meeting took place in the Pakistani city of Peshawar, and was arranged through a friend in the police service, who confirmed to me that his contact was neither any longer an active insurgent nor someone on the payroll of any official organization in Pakistan. As part of an attempt to understand what inspires some militants to quit their extremist activities, I was particularly interested in talking to a few people who had given up their membership of a militant organization.

Omar Khan welcomed me to his home in the Hayatabad area, a well-to-do and relatively secure locality in the provincial capital. I was told that he had voluntarily left his old organization and had slipped into Pakistan around 2008, though he remained true to his conservative religious views and believed that the Taliban does have a role in Afghanistan's future. Frankly, his refined demeanour and articulate expression came as a surprise to me. I had a different image of the Taliban.

Omar maintained that very few of the 'real Taliban' were on the battlefield in Afghanistan, as criminals, drug dealers and thugs were now spearheading the insurgency. He added that ordinary Afghans disaffected with the general state of affairs were readily available to these forces as foot soldiers. This was especially so in the rural areas, he explained. As to where the 'real Taliban' were hiding, he told me that was an open secret, and hinted that mostly they were in Pakistan. He was very careful though, given the perceived reach of the Pakistani intelligence services, which are widely believed to have close contacts with the Afghan Taliban. He also shared with me the information that some construction companies have been found to be involved in attacks on schools, since this meant more reconstruction business for them. This was the first time I had heard this, but later a US government official confirmed that he was aware of investigations along these lines.

Omar surprised me with yet another revelation. He linked suicide bombers with drug business interests, arguing that chaos and lawlessness were necessary conditions for growth of that nefarious business. He even quoted a case where President Karzai had presented a few trainee child suicide bombers on television, the youngest eight years old, who narrated how other kids were drugged before suicide operations.[9] Omar was not suggesting that this hideous method explained all the cases of suicide bombings, as among the older bombers a mixture of religious radicalization and brainwashing would do the trick. He blamed Al-Qaeda for introducing the practice into the region, and even tried to absolve the Taliban, pointing out that there had been no suicide bombings against the Soviets during the Afghan Jihad years or during Taliban campaigns in the 1990s. He was quite right about the history, and in fact Al-Qaeda acknowledged as much around 2007, when it took credit for popularizing this deadly weapon in Afghanistan, declaring that: 'While suicide attacks were not accepted in the Afghani culture in the past, they have now become a regular phenomenon!'[10]

This discussion reminds me of Chicago University Professor Robert Pape, who, in his revealing 2005 book *Dying to Kill*, makes a case that foreign occupation is the leading cause of suicide bombing. His updated research in 2010 shows that around 90 per cent of all worldwide suicide attacks are now anti-American, and his data confirms that 90 per cent of suicide attacks in Afghanistan involve Afghans.[11] Equally startling are the results of another study conducted by a pathologist who researched the background of a hundred suicide bombers in Afghanistan. It shows that 80 per cent were missing limbs before they blew themselves up, or else were suffering from serious and terminal diseases, such as leprosy and cancer.[12] This is a reflection of the mentality of those who choreograph the attacks.

As I was leaving Omar's home (a process which in the South Asian tradition can take some considerable time), I asked about economic growth in Afghanistan and whether it created more hope for the future of the country. In reply, he told me a joke about the famous Mullah Nasruddin – a legendary thirteenth-century Asian character, known for his funny but meaningful tales, who is claimed by Turks and Iranians, as well as Afghans. This is the story he told:

> Mullah Nasruddin visited a clothes shop to buy some trousers. After picking out a pair that fitted him perfectly, he suddenly changed his mind and decided to purchase a cloak instead. The two were of similar price. The mullah handed the trousers over to the shopkeeper, put the cloak in his bag and left the shop. 'You have not paid!' shouted the shopkeeper after him. The mullah turned back to him: 'I left you the trousers, which are the same value as the cloak.' 'But you didn't pay for the trousers either', the irritated shopkeeper reminded him. 'Why should I pay for something that I did not want to buy?' responded Mullah Nasruddin.

We laughed out loud at the story, but it got me thinking how best to interpret it in relation to my question. Maybe Omar wanted me to think about the gap between the Western economic policies and local requirements.

This chapter analyses how various economic factors have influenced the Taliban insurgency in recent years. The ideological and political roots of the insurrection are definitely important, but my interviews and interactions in the region over the years have taught me the critical nature of the economic variable in this case. In fierce competition for political power, individuals have used religion or tribal linkages, depending on which would work in a given situation. Irrespective of the choice, illicit taxation of transport and a levy on poppy sales were seen as legitimate avenues for revenue generation. This was especially the case in the south and east of Afghanistan, where Taliban resurgence was more vibrant. This feature deserves particular attention, as it provides an insight into the workings of the political economy of the Taliban revival.

Historically, Afghanistan's perennial lack of economic self-sufficiency forced it to rely on foreign sources of income to subsidize its domestic patronage network. This would prove a determining factor in the relations that Afghan rulers had both with their neighbours, and with their domestic elites. For the ruling clique in Kabul, bringing local elites into the taxation net and earning their resentment was not seen as a price worth paying to get them under government control. As insightfully summarized by Angelo Rasayanagam:

> In Afghanistan's programs of development, it became almost entirely dependent on foreign aid ... this dependency made Afghanistan a 'rentier state', to an extent without parallel elsewhere in the world.[13]

Corruption was simply a by-product of this dynamic. The historical trend by and large survived the latest international intervention in Afghanistan. For instance, a 2011 Asia Foundation survey showed that 76 per cent of Afghans believe corruption to be a major problem nation-wide, while 87 per cent regard it as a problem in their daily lives.[14] For any group opposed to those in power in Kabul (i.e. in this case the Taliban), this opens up a great opportunity to win over the disgruntled and disenfranchised.

The opium factor

The notorious and well-entrenched drug barons of the region had been waiting since 2001 to dominate the weak Afghan state structures just as soon as it became feasible. And they did not have to wait very long. It is nothing short of ironic that after a decline in drug production in 2001, production levels picked up in 2002, making Afghanistan the world's largest producer (accounting for almost three-quarters of global opium production).[15]

The problem is, of course, an international one, as demand drives the illegal opiate market. Contrary to the general view that opium was only produced in the Pashtun-dominated areas, in fact it was cultivated by several ethnic groups in the south (Helmand), east (Nangarhar) and north (Badakhshan). The opium trade was certainly not a new problem in Afghanistan, but the challenge grew as a consequence of the degradation of the agricultural and economic infrastructure. An Afghan from Helmand told me once that many drug dealers were local heroes in some areas, because they brought back income to their villages and took care of the impoverished. In the absence of other economic activity, this production and trade in opium was likely to continue. However, this common-sense assessment apparently evaded the policy planners sitting in Kabul in the early years of the Karzai government.

The trade depends not only on farmers in the field growing opium, but also on heroin laboratories and traders with regional networks and ready access to the international banking sector. Even more importantly, connections with high officials in government and (especially) in law enforcement organizations are critical for the business to survive. Mirwais Yasini, chief of Afghanistan's Counter-Narcotics Directorate, reported as early as May 2004 that he was personally aware of at least two millionaire drug smugglers supplying Taliban fighters with ammunition and communications equipment in the south.[16] How all of this could have escaped the attention of the international forces and the powerful intelligence agencies that were operating in Afghanistan with unprecedented freedom raises some serious questions.

The Taliban clearly became a major beneficiary of this dreadful business. There is ample evidence to show that by 2009, a raging Taliban-led insurgency was intersecting with a thriving opium trade, so that 'it was no more possible to treat the insurgency and the drug trade as separate matters'.[17] From 2005 to 2010, the Taliban's share of opium production and trafficking is put at between $90 million and $160 million a year, according to the UN Office on Drugs and Crime.[18] In some areas, they taxed opium farmers' profits; in other areas they levied a 'protection fee.' In an alarming trend, opium poppy cultivation rose substantially in 2012, meaning higher profits and consequently a more vibrant insurgency. Higher production was driven by high prices for the crop, as well as by increased instability in the growing areas, making it easier for illicit networks to operate more freely.[19] The Taliban are also now increasingly reliant on drug money, as the conflict in Syria is absorbing the dollars of their friendly donors. A host of counter measures were introduced by Kabul with the help of donors, but these made not a dent in the trend.

The money thus generated was enough to run an effective insurgency in the country. But it is a moot point whether the Taliban are inspired to earn drug money in pursuit of their insurgency cause, or whether the money itself has become the ultimate prize. A 2009 US Institute of Peace report indicates that, according to Afghan perceptions at the time, the Taliban was fighting for profit rather than religion or ideology. The report supported this assertion with reference to a NATO intelligence assessment, which said that as little as 5 per cent of insurgent commanders fought for ideological reasons.[20]

As Dov Zakheim, a thoughtful former US Defense Department official in the Bush administration, said: 'Drugs could move by donkey; but the legitimate economy could not grow without a viable road network.'[21] Indeed, an alternative economic model was not given any real chance to transform Afghanistan. Insufficient reconstruction assistance, especially in the fields of agriculture and infrastructure development, meant, in the words of Zakheim, 'that the country was ripe for a Taliban revival'.

At the end of 2013, total US investment since 2002 in tackling opium problem was in the range of $7 billion, yet counter-narcotics experts maintain that the 'opium market is booming, propelled by steady demand and an insurgency that has assumed an increasingly hands-on role in the trade'.[22] Opium farming in Afghanistan in fact hit a record high in 2013, with farmers harvesting a crop worth nearly $1 billion.

According to Russian officials, by late 2013 'almost 1,900 organized criminal groups and 150 major drug cartels in Central Asia [were] trafficking illicit drugs from Afghanistan to Russia' – and that is a good indication of the volume involved.[23] This is bound to have a negative impact on Afghanistan's future, and in the words of Jean-Luc Lemahieu, the former head of the UN office on drugs and crime in Afghanistan, 'If no appropriate action is taken, then Afghanistan runs the risk of becoming a fragmented criminal state, ruled by an illicit economy.'[24] The Counter-Narcotics Police of Afghanistan, which has dealt with the menace since its inception in 2005, requires a massive upgrade to be really effective.

Crime and punishment

Hardline Afghan Taliban always believed in enforcing their politically oriented ideology and worldview, rather than in building roots within the society for change. This mindset needed strong-arm tactics, which naturally brought the Taliban closer to criminal elements that likewise employ harassment, violence and ferocity in their day-to-day dealings. In the absence of an effective law enforcement and criminal justice system, criminals had a field day in many parts of Afghanistan, as the international forces settled down and contemplated their priorities in the country. Organized crime benefited from this vacuum, which has also fuelled corruption.[25]

The US policy makers missed this point altogether. To avoid blame, it has even become fashionable in Western capitals to argue – wrongly – that corruption is a cultural issue in Afghanistan. Smuggling, extortion and kidnapping – the central features of organized crime – generate funds and spread fear, at the same time as they nourish criminal networks. Breaking this cycle is certainly not easy, as it takes decades (and in some cases generations) to establish the rule of law. Early initiatives to control crime by building and strengthening the necessary institutions are thus essential in situations like the one the international community faced in Afghanistan. Otherwise, as expert

Robert Perito rightly suggests, it is likely that 'Lawless, war-hardened networks will cement their informal power bases', establishing their dominance through criminal syndicates and nourishing the black market economy.[26]

It is surprising how many of the important lessons from various world conflict zones have been criminally ignored in the case of Afghanistan, with terrible consequences. A 2010 study report by West Point's Combating Terrorism Center argued that organized crime funded the militants.[27] It further expanded on the theme by explaining that this nexus not only amplifies and sustains the conflict by spreading insecurity and corruption, but also slows development and seriously damages the credibility and effectiveness of local governments. Nothing can be more corrosive for a nation-building endeavour, because it strikes at the core of the mission.

When criminals realized that their excesses were going largely unnoticed, they expanded their activities. Robberies and attacks on supply convoys started occurring more frequently. Rather than generating more investment in law enforcement bodies, this led to informal security contracts for groups that sought to ensure the safe movement of goods. In some cases, these groups were Taliban fronts.[28] A US congressional investigation revealed that some of the guards hired by US trucking companies to escort their convoys in fact bribed the Taliban not to attack them, so the US was inadvertently funding the very people it was fighting.[29] Secretary of State Clinton did not mince her words when giving evidence in November 2009: 'one of the major sources of funding for the Taliban is the protection money'.[30] American taxpayers were literally being taken for a ride.

The Taliban showed more adaptability during the insurgency years than when they were at the helm of affairs in Kabul. Their victories in the early to mid-1990s were achieved mainly through conventional warfare and the use (and misuse) of Islamic slogans. After 2001, they were resurgent thanks to different means, mainly guerrilla warfare, improvisation and galvanizing people in the name of resistance to invasion.

During this later phase, they also compromised on their principles, which was not the case when they held the reins of government. Arguably, economic and religious factors influenced this metamorphosis. For instance, the Taliban were understandably opposed to the creation of new schools, as they suspected that education would modernize Afghanistan and render them irrelevant. They were right. However, according to research by Antonio Giustozzi of the London School of Economics, their position started to change in 2008–09, as the 'Taliban made deals with local school headmasters, allowing teaching to continue, but with changed curricula and the incorporation of mullahs among the school staff, tasked to monitor the proper behavior of the teachers'.[31] This shared control of sorts led to the opening of around 80 schools (including some with girl students) in Kandahar, Helmand and Uruzgan provinces. Though some analysts dubbed it a sign of the Taliban's soft power, the compromise not only helped the Taliban's image but saved them money, too, as they would have had to establish schools in areas under their control for ideological purposes and maybe in some cases to cater to public demand.[32]

Direct financial dividends from criminal activities became so enormous that the Taliban leadership referred to them specifically in its 2009 Code of Conduct, which was later updated in May 2010. Field commanders were given strict instructions on money matters, with explanations for how profits and income were to be shared in the local and provincial Taliban hierarchy.[33] A substantive addition covered contractors who provide workers to 'the enemy': a death warrant was issued for such people, but on the ground it led to a rise in the rates for 'protection services'.

An efficient 'rule of law' infrastructure was needed to effectively tackle these criminal enterprises. Even though the need to build a police force with both investigative and crime prevention capacity was belatedly realized, this alone could not deliver results. Functioning courts, at both the local and the national level, and modern corrective facilities were equally important. For Western states involved in state-building in

Afghanistan, this 'rule of law' paradigm is not rocket science at all, and that is what makes it so amazing that an understanding of even the most basic elements of a criminal justice system eluded the strategists and planners of the Afghan reconstruction. A UNDP-sponsored strategy for justice sector reform was introduced early on, but it largely remained on paper in the initial years of the international effort, so that a crucial window of opportunity was missed. However, some infrastructure progress started to become visible by 2011. New courthouses were built, new laws promulgated, and – most importantly – about a thousand judges were trained to run the system.

Inevitably, it was not easy to introduce and establish the foundations of a new judicial system. Various views about the role of Islam in the legal arena were put forward when the project was considered, and needless to say it is a highly sensitive subject. Nevertheless, the ten-year plan for justice sector reform, framed in 2004–05 with help from Italy (the lead nation for this task), suggested that 'modern, market-based democracies' were the most appropriate model for bringing change to this sector.

Anyhow, the newly established Afghan Judicial Commission, which had significant Afghan representation, was hardly consulted as work on developing new codes, laws and regulations was expedited after 2005. The most important task was to devise a new criminal procedure code – the backbone of a criminal justice system. The Italians were criticized for being 'slow and passive', but even more problematically they seldom engaged with Afghans in developing this code, and paid little heed to Afghan laws and traditions.[34] When it was finalized in June 2009, the code appeared so irrelevant to Afghan society that Karzai refused to sign it into law. Rather than revising it, the Italian diplomats withdrew their cooperation and threatened to withhold their funding for this sector. Karzai was forced to compromise and the colonial-like project continued. US Department of Justice officials did something similar in 2006, when they drafted a law on terrorism for Afghanistan that simply copied large chunks of the US Patriot Act; but in this case the opponents of this idea won through and a draft law prepared by Afghan experts was adopted. The question is whether any authority was over-seeing this whole law-making process.

To be fair, a 2007 conference in Rome did assess the judicial reform effort in Afghanistan and duly exposed the huge gaps, pointing out that such key issues as the role of informal or traditional structures of justice, legal aid, access to justice and oversight of the National Directorate of Security were not addressed.[35] For an ordinary Afghan, what was the guarantee that the future of the internal security project in Afghanistan would be any better? Dozens of reports, meanwhile, were commissioned by policy circles in the US and the EU, though I seriously doubt if these influenced the policy makers to be more responsible in dealing with such issues. By then the Taliban were focusing on the provision of quick justice (as brutal as it was) in areas under their control, thus making a mockery of the Western promises.

According to Professor Astri Suhrke, a more effective 'rule of law' strategy that drew lessons from Afghan and Islamic traditions was only advocated after 2010, and that 'with strong US military backing.'[36] A Western military official tasked with supporting the capacity building of the Afghan judiciary told me in a 2013 interview that 'rule-of-law effort was certainly an afterthought'. She lamented the inadequate allocation of resources for this sector. Asked if Afghans were even ready to handle a modern court system (since an informal justice system like *jirga* remains in vogue in the countryside), she surprised me by saying that there was a lot of interest, and the understaffed and poorly funded judicial institutions of the country were begging for support, but the requests were mostly falling on deaf ears. It was a pleasant surprise to hear from her that about 10 per cent of Afghan judges are women, and that in a 2012 training programme for new judges, 13 of the top 15 were women. I trusted her implicitly, but to me the figures sounded too good to be true. When I tried to verify them, I was delighted to come across a 2012 USAID report on its judicial training programme, which confirmed that: 'Most remarkably, and for the second consecutive year, the overwhelming majority of the top graduates in the class are female.'[37] Time and again Afghans have shown that they respond well to sensible development and reform projects; but the international efforts to rebuild Afghanistan took a long time to start looking really meaningful.

Modern technology and media

For all the security challenges, regional power play and growing insurgency, Afghanistan has undoubtedly come a long way since 2001. Back then, the country's GDP was $2 billion; by 2013 it stood at $20 billion (even though a large part of that is due to international aid). There are dozens of newspapers and private TV channels serving the country, and access to modern technology is also quite widespread. For instance, in 2006 there were 200,000 internet users in Afghanistan, a figure that had increased to about 1.3 million in 2013; mobile phone users increased from 1.7 million to over 16 million in the same period.[38]

This is a substantial achievement in a country that, over three decades of conflict, has undergone massive destruction of infrastructure, huge displacement of people and intense disorientation in religious terms. It is another matter that the Taliban have also caught up fast and are making use of the new tools to project and propagate their goals.[39]

There has been a rise in the Taliban's text-message intimidation to coerce the rural population into cooperating with them and to undermine the central government.[40] The Taliban official online magazine, *Al Somood*, besides skilful marketing of its ideas, provides detailed information about its print publications.[41] Al Emarah, the official Taliban website, offers material in five different languages: Dari, Pashtu, Urdu, Arabic and English, signifying the various regional and local audiences being targeted by the Taliban media cell.

Attempts have been made by various Western agencies to shut down Al Emarah and other Taliban-supportive sites, but it is no easy matter, given the endless number of servers and domain names available. Interestingly, Taliban sites are often found to be unconsciously hosted by American technology firms: one Texas company, The Planet, realized in 2009 that it been a conduit for Al Emarah for over a year.[42] The

Taliban are now increasingly communicating with journalists and news agencies via email, making themselves more accessible.

Another sign of rapid Taliban adaptation to (relatively) modern technology is the mass production of cassette tapes and CDs with songs and religious chants, evoking nationalistic and cultural images that serve as reminders of the indignities of occupation. These are especially effective in rural areas, where most of the people are illiterate and lack access to television and internet. For this audience, the Taliban's video documentation of violent acts also helps with recruitment. An Afghan police official told me that the widespread availability of these tapes does not necessarily indicate more popularity: some people carry these tapes in their vehicles as a form of protection, believing they could be useful while passing through a Taliban-controlled area! However, their purchases mean that the Taliban media cell can raise enough funds for future productions. It is instructive how a regime that banned music, photography and television while in power has embraced the modern forms of communication and shown unexpected flexibility.[43] The taste of power can be truly transformative!

There is perhaps only one sector where the Taliban capacity has declined – and that has apparently been a strategic decision. The Taliban have downsized from their prestigious Toyota Hilux pickups and instead have adopted motorbikes as their vehicle of choice.[44] According to Michael Semple, this decision was geared towards empowering marginalized Afghan youth. Given the appalling roads in Afghanistan's south and the Taliban's dire need to reach out to underdeveloped villages at the end of uncharted pathways in the Pashtun heartland, the choice was both cost effective and smart.

International funds versus Taliban fund raising

The reconstruction of Afghanistan has been a long, arduous and very expensive business, rendered even more difficult by a lack of vision as to the achievable end goal. Up to the end of 2013 the US had spent $650 billion on securing and rebuilding Afghanistan.[45] Security sector paraphernalia and corruption consumed a large proportion of that. Mismanagement, wastage and poor prioritization of projects led to inflated budget requirements, and in the absence (for the most part) of effective and independent monitoring there was little timely recognition that something was terribly wrong. From 'Viagra diplomacy' in Helmand, where local mullahs were gifted the blue pills by British officials as a reward for cooperation, to regular MI6 and CIA cash handouts to Karzai that helped him sustain and groom his patronage network, wastage of financial resources has been endemic.[46]

According to the World Bank, 92 per cent of Afghanistan's operating budget comes from foreign aid (most of it originating in the US), and the country will need this support to continue for years in order to sustain what has already been built.[47] More than anything else, the crippled Afghan justice system needs reform and greater capacity, so that it can prosecute insurgents and criminals; but funding for such purposes has been scarce (as discussed above). It is also highly questionable why investment in civilian law enforcement institutions, such as the Afghan National Police and the Afghan Local Police, has been seen as less important than building the Afghan National Army.

A misplaced assessment of local needs and of the allocation of funds lay at the heart of the problem. For instance, during a January 2013 inspection, most of the infrastructure at five Afghan Border Police facilities in Kunduz and Nangarhar provinces was found to be either unoccupied or used for purposes for which it was never intended: one building housed a poultry farm.[48] Still, there is a possibility that the infrastructure will be utilized in the future, hopefully once trained Afghan security forces are ready for the job.

What is frankly hard to fathom is why a brand-new, modern, well-equipped building in Helmand that was built for military purposes at a cost of $34 million should be scheduled for demolition by the US. Reportedly, work on its construction continued even after it was realized that there was no need for it, and now it is deemed too expensive for the Afghans to maintain and run. Some senior US officials told a *Washington Post* journalist, Rajiv Chandrasekaran, that this is 'the whitest elephant in a war littered with wasteful, dysfunctional and unnecessary projects funded by American taxpayers'.[49]

An alarming exposure of mismanagement and misappropriation of development funds in Afghanistan is provided by US Special Inspector General for Afghanistan Reconstruction (SIGAR) John Sopko. SIGAR produced its first report only in late 2008, after the US Congress belatedly instituted the body earlier that year to promote efficiency of reconstruction programmes, detect fraud and prevent abuses. It was supported by the excellent investigative skills of various US civilian law enforcement agencies, including the Federal Bureau of Investigation and Immigration and Customs Enforcement.

On the administrative side of things, many official US reports explained away the situation in Afghanistan by emphasizing the 'adaptive' and 'significant regenerative capacity' of the Taliban, thus absolving themselves of their lack of vision in conceiving and implementing development plans that could have circumscribed Taliban activities. Money was not a problem; competence was. By mid-2013, the US government alone had provided around $25 billion to support governance and stimulate economic development in Afghanistan.[50] And yet many important energy and infrastructure projects remained incomplete, and some had even been abandoned midway.

Vital time was also wasted due to US inter-departmental squabbles in Afghanistan over the best approach to take. This might have been understandable in 2002–03, but the fact that such differences lingered on for over a decade is evidence of lack of direction. One such challenge was how to provide a reliable supply of electricity to Kandahar, in order to deny the Taliban space. This was rightly deemed to be of paramount importance for stabilizing the south. Still, in 2010, General Stanley A. McChrystal and Ambassador Karl W. Eikenberry locked horns over how to achieve this. McChrystal's team wanted to spend $200 million on purchasing more generators, plus millions of gallons of diesel fuel; but Eikenberry considered this 'expensive, unsustainable and unlikely to have the counterinsurgency impact desired'. He preferred a long-term approach based on infrastructure development, such as construction or building additional capacity of dams, etc.[51] In the end, a combination of the two ideas was attempted. As a result, Kandahar today needs 100MW of electricity, but has access to only 40MW. Some of the blame for this rests with the Afghans, as certain government departments and influential citizens refuse to pay their electricity bills.[52] But the upshot is that the need to deny the insurgents space in the Kandahar area is today more acute than ever.

Charity money flowing from Gulf and Arab states is another factor that contributes to the Taliban cause in Afghanistan, though its extent is disputed. The US ambassador in Abu Dhabi clearly stated in 2009 that 'Taliban financing originates in and transits the UAE to Afghanistan' and 'cash couriers are believed to carry the majority of illicit funds to and from Afghanistan'.[53]

The late Richard Holbrooke, special US envoy to Pakistan and Afghanistan, once remarked that funding from the Gulf region 'outpaces the cash gathered from Afghanistan's multibillion-dollar exports of opium and heroin'.[54] Maybe that was a slip of the tongue. An Afghan intelligence official told me in June 2013 that according to official Afghan estimates, less than 10 per cent of the Taliban's total funds come through Gulf and Arab-based Islamic charity channels. A former British ambassador to Afghanistan, Sir Sherard Cowper-Coles, substantiates this, maintaining that any potential contributions from the Gulf and Saudi Arabia could not provide the financial foundations of the insurgency.[55] Reports from 2012 onwards show that the growing flow of gold and cash is in fact originating in Kabul and being laundered in Dubai. In a country where 'nearly 90 percent of the financial activity takes place outside formal banks', it is extremely difficult to track money flows, making it an uphill task for government forces to cut off the Taliban's financial connections and to track wealth generated through corruption.[56]

The total amount spent by the US in Afghanistan would suggest to anyone that there was no dearth of money for the country. Yet surprisingly, in areas where economic frustration has been highest – such as Pashtun-dominated regions – the provision of funds to create jobs and pursue development projects has been inadequate. Many astute researchers with field experience in Afghanistan say Taliban fighters are mainly motivated by local grievances, which invariably revolve around economic factors.[57] The Taliban have deftly manipulated this widespread feeling of economic distress to their political advantage. By the same token, investment in the economic viability of Afghanistan would have sealed the Taliban's fate.

The policy challenge

By 2010, the Taliban had regained a large chunk of lost territory in the east and south of Afghanistan – more in terms of influence than direct political control – and had become so strong on the ground that a US national intelligence estimate focusing on the war in Afghanistan could not but present a 'gloomy picture', warning that 'large swaths of Afghanistan are still at risk of falling to the Taliban'.[58] It was an honest assessment, but slightly outdated: the Taliban were in the ascendant.

One measure of that was the considerable increase in violent activity. Between 2008 and 2010, the average number of suicide bombings per year rose to 142, from an earlier average of 108 in 2005–07.[59] Similarly, there was a sharp rise in the number of devastating IED attacks.[60] Most debilitating, however, was the assassination campaign run by the Taliban against district governors, police chiefs and other government officials. For this, the Taliban especially focused their energies on the southern provinces, especially Kandahar, Helmand, Paktika, Zabul and Ghazni.[61] Nothing could be more discouraging for those who wanted to build a new Afghanistan. It shattered civilian confidence in the new system and in the capacity of the US-led coalition to provide public security. That was just the depressing environment that the Taliban were seeking to create.

Joining the Afghan government became a crime – with potentially deadly consequences. Teachers and doctors were not spared, and (surprisingly for many) *ulema* (clerics) were also in the line of fire. Maulvi Fayyaz, who had courageously stripped Mullah Omar of his self-proclaimed *Amir ul Momineen* (Commander of the Faithful) status, was killed as early as 2005, but this pattern picked up pace as time went on. For the Taliban, any challenge emanating from the religious authorities was particularly damaging. By 2010, 23 out of 50 members of the Kandahar Ulema Council had been assassinated.[62] This speaks volumes for the Taliban's gains and their mounting confidence.

This was sufficient to force a rethink in US policy circles. America's Afghan campaign was in serious jeopardy. President Obama, for whom this was a 'good war' (unlike the Iraq war), was apparently in two minds after moving into the White House in January 2009 as to whether to agree to the recommendation of his military advisers (who were seeking a troop 'surge' to defeat the Taliban insurgents and Al-Qaeda remnants militarily) or to consider drawing down forces and start looking for an exit strategy. He ultimately opted for a surge, as he also wanted to look tough on national security. Relative stability in the north, west and centre of Afghanistan was a positive sign, but this was balanced by increasing insurgent activity in the Pashtun-dominated south and east. Obama's shift in strategy became obvious in December 2009, when a decision to send an additional 30,000 troops was announced. This pushed the total number of US troops in Afghanistan over the 100,000 mark.

The Taliban remained focused on their own surge. On 30 December 2009, eight CIA officials were killed in a devastating suicide attack inside Forward Operating Base Chapman, in Afghanistan's Khost Province. The bomber was one Humam Balawi, a Jordanian physician who had originally been recruited by the Jordanians to spy on Al-Qaeda and then handed over to the CIA as an intelligence asset. He left a video message that sent shudders through the security analysts both in the US and Pakistan. In it, he sat beside Hakimullah Mehsud, leader of the Tehrik-i-Taliban Pakistan (TTP), based in Pakistan's tribal areas adjacent to Afghanistan, and referred to this as a revenge attack for the killing of former TTP chief Baitullah Mehsud in a US drone strike a few months earlier.[63] Balawi could access the military base, as he had promised CIA officials crucial information about Bin Laden's whereabouts. The convergence of interests and the sharing of resources between the

Afghan insurgency, the Pakistani Taliban and Al-Qaeda had matured over the years.

It had taken unduly long for the Obama administration to review US strategy in Afghanistan and decide in favour of the military surge option; but surprisingly it had also simultaneously declared that forces would start to be drawn down in July 2011. This later pronouncement was music to the Taliban's ears, as they could now plan their strategy accordingly. Realizing the potential significance of the miscommunication, senior Obama administration officials quickly dispelled the impression that a rapid withdrawal after the surge was on the cards and linked the original Obama statement to a new plan to expand the Afghan army and police.[64]

Though some damage was caused by this fiasco, the focus on strengthening the Afghan security forces was a smart (albeit belated) way of approaching the issue – so long as the resources were adequate and the requisite patience was displayed. The 'surge' was, in essence, a booster shot to knock the Taliban back on its heels and give Afghans enough respite to take over the fight. It was also meant to be a wake-up call for Kabul to get its house in order and prepare to take full charge of the situation.

Still, America had no magic formula that could overnight discourage and deter the corruption in Afghanistan, which had now become rampant. Building institutional culture and inculcating a good work ethic takes decades, whereas in the new Afghanistan no one had any clear idea when the aid tap would be turned off. In such an environment, corruption could only grow. Those with greater awareness of the troubling global economic trends and the poor prospects for sustainable local revenue generation were more prone to panic – and more prone to involvement in corrupt practices. They were incompetent, but knew well that America was not going to invest in Afghanistan forever.

Failing as it was to provide effective economic and social services, the Karzai government struggled to win the public trust needed for a national political consensus to resolve the complex challenges. To give just one example, Afghanistan's electricity generating capacity almost quadrupled from 2002 to 2012; but despite that, only 6 per cent of the population had reliable access to electricity in 2012.[65] Karzai had indeed won a second presidential term in 2009, but the process had been controversial and was marred by charges of fraud. Nepotism and his resulting armlock on the Afghan bureaucracy had helped. To give him his due, none of the other candidates enjoyed nationwide acceptability at the time; nevertheless, the serious governance problems could not be wished away. By failing to offer any real solution to the crisis that was fuelling the insurgency, Kabul in many ways was itself a reason why the insurgency was gaining ground.

The American presence on the ground – both military and civilian – had the means to monitor financial transactions and to track who was accumulating assets in the Gulf states through corruption. The problem was that those selfsame folk were American partners in Afghanistan. Ordinary Afghans consequently started to lose hope in the new bureaucratic and political elite that was at the helm of affairs. The Taliban lost no time in making their moves, with terror attacks in and around Kabul creating more insecurity.

The Taliban were no longer just a rural phenomenon: they were now bringing the fight into urban centres, successfully creating the impression that no part of the country was beyond their reach. A spectacular assault in the heart of Kabul by a group of Taliban militants, equipped with suicide bombers, in mid-January 2010 further demoralized Afghans as Pashtunistan Square, a traffic circle where the presidential palace, the Ministry of Justice and the Central Bank are all located, became a battleground between security forces and the Taliban.[66] This audacious attack was not the first of its kind in Kabul, but a deadly new pattern was emerging.

The following years showed not only a continuation of the heightened violence, but even more sophistication. Coordinated suicide attacks and assaults on embassies and government offices jumped in 2011–12.[67] A daring Taliban attack on an important US airfield in eastern Afghanistan in December 2012, during which the attackers were disguised in US army uniforms, caused over $200 million in damage.[68] Security arrangements around government institutions were revamped, but the attacks did not subside.

A major assault on a courthouse in Farah Province in western Afghanistan in a bid to free Taliban in police custody caused 53 deaths in April 2013. And there was a series of insurgent attacks targeting the Afghan National Police in both eastern and western parts of Afghanistan during August 2013. These incidents indicate a further trend, showing that the Taliban are cognizant of the new 'rule of law' structures being built and consider these to be detrimental to their own goals.[69]

Some American miscalculations also added fuel to the fire. Between 2009 and 2013, there was an upsurge in lethal American 'night raids', which led to high 'collateral damage' and civilian detentions: by early 2011, there were 19 raids a night on average.[70] These sparked a major backlash in Afghanistan, so much so that Karzai went berserk, strongly condemning the raids in which there were non-combatant civilian casualties.[71] For the US military, the raids were the linchpin of their mission in Afghanistan; but among the people they were highly unpopular. Taliban support grew by leaps and bounds in areas where the raids went awry. Reacting to the impact on public perception, in April 2012 US commanders on the ground agreed to hand over control of the raids to Afghan forces.[72]

The significant US investment in building the Afghan National Army (ANA) in the post-2009 policy shift has meanwhile had mixed results. Now almost 350,000 strong, the ANA will need years before it can transform itself into a professional army. This is not actually anybody's fault: it is not possible to forge quickly a professional army with strong organizational culture and discipline. But nepotism and a tangible tilt in favour of non-Pashtuns in recruitment and promotion to senior ranks do pose a serious challenge. Many Afghans who hold senior positions in the military are known more for their close political connections in Kabul than for their brilliance as military strategists or for any gallantry displayed on the battlefield. The younger officers I have met show much more promise and dedication.

Somewhat predictably, Pakistan has regarded the rise of the ANA critically. Islamabad touts it as a Northern Alliance militia dominated by Tajiks; but this view runs counter to official figures, which show that average Pashtun representation in all ranks hovers around 45 per cent – close to the ethnic group's population ratio.[73] According to the eminent scholar Vali Nasr, Pakistan's former army chief, General Ashfaq Parvez Kayani, advised the US not to invest in building an Afghan army, warning: 'You will fail . . . then you will leave and that half-trained army will break into militias that will be a problem for Pakistan.'[74] Interestingly, Pakistan itself also offered assistance in training the Afghan military, but Karzai ignored it.

To the surprise of many, Karzai became quite keen to reach out directly to the Afghan Taliban during his last full year in power, and tried to avoid saying anything that could sow discomfort in the minds of the Taliban. His refusal to sign the Bilateral Security Agreement (BSA) with the US was a part of this strategy. In October 2013, in an attempt to woo the Taliban, he even argued that foreign intervention did Afghanistan no good.[75] But many saw it as a tasteless joke when he declared that Afghan women should have nothing to fear from the Taliban. This was all a way for Karzai to distract media attention from the rampant corruption in his government. I heard it repeatedly from many Afghans that corruption is an even bigger threat than the one posed by the Taliban.

The Taliban attacks continued in 2013 with their trademark ferocity; but for all that, they have failed to take control of any population centres, even in those areas where they are relatively strong.[76] Still, according to a UN report, the really troubling sign for the future is that Taliban bomb-makers have acquired access to high-grade industrial explosives, and their weapons are becoming 'increasingly sophisticated and technically advanced', as they have refined their IED-making skills over time for instance. In some instances luck smiled on the Taliban, too, as in a case in Kunar Province in October 2013, when Monsif Khan, an Afghan army special forces commander, defected to Hizb-e-Islami, now allied with the Taliban insurgents, in a Humvee truck packed with his team's guns and high-tech equipment.[77] In Ghazni Province in late 2013, some 'entrepreneurial' Afghan security officials were found selling – or in some cases offering as 'tribute' to the Taliban – ammunition and equipment, including solar panel systems.[78] Such improvements in their arsenal, according to the UN findings, had recently been accounting for 80 per cent of Afghan army and police casualties.

It looks as though 2014 will be no different, as some Afghan officials are busy cutting deals with Taliban groups operating in their areas while calling these 'ceasefires'. On other fronts, the pitched battles between the Taliban and Afghan security forces in early 2014 show a continuation of the overall destabilizing trend. In fact, Afghan security forces have remained continuously in the line of fire. It is an overlooked fact that nearly 14,000 Afghan police and military officials have been killed and around 16,500 wounded since 2002 – most losses occurring since 2011.[79] According to a January 2014 SIGAR finding, almost half of Afghan security forces could not read or write, exposing poor recruitment standards. How they could be professionally trained, especially the police, with this decapitating handicap is puzzling. It is nothing short of criminal negligence.

CHAPTER NINE

Empowering the Taliban revival?
Impact of local politics, regional rivalries and drone strikes

For years, Pakistan routinely and inaccurately attributed the rise of terrorist activity in the country to 'outside forces' – a phrase that almost always implies India. Pakistan was slow to recognize that it was sons of the soil who had radicalized to the extent that terrorism had become their bread and butter. By 2013, the TTP and other terrorist groups, such as Lashkar-e-Jhangvi (Militia of Jhangvi), had emerged as the most dangerous threat to Pakistan. Army Chief Kayani, in an address on the nation's independence day in August 2013, rightly asserted that the 'internal threat to Pakistan is now greater than any external one'.[1]

This is a crucial recognition – and a result of institutional rethinking in army circles in Pakistan – but a corresponding impact on Pakistan's counterterrorism policy is hardly visible. The country has shied away from investing in building a modern police force that could analyse, investigate and develop solid evidence about terrorists.

Benefiting from an Asia Society grant, I worked with 20 leading Pakistani police officers (both serving and retired) during 2010–12 to assess the capabilities of Pakistan's law enforcement infrastructure and to brainstorm to reform it. In a nutshell, our findings showed that there was tremendous potential in the Pakistani police, but that political interference in police work, totally inadequate resources and poor training facilities were hampering its prospects of contributing towards stability and security in Pakistan. The US, which is the major donor in Pakistan's counterterrorism capacity building, seemed oblivious for quite a while to the fact that a criminal justice system even existed in the country.

Pakistan loves F-16s (what air force doesn't?). But the country needs training and equipment for its police forces more than it requires big-ticket military hardware. Poor priority setting unsurprisingly haunts Pakistan. Meanwhile US policy makers take cover under the Kerry–Lugar legislation of 2009, which tried to change the equation and focus more on aiding the civilian and development sectors in Pakistan. Yet there has been very little that has trickled down to the institutions associated with the 'rule of law', such as the judiciary and police forces. Extremists are bound to thrive in an environment where the criminal justice system is faltering.

Mainstream democratic forces gained considerably in the 2008 national elections. But the people of Pakistan – distressed by frequent electricity shortages, burdened by the economic downturn and frightened at the rising insecurity – have become increasingly disillusioned with their political leaders. As a result, in the May 2013 national elections they voted for a right-of-centre party, the Pakistan Muslim League, led by Nawaz Sharif. The experienced leader, who had twice served as prime minister and had enjoyed some quality time to think about Pakistan's drift while in exile after the 1999 military coup, now found himself at the helm of affairs again at a very critical juncture in his country's history. His strategy for progress is built around economic growth and improving trade relations with India, but his policy declarations on counterterrorism sound vague and unclear. His party's political alliances with some religious extremists arguably caused this hesitation. Sharif is not the only political leader with a soft spot for Taliban-like groups. In an effort to negotiate with TTP, he empowered many of the country's 'stalwarts' of the religious right.

The politics of Imran Khan, the handsome cricketer turned politician, also came of age in recent years. His party – Pakistan Tehrik-i-Insaf (PTI – Movement for Justice) – was formed in the mid-1990s, but it lacked mass appeal at the time. He was adored for winning the

Cricket World Cup for Pakistan in 1992, but (even though South Asians are crazy about cricket) that was not enough to win votes. But Khan persisted and was able to galvanize the younger generation of Pakistanis, who came out in big numbers at his rallies across the country, especially in the politically important urban centres of Lahore, Karachi and Peshawar. He ran on the slogan of 'change' and sounded genuinely committed to reforming the dysfunctional and corrupt state institutions. Many Pakistanis saw him as someone who could transform the country. His successful philanthropic projects were seen as an indicator of his good management style, and being seen as an honest politician further bolstered his image. The Pakistani media's fondness for him catapulted him to among the top contenders for the office of prime minister. He failed in this in 2013, but the PTI did emerge as a major party on the national scene, and won enough seats to form a government in the Pashtun-dominated Khyber Pakhtunkhwa Province (KPK). The popularity of Khan's anti-drone stance did wonders for him, too. Where he disappointed many Pakistanis was in his Sharif-like confusion over the Taliban. He in fact went a step further than Sharif and avoided every opportunity to condemn the Taliban and other militant groups operating in Pakistan. For this, his critics dubbed him 'Taliban Khan'.[2]

During the 2013 election campaign, the Taliban systematically targeted relatively liberal and left-wing parties, especially the Pakistan People's Party, the Awami National Party and the Muttihada Qaumi Movement (MQM) – to the extent that there was an impact on the election process and those parties were forced to significantly trim their campaigning. Sharif's Muslim League and Khan's PTI campaigned freely, as they faced no such targeting or threats to their leaders.

The elections were far bloodier than any previous polls. The newly elected Sharif government was well aware of these undercurrents and argued in favour of developing a national consensus on dealing with terrorism – a very hard thing to ask for in a country that is polarized on the subject. The government would prefer a negotiated settlement with the Pakistani Taliban – and openly said so both before and after taking power. The problem is the Pakistani Taliban, who oppose the idea of Pakistan and refuse to accept its constitution. Their training centres preach that Pakistan's founding father Jinnah, being a Shia and secular – two unforgivable sins in the eyes of the Taliban – is unworthy to be emulated.[3] The TTP cannot be expected to accommodate Islamabad's interests. It is not mere chance that, when Hakimullah Mehsud was killed in a drone strike in November 2013, the Pakistani Taliban picked hardliner Mullah Fazlullah, who since 2010 had been operating from his base in Afghanistan, as the new TTP commander. Fazlullah, mastermind of the reign of terror in the Swat Valley, was not someone who would come to the negotiating table to compromise on his abhorred principles. Interestingly, he was the first top leader of the organization who was not a member of the Mehsud tribe, the dominant group under the TTP umbrella.

Though the Sharif government publicized its dialogue with the TTP while Hakimullah was alive, there is hardly any indication that the process actually moved beyond statements. When the TTP blamed the Sharif government for being hand in glove with the US in coordinating the attack that killed Hakimullah, the administration sheepishly shifted the blame onto the US – and even described the drone strike as an attack on its 'peace initiative' with the TTP. It is inconceivable that the government had totally forgotten that Hakimullah had personally butchered dozens of Pakistani soldiers, including the legendary commando Brigadier Tarrar ('Colonel Imam' – see above), and was responsible for killing thousands of Pakistani citizens. Islamabad was just too scared to call a terrorist a terrorist.

Munawar Hassan, head of the Islamic political party Jamaat-e-Islami, went a step further and declared Hakimullah Mehsud a martyr. He also argued that those dying for 'the US cause inside Pakistan', including military personnel, were not martyrs. This justifiably irked the Pakistani army, which duly called for an unconditional apology from Hassan. The discourse reflects the nature of the polarization that is shaping up in the country. Unless treated immediately, this schism has all the potential to widen.

Use of force can serve as an antibiotic for the serious infection that has overtaken Pakistan; but there will be no recovery without a range of remedial measures. Pakistan requires a lot of energy, vigour and strength to utilize its potential to the full. One critical path on this journey would be the development sector, bringing an emphasis on modern education, leading to economic growth.

Tackling militants in FATA: No easy answers[4]

Unlike in Afghanistan, where security-related initiatives were introduced almost in parallel with political moves and development projects sponsored by the international community, the Pakistani tribal belt faced a military onslaught first, and development was an afterthought. Meanwhile concrete signs of political development are still few and far between. By the time development projects were introduced, the security situation had deteriorated to such an extent that people were unable to respond positively. Conventional wisdom has it that development helps defeat militancy, create stability and promote security. In principle, this could also aid reversal of the Talibanization trends in South Asia, especially in Pakistan's FATA. With this goal in mind, the US pledged $750 million of development aid to Pakistan between 2007 and 2011 for FATA, and various US and UK agencies continue to support implementation of development projects in the region, with the objective of helping Pakistan increase its credibility and improve economic activity in the area.[5]

In Pakistan, the idea of development as a cure for militancy contends that providing economic opportunities and delivering services to civilians discourages rebellion by increasing its opportunity cost, while simultaneously allowing the government to win over insurgent tribes. One only wishes it were that simple. Development and security have a paradoxical relationship: developmental efforts are often thwarted by the very insecurity they are meant to remedy. The bombing of 460 schools in FATA between 2008 and 2012 is a case in point.[6] Thus, while development will be crucial to bringing stability to the tribal areas in the long run, it remains dependent on first ending militancy in FATA and achieving a return to relative normality.

The major assumption undergirding the case for development is that those who rebel are overwhelmingly poor, and the financial benefits provided by insurgents outweigh what the Pakistani government offers. The Pakistani Taliban's recruitment pattern, however, reveals that they use a variety of tactics, and financial inducements are only one of several factors in play.[7]

As discussed in earlier chapters, Pakistan's Taliban insurgency is a complex conflict, featuring not just anti-state conflict, but also inter-tribal warfare. First of all, there is the tribal dynamic, which has its own push and pull factor. Wazir and Mehsud tribal groups have a long history of mutual distrust, battles and assassinations. Taliban factions that recruit heavily from these tribes inherit this rivalry and animosity. Mehsud representation in the TTP is currently quite significant, so to counter it Pakistan has been trying to build bridges with Wazir tribesmen in order to 'squeeze' the Mehsuds. In some cases this has been done by economic blockade and road construction in Wazir areas, so that the people can bypass Mehsud areas, thus lessening their dependence on the Mehsuds.[8] The Pakistan Army has also armed militants of the small Bhittani tribe (who are despised by the Mehsud) in areas leading to Khyber Pakhtunkhwa Province, so as to discourage Mehsud incursions.[9] Thus, this aspect of Pakistan's counterterrorism model inadvertently further empowers tribalism, which is no less problematic. The Taliban recruitment drive also benefits by targeting the tribes under stress at any given time.

The TTP also attracts potential recruits through social networks, by providing social prestige. Recruiters have reportedly invited young men for informal conversations and to offer them company. The interaction is used to glorify war and martyrdom, gradually to give the individuals concerned a sense of belonging to a peer group, and ultimately to convince them to volunteer for combat.[10] Furthermore, in Swat, militants have recruited young men by offering them the opportunity to ride in pick-up trucks and to hold weapons. This all confers social prestige and authority, while political backing from the Taliban offers clout.[11] The TTP has similarly attempted to use Facebook as 'a recruitment centre', organizing a virtual community of radicals.[12]

Revenge and reaction are yet another potent driver of recruitment. Contrary to general assumptions about the Taliban's worldview, they cleverly employ those elements of classic *Pashtunwali* code that suit their recruitment objectives. For instance, on both sides of the Durand Line the Taliban have exploited the notion of *badal* (revenge) to recruit new fighters after civilian deaths caused by military strikes and drones.[13] Taliban militants regularly visit refugee camps and recruit those who desire to avenge the death of family members killed by the Pakistani military or who are frustrated by the government's lack of basic human facilities in these camps.[14]

Forced conscription was also used as a recruitment tool. For example, in Swat militants have kidnapped boys from school and coerced them into joining their movement. The Taliban used to enforce the rule that locals either provide monetary support or supply a male member of the household to the movement.[15]

Finally, the Taliban do indeed provide financial incentives to recruits, both directly and indirectly. Senior law enforcement and government officials in FATA and Khyber Pakhtunkhwa Province told me that, according to their investigations, the Pakistani Taliban make regular payments to their core membership of between $250 and $500. The Pakistani Taliban's indirect provision of financial benefits comes from partnering with local criminal networks and profit-sharing. In practice, this amounts to sheltering criminal activities and taking a financial cut for this service. For example, in Khyber and Orakzai agency there is a clearly defined commission system that covers the drug trade and kidnapping activities, and that rewards local Taliban commanders and other fighters.[16] This new reality of the militant–criminal syndicate was captured well by Declan Walsh of the *New York Times*, who reported:

> The business is run like a mobster racket. Pakistani and foreign militant commanders, based in Waziristan, give the orders, but it is a

combination of hired criminals and 'Punjabi Taliban' who snatch the hostages from their homes, vehicles and workplaces.[17]

The work is delegated to various groups according to their expertise, knowledge of the area and capacity to securely transport victims to tribal areas.

These opportunities attract many young men to the Taliban's cause, while allowing them to maintain some independence from the strict religious discipline that the Taliban may impose on their fighters. This approach has helped the Taliban expand from FATA to parts of KPK and even far-off Karachi, but has also served to loosen their command and control.

Haider Abbas Rizvi, a senior politician in the MQM, knows Karachi very well:

Actually the Taliban are using Karachi as a source of money and they are involved in different crimes like extortion, heavy bank robberies, kidnapping for ransom, land grabbing, drug and weapons smuggling and it is big-time, very huge involvement.[18]

This collaboration between organized crime and terrorist groups is a potent factor behind the increased violence in Pakistan, though the Taliban had officially sanctioned kidnapping as a legitimate weapon for their cause as early as March 2008.[19] Crime trends in Afghanistan indicate that this source of finance is becoming popular among the Afghan Taliban as well, and the TTP likely learnt of its utility from them.[20]

The crux of the larger argument here is that the Taliban are now intricately connected to the privatization of violence in both Pakistan and Afghanistan. Operating on both sides of the Durand Line, their activities fuel each other's economic interests – especially as regards movement of drugs and weapons. In the absence of a collaborative effort between Pakistan and Afghanistan, peace is likely to remain elusive.

It is clear that the causes that have given rise to the Taliban resurgence in Afghanistan and the Taliban emergence in Pakistan are varied, but at their heart reside economic distress, insecurity and a perception of injustice among the people – factors that the Taliban exploit to the full. The Taliban's only creativity lies in adding a religious tinge to these concerns. Otherwise the rest falls in place quite neatly in a land that has been devastated, and among people who are desperate to cling onto any idea that offers them some hope. Night raids and drone strikes only add fuel to the fire.

Do drone strikes create more terrorists than they kill?[21]

The US drone strikes that target terrorists in the restive Pashtun tribal belt are highly controversial in Pakistan. For US policy makers, it is an effective counterterrorism tactic; but for Christof Heyns, the UN special rapporteur on extrajudicial, summary or arbitrary executions, they are a major challenge to the system of international law.[22] There are several studies available on the accuracy, reliability and ultimate effectiveness of this tool of war; using the same data, analysts can come to very different conclusions depending on their particular point of view.[23]

For some, the percentage of civilian deaths is the criterion; for others, denying the terrorists sanctuary is a critical benchmark. One problem is a lack of credible data on exactly how many terrorists have been killed by drone strikes and on who those terrorists are.[24] According to the New America Foundation, a credible source of information on the subject, during the first five years of the drone campaign (2004–08), there were 46 such strikes; in the next five years (2009–13) there were 321.[25]

Depending on various claims, between 2,000 and 3,500 individuals are estimated to have been killed in these attacks, but it is not clear how many of these were terrorists. Credible Pakistani security analysts with knowledge of the area maintain that they know the names of around 70 highly trained and dangerous terrorists who were among those killed.[26]

Based on my interviews in Pakistan during 2012 and 2013, I believe that Al-Qaeda and its affiliates are certainly on the run due to drone strikes. I also believe that (for the most part) Pakistan's government, both its military and its civilian power centres, are fully on board. Many mainstream and moderate Pashtuns in Pakistan are largely supportive of the campaign, because it accomplishes what they and the Pakistani security forces could not achieve. It must be admitted, though, that this view is often expressed behind closed doors and in private.

On the flip side, a significant number of drone victims – believed to be around 50 per cent according to local estimates – have been civilians, including women and children. It is this 'collateral damage' that helps militant groups recruit.[27] In many cases, the network of local CIA spies who identify targets on the ground have their own ethnic, tribal or political vendettas to settle as well. The CIA station chief in Islamabad believed that the drone strikes in 2005 and 2006 'were often based on bad intelligence and resulted in many civilian casualties'.[28]

The inherently secret nature of the weapon creates a persistent feeling of fear in the areas where drones rend the sky, and the hopelessness of communities that are on the receiving end causes a severe backlash – in terms of both anti-US opinion and violence. The response to drone strikes comes in many forms. First, there is revenge – targeted at those within easy reach of the insurgents and militants. But the targets of those revenge terrorist attacks also consider the drone strikes to be responsible for the mayhem. Consequently, the terrorists and ordinary people are drawn closer together out of sympathy. And yet a critical function of any successful counterterrorism policy is to win public confidence, so that ordinary people join in the campaign against the perpetrators of terror. Poor public awareness about terrorist organizations (often a function of inadequate education) indeed plays a role in building this perspective. Thus public outrage at drone strikes indirectly empowers the terrorists. It allows them space to survive, move around and manoeuvre.

Second, anti-US feeling in Pakistan has increased substantially, weakening the US–Pakistan counterterrorism cooperation. Some of the facts sound contradictory, and indeed they are. The truth is, we do not know whether US drone strikes have killed or spawned more terrorists. But regardless, killing terrorists is only a stop-gap arrangement. There is a desperate need for a corresponding and parallel development strategy to bring the tribal areas into mainstream Pakistan, in order to empower girls like Malala Yousafzai, who challenged the Taliban world-view by standing up for education (see above). This inclusiveness has long been the missing component in US policy, and tragically it remains so. Dismantling the Al-Qaeda network is a worthwhile goal, but de-radicalization is equally important.

It is not that there has been no US investment in education; rather, the dilemma is lack of balance in the use of 'hard' and 'soft' power. Up to the end of November 2013, there had been roughly 350 drone strikes in the tribal areas since 2004. The cost has been exorbitant, even though drone strikes offer a cheaper alternative than 'boots on the ground'.[29] But how many schools were opened in the region over the same period of time? The answer is distressing: the number of schools actually declined sharply.[30] The damage done to hundreds of schools throughout the tribal belt at the hands of the Taliban has in fact displaced 62,000 children, including 23,000 girls, from school.[31] It does not take much to realize the kind of future that awaits these kids in the absence of schools and with an increase in violence. Drone strikes may knock out some of those who destroyed the schools, but that is hardly a sustainable solution to the larger problem of Talibanization and militancy.

The value of drones in the arena of intelligence gathering and secret surveillance of foes is unmistakable. In war zones, too, drones can support ground operations in significant and even decisive ways. What is debatable is their use as a counterterrorism instrument in theatres that are not declared war zones and where a sovereign state is not fully and publicly on board with the policy. The lack of transparency over the regulations that govern this new type of warfare, the unverifiable nature of the targets and the questions over the credibility of the intelligence only complicate matters.

The wider socio-political impact and indirect costs of drone strikes must be accounted for when evaluating their efficacy. In Afghanistan, too, the high civilian casualty rate in drone strikes is emerging as a serious issue. A study conducted by a US military adviser has found that drone strikes in that country during 2012–13 caused ten times more civilian casualties than strikes by manned aircraft.[32] The figure becomes even starker if the total number of drone strikes in Afghanistan is borne in mind: in 2012 alone, there were 447 drone strikes – up from 294 in 2011 and 278 in 2010.[33] The impact of this policy is evident from a highly credible 2013 field study, based on interviews in 200 Afghan villages. It shows that 'harm inflicted by the International Security Assistance Force is met with reduced support for ISAF and increased support for the Taliban, but Taliban-inflicted harm does not translate into greater ISAF support'.[34]

Drone strikes that specifically target hard-core terrorists can be effective, provided they are supported by a parallel PR exercise to challenge the ideas projected by those terrorists. In combating terrorism, the physical elimination of the enemy matters, but it is not decisive. Hitting at the mindset of the terrorist and discrediting the ideas that generate terrorism is the really big prize. Law enforcement action that flows from a 'rule of law' paradigm, involving thorough investigation and prosecution in courts, is likely to be far more damaging to the ideas that the terrorists stand for. The limited and internationally regulated use of drones to target the most wanted terrorists may be part of this comprehensive approach – it may take longer to deliver, but it will be more sustainable and the results will be more durable.

US Secretary of State John Kerry eased the mounting pressure on the Pakistani government when, on his trip to Pakistan in August 2013, he hinted that the programme of drone strikes could end soon after it achieved its major goals.[35] The number of strikes has indeed declined significantly since mid-2013. Rumour has it that the US agreed to show restraint for a year, during which Sharif could make a concerted effort to deal with the issue – through talks or otherwise.

In regional capitals, though, especially Kabul, New Delhi and Tehran, the US drone policy has only brought relief, as the strikes have eliminated many terrorists focused on regional targets.

The India factor

External interference has rarely worked in Afghanistan's best interests, and the India–Pakistan antagonism and mutual distrust continues to exacerbate the security challenges in Afghanistan. India often blames Pakistan for repeated attacks targeting its embassy in Kabul and its consulates in the south of Afghanistan, and Pakistan frequently claims that India is supporting anti-state elements in its Balochistan Province. The India–Pakistan mutual hostility lies at the heart of both states' policy towards Afghanistan – and that does not bode well for prospects for peace in the region.

Pakistan's rivalry with neighbouring India is neither new nor easily resolvable, given the long-standing and seemingly irreconcilable differences over the disputed Kashmir region. Both countries have a track record of poking their noses into each other's internal affairs. India is the world's largest democracy and has a commendable economic growth record, but it often behaves childishly when it comes to Pakistan. During a trip to India's capital New Delhi in 2010, a local friend 'informed' me of an area in the suburbs of the city that was under the control of Pakistan's Inter-Services Intelligence – a ridiculous assertion at best. Pakistan, too, suffers from an insecurity complex when it comes to India.

The Obama administration was well aware of the importance of India–Pakistan relations to peace prospects in Afghanistan. In June 2007, the then Senator Barack Obama had written in one of his early policy papers: 'I will encourage dialogue between Pakistan and India to work toward resolving their dispute over Kashmir.'[36] After being elected as president of the United States in a historic election, he went a step further in a *Time* magazine interview, arguing that Pakistan would not fully commit to fighting the insurgency it shares with Afghanistan until it sheds its historic insecurities toward India; resolving the Kashmir conflict, he said, will be among the 'critical tasks for the next administration.'[37] Nothing substantive came of this assertion.

The competition between India and Pakistan in Afghanistan continues, and the Afghan Taliban are more empowered in the process.

India is haunted by the thought of the return of the Taliban to Kabul, and Pakistan is none too keen to see such an outcome of the 'war on terror' either; yet there is a fundamental difference in how the two countries view the future of Afghanistan. India, besides its pure economic interests, wants to keep Afghanistan within its zone of influence. It has some legitimate reasons for this line of thinking. It learned the hard way that Kashmir-focused armed groups benefited from sanctuary in Afghanistan while the Pakistan-friendly Taliban were at the helm. Indian investment in the Northern Alliance, through financial support and military training facilities for its supporters during the 1990s, paid off well in the post-2001 scenario. It was wise of India to build on that strategy through economic and development projects, which it did with the support of the US and Iran. India's security interests were naturally served by this 'soft power' approach. It also kept Pakistan under pressure, but without any military projection.

For Pakistan, the rise of the Afghan Taliban in the 1990s was a guarantee that its Pashtun connection would bear fruit and that Indian influence in Afghanistan would remain nominal. Everything else was immaterial to Pakistan. Things changed with the advent of the age of modern terrorism, and Pakistan now wants a stable Afghanistan; but its security concerns vis-à-vis India have also become more intense. It distrusts non-Pashtuns in Afghanistan and wants Pashtuns in whatever shape or form to play a dominant role in the country. This is not only unfair, but counterproductive, too; however the myopia of Pakistan's security strategists blurs its vision. The Afghan Taliban, especially the old cadre led by Mullah Omar, is still the favourite of Pakistan's military. In this case old ties matter, and it is expected that the hospitality that Pakistan provided to many of its stalwarts since 2001 will pay off. It is unlikely that the Taliban insurgents on the ground in Afghanistan are getting direct support from Pakistan's security services, but these fighters are expected to fall in line if and when Mullah Omar returns to Kabul in triumph. Pakistan continues to maintain its links with some Taliban-affiliated insurgent factions, such as the infamous Haqqani group, in order to remain relevant to the future of Afghanistan.

Pakistan's policy, too, like that of India, seems well thought-out, bearing in mind the security threat it perceives from India and its expanding influence in Afghanistan, which it considers to be its backyard. In pursuit of this agenda, Pakistan lost the hearts and minds of ordinary Afghans, but it is unwilling to accept that.

All of this may sound a bit simplistic, but my extensive interaction with Indian and Pakistani security officials convinces me that these issues explain the core of the problem. A strategic partnership agreement between Afghanistan and India signed on 4 October 2011 further convinced Pakistan that its worst fears were being realized. Karzai made this move quite deliberately, to poke Pakistan in the eye, after having failed to receive Islamabad's support in reaching out to Taliban leaders.

Referring to a trilateral meeting between Pakistani, British and Afghan leaders in England in early 2013, an Afghan Foreign Ministry statement criticized the 'delusional tendency of some in Pakistan who choose to ignore Afghanistan's sovereignty . . . and continue to want to . . . re-exert control in Afghanistan through armed proxies'.[38] Pakistan has its own set of complaints against the Afghan government for supporting certain Pakistani terrorists, especially Mullah Fazlullah, who between 2010 and 2014 operated from the Kunar or Nuristan area of Afghanistan and conducted repeated raids inside Pakistan.[39] ISAF advisers believe that the 'Afghan army is allowing the Pakistani Taliban to operate in retribution for Pakistan not doing enough to stop cross-border rocket attacks and armed infiltrators using Pakistan as a haven'.[40]

Afghanistan has also been providing space to some Baloch insurgent leaders as well, thus raising the stakes. In one important case – that of Brahamdagh Bugti – even an effort by the CIA station chief in Pakistan to find an amicable solution between the two states failed.[41] There is a long history of both states offering sanctuary to the other's opponents, but in this specific case Pakistan earnestly believed that the Karzai government was hand in glove with the Indians. Though nothing can actually be ruled out, official US sources maintain that they have seen no evidence of such Indian interference.[42] However, Christine Fair, a noted American expert on South Asia, aptly comments:

Although India downplays its interests in securing and retaining Afghanistan as a friendly state from which it has the capacity to monitor Pakistan, and even possibly cultivate assets to influence activities in Pakistan, it most certainly has such aims.[43]

Pakistan's encirclement fears in turn drive its security policy. Pakistan is also very sensitive about Balochistan, as a low-intensity insurgency has been gaining steam there in recent years. This underdeveloped and impoverished province shares a 500-mile or so border with Iran. Aside from Taliban remnants (the Quetta Shura) based in the provincial capital of Quetta, various terrorist organizations operate freely in the countryside. Some religious extremist groups moved into the province (with the connivance of the state's security services) with the aim of defeating the secular insurgency.

One of the militant groups operating in the province is Jundallah, a terrorist outfit that is solely focused on Iran. Its members move in and out of Iran through smuggling routes. *Foreign Policy* magazine revealed in early 2012 how 'Israeli Mossad agents posed as American spies to recruit members of the terrorist organization Jundallah to fight their covert war against Iran', and in the process 'Israel's activities jeopardized the [Bush] administration's fragile relationship with Pakistan.'[44] For Pakistan, this was shocking and the Iran–Pakistan relationship also took a jolt. Whether a half-truth or a psychological-warfare operation intended for a different audience, it gave some legitimacy to Pakistan's security concerns.

After the fall of the Taliban in 2001, India quickly devised an arsenal of economic, developmental and security tools in its pursuit of a more coordinated strategy, as it could see an extraordinary opportunity. Lack of a common border did not get in the way of Indian plans. India has contributed close to $2 billion in aid, making it Afghanistan's fifth-largest bilateral donor.[45] The fingerprints of Indian development policy can be seen from school benches and public buses to the very parliament building where the fledging democracy is supposed to be taking shape. The Indira Gandhi Hospital, built by Indians, was the only hospital in Kabul to treat women and children. Medical support in Mazar-i-Sharif, Jalalabad and Kandahar was also significant. Though India maintained a light military footprint in Afghanistan, it regularly offered training and support to the Afghan National Army, as well as Afghan intelligence. For Pakistan, this was like a red rag to a bull.

Within Pakistan, many exaggerations about the Indian role have been popularized. The most widely believed theory is that India has established 14 (or some say 21) consulates in areas close to the Pakistan–Afghan border and that these offices are run by Research and Analysis Wing, India's premier intelligence service. In reality there are only four Indian consulates in the entire country (Jalalabad, Kandahar, Herat and Mazar-i-Sharif), though it is likely that these offices do also have intelligence functions. Perceptions, at times, are more powerful than reality.

Stanley McChrystal, the top US general in Afghanistan in 2009–10 was quick to grasp these regional undercurrents: 'While Indian activities largely benefit the Afghan people, increasing Indian influence in Afghanistan is likely to exacerbate regional tensions and encourage Pakistani countermeasures in Afghanistan or India.'[46] In 2011, Chuck Hagel, who later became US secretary of defence, was more blunt when he spoke at a university event on the subject: 'India for some time has always used Afghanistan as a second front, and India has over the years financed problems for Pakistan on that side of the border.'[47]

Irrespective of Indian motivations, the Taliban targeted India on account of its active reconstruction role in Afghanistan. On a few occasions, India directly blamed Pakistan's ISI for orchestrating the attacks. And in the case of the July 2008 bombing of the Indian embassy in Kabul, the US intelligence assessment, based on intercepted communications, concluded that ISI agents had been involved in planning the attack.[48]

I asked a Pakistani general for his response to these allegations. After the standard lines calling it Indian propaganda, he argued more seriously that the 'Taliban in Afghanistan are attacking all outsiders who are collaborating with ISAF and so they need no special provocation from Pakistan to target Indians'.[49]

According to a range of independent studies and intelligence assessments, Pakistan certainly has a soft spot for (and association with) the Haqqani group, which is actively assisting the Taliban insurgency in Afghanistan.[50] This militant group has camps and support in the North Waziristan tribal area of Pakistan, but its primary area of recruitment, support and influence lies within the Afghan provinces of Khost, Paktia and Paktika (together known as Loya Paktia).[51] The group draws its name and strength from the career of Jalaluddin Haqqani, a legendary Afghan commander of the anti-Soviet Afghan Jihad years. According to Steve Coll, his other accomplishments include the following:

> He raised money during Haj visits to Saudi Arabia, accepted cash subsidies as a 'unilateral' asset of the Central Intelligence Agency, and at the same time made himself indispensable to Pakistan's principal intelligence service . . . ISI.[52]

He offered his services to Osama bin Laden, as well as to Mullah Omar, and, as mentioned earlier, joined the Taliban cabinet in the late 1990s. Today his family members, especially his son Siraj Haqqani run the show and are considered untouchable in Pakistan. His status as an intelligence asset for Pakistan is due to two important reasons. First, in an environment where many other militant groups have turned their guns in the direction of Pakistan, this is one influential group that is not involved in terrorist attacks inside Pakistan. Second, given the uncertainty in Afghanistan, Pakistan is hedging its bets by maintaining good relations with the group.

A second layer of reality, however, also exists. The Pakistan–Haqqani group nexus is far more complicated than it may appear on the surface. After all, Haqqani group militants have not helped Pakistan to defeat the Tehrik-i-Taliban Pakistan, which is a declared enemy of Pakistan and has been directly responsible for dozens of suicide bomb attacks on military convoys and even ISI offices. Pakistan's military leadership must have asked for Haqqani group support, as the TTP and Haqqani group militants operate from the same area. Based on my own interaction with many Pakistani military and intelligence officials, I conclude that in fact the Haqqani group deals with Pakistani intelligence on its own terms, and in many cases operates quite independently. It knows Pakistan's security vulnerabilities and long-term interests in Afghanistan and blackmails it. Pakistan plays along – at times even happily.

Leaving aside the rhetoric asking Pakistan to 'do more' on the counterterrorism front, I suspect the US has reached a similar conclusion. Otherwise, it makes little sense for the US to continue military aid to Pakistan. ISAF and Afghan forces must also share the blame for not dealing with the Haqqani group effectively on the Afghan side of the border. The possibility that the Afghans exaggerate the role of the group in fuelling Taliban insurgency is also worth considering.

None of this justifies Pakistan's links with this terrorist outfit, and if history is any indication, sooner or later the policy is likely to blow up in Pakistan's face. Islamabad's misplaced regional interests have indeed clouded its vision.

Wider regional rivalries

A stable Afghanistan is good for everyone in the region, but in practice this view does not seem to have really influenced the policies of the states involved. It is truly amazing how many countries have expended their resources and energies in Afghanistan, but with little planning and coordination. Teamwork among nations has been woefully missing, which has led to over-competitiveness and the pursuit of divergent agendas – all in the name of helping Afghanistan. Retrogressive forces, including the Taliban, have been direct and immediate beneficiaries of this incompetence and ineffectiveness.

One obvious example is the missed opportunity to involve Iran in the international effort to ameliorate Afghanistan's problems. Ambassador James Dobbins, the US special representative for Afghanistan and Pakistan (SRAP) since April 2013, represented the US during the Bonn Agreement proceedings in late 2001. Afterwards he openly acknowledged the helpfulness of the Iranian delegates, who had made two 'memorable contributions' to the Agreement text, namely the inclusion of 'democracy' and 'war on terror' as goals that the new government in Afghanistan must commit to.[53] The prospects for a renewed relationship only declined when President Bush listed Iran among the 'axis of evil' countries during his state of the union address in January 2002. To dispel any US and Afghan misgivings, Iran even expelled Afghan warlord Hekmatyar from Tehran in February 2002 after he criticized the nascent Karzai government.[54] His political office was also closed, and his bank accounts frozen.

Former Iranian President Mahmoud Ahmadinejad visited New York in 2008 and 2009 to speak at the United Nations General Assembly sessions. At a small gathering organized by the Iranian UN mission, I had an opportunity to ask Ahmadinejad about the potential of positive US–Iranian engagement in Afghanistan to help defeat the militancy. He surprised many of us by not only acknowledging such a need, but sounding ready to give such a partnership a real chance.

It may be politically incorrect to say this in Western capitals, especially Washington, but the reality is that a collaborative arrangement between the US and Iran would have helped build Afghanistan. The late Richard Holbrooke, the talented diplomat appointed by President Obama as the US SRAP in 2009, and his able adviser Vali Nasr, presented this idea to top US policy makers; but the US differences with Iran over the latter's nuclear programme meant their attempts were fruitless.[55]

However, this did not stop the Iranians from making inroads into Afghanistan, both literally and figuratively. As a landlocked state, Afghanistan is heavily reliant on its neighbours for trade. Its 600-mile border with Iran and the historical, cultural and religious connections between the two states mean it is of particular importance. Dari, one of the two official languages of Afghanistan and the lingua franca of the Afghan elite and intellectuals, is an Afghan dialect of the Persian language. Culturally, Herat, the third-largest city in Afghanistan, is closer to Tehran than it is to Kabul – and historically it remained part of Iran and the Persian Empire for centuries, until the middle of the nineteenth century.[56]

In 2002, Iran pledged $560 million at the Tokyo conference on the reconstruction of Afghanistan, and over time Tehran has emerged as Afghanistan's leading donor in terms of per capita income. Regular Iranian investments have raised the value of bilateral trade to around $1.5 billion.[57] Iran also accounts for at least 30 per cent of Afghanistan's oil supply.[58] A newly built 76-mile road linking Herat to the Dogharoun region of Iran is also strategically conceived, while Afghanistan is being linked to the Iranian port of Chabahar via another new road, which seeks to lessen Afghan dependence on the Pakistani port of Karachi. Tellingly, perhaps, India has been financially supporting this road network expansion between Afghanistan and Iran.[59] To further encourage Afghan traders, Iran has granted Afghan exporters a 90 per cent discount on port fees and a 50 per cent discount on warehousing charges, and has given Afghan vehicles full transit rights on the Iranian road system.[60] The whole undertaking has not been plain sailing, however, given the staunch Taliban opposition to increased ties between non-Pashtun areas and Iran, and the road project particularly has been 'attracting suicide bombers like flies'.[61]

For its part, the US realized soon after 2001 that Afghanistan needed a viable road network, and a consortium of donors was put together, featuring USAID, the Asian Development Bank and Saudi Arabia. This resourceful group committed itself to building a ring road around the country, at the same time as Iran started building a road network linking Herat with Iranian cities. The Iranians completed their project in 2005, but the other one moved at a snail's pace because, in the words of US Defense Department's chief financial officer, Dov Zakheim, the 'Saudis simply did not come up with the money they had promised' and the USAID contractor picked for the project had little experience of working in a security-challenged environment.[62]

But that does not mean Iran has hit a home run. Two serious challenges plague its relationship with Afghanistan. First of all, around half of Afghanistan's illicit opium production is smuggled across the

Iranian–Afghan border.[63] Although Iran's role in this is as a transit point for this poisonous commodity, the number of its own opiate addicts has risen considerably in recent years.[64] An effective counter-narcotics strategy – with an annual budget of $1 billion – has lately started to have an impact in Iran (so much so that a similar model is being touted for Afghanistan), but it still faces massive obstacles.[65] Second, the pitiful plight of the million-plus Afghan refugees in Iran poses a challenge in terms of both the economic burden placed on Iran and the way in which ordinary Afghans view Iran through that lens. The Iranian government has, on a few occasions, threatened to expel all Afghans living in Iran, apparently to remind Kabul that it needs Tehran's goodwill.

But Iran needs a friendly Kabul, too, as the two countries share a flow of water that originates in Afghanistan. So Iran is vulnerable to Afghan policies. The issue has been a bone of contention for over a century. Iran's southeast provinces are dependent on water from the Helmand River, which rises in the Hindu Kush Mountains northwest of Kabul and flows 750 miles into Iran's Sistan-Balochistan Province. A 1973 agreement provides for a water-distribution mechanism, but every now and then differences arise as to its implementation. Iran can never forget that in 1999 the Taliban cut off the water flow to Iran, resulting in an environmental disaster in and around the Lake Hamun region.[66] The issue was tentatively resolved with the intervention of Iranian President Khatami and Karzai in 2002, but Iranian fears linger on. In one case Iran pressurized India to stop funding for the $150 million planned reconstruction of the Salma Dam in Herat, as that would have obstructed the flow of water to Iran.[67]

Aware of the stakes, Iran made a huge investment in the Afghan media to aid its image building and profile. Some believe that around 'a third of Afghanistan's media is backed by Iran, either financially or through providing content'.[68] From my own observations, Iranian media sources are generally critical of Taliban activities, but disapproval of the US presence in the region is just as enthusiastic. The election in 2013 of Mohammad Hasan Rouhani, a reformist cleric, as president of Iran has led to improvement in Iran's relations with the West, especially the US, and that could potentially lead to a convergence of Iranian and American interests as regards stability and peace in Afghanistan.

Back in the 1990s, Iran sided with and funded the Northern Alliance, while Saudi Arabia, its ideological nemesis, was one of only three countries in the world that recognized the Taliban regime. But today the dynamic has been transformed: as Iran builds highways in Afghanistan in collaboration with India, Saudi Arabia's trademark project is a $100 million Islamic centre that is under construction on a hilltop in Kabul and will be run jointly by the sponsor and the host country.[69]

The Iran–Saudi Arabia contest in Afghanistan becomes hot whenever news of negotiations with the Taliban comes up in the media. Saudi royals were expected to play a part in moderating the Taliban and even in bringing them to the negotiating table; but the Saudis have been deliberately cautious in this domain, as they have limited influence over the modern-day Taliban insurgents. Still, they will likely support any Pakistani initiatives for 'reconciliation' with Taliban – both morally and financially.

Iran meanwhile remains focused on its traditional allies in Afghanistan – who are invariably non-Pashtuns. President Karzai admitted in October 2010 that his office regularly received suitcases of cash from Tehran, with as much as $1 million in euro banknotes stuffed inside, in exchange for 'good relations'.[70] A similar revelation about CIA cash support for Karzai's office emerged in 2012, but it is not known if the CIA cash is in place of Iranian cash, or if both channels operate in parallel. The latter scenario is more likely. That would not be too difficult for any Afghan leader to pull off, given the historical precedents.

The role of Central Asia has assumed greater significance for Afghanistan during the past decade. Though all five Central Asian states – Turkmenistan, Uzbekistan, Tajikistan, Kazakhstan and Kyrgyzstan – are seriously concerned about the fate of Afghanistan, the first three share a border with Afghanistan and are more vulnerable, due to their ethnic connections. Luckily for them, Talibanization has not really expanded in their direction, but since 2010 remnants of the Islamic Movement of Uzbekistan, a militant group known to have a good rapport with both the Afghan and the Pakistani Taliban, have shown some signs of revival.[71]

Central Asia has the world's largest untapped reserves of oil and gas, and that is enough to attract global interest. The US Department of Energy estimates that 163 billion barrels of oil and up to 337 trillion cubic feet of natural gas are to be found in the Caspian region. And Kazakhstan has been found to have the second-largest reserves of gold in the world.[72] Afghanistan's stability is important for the safe and reliable transportation of these resources to the world's main markets. Planned projects such as the Turkmenistan–Afghanistan–Pakistan–India (TAPI) gas pipeline hold the key to meeting the future energy needs of the region. The return of the Taliban to Kabul could throw a spanner in the works.

Afghanistan's future is inextricably linked to that of its neighbours. Regional tensions and rivalries continue to haunt Afghanistan, just as much as instability in Afghanistan troubles the region. The export of arms, drugs and ideology must give way to constructive partnerships that can lead to capacity building, economic development and religious harmony. A 'New Silk Road' vision of regional and economic connectivity through a network of railway lines, roads and energy infrastructure has been marketed by the US State Department since 2011. It looks very good on paper, but without regional collaboration and understanding is more akin to a pipedream.[73] The prospects for such a transformation remain dim so long as there is no effort to resolve the regional and civilizational fault lines in and around Afghanistan.

Though very active in pursuing its economic and security interests in Afghanistan, China is not interested in assuming any responsibility for what has gone wrong there – and perhaps rightly so. In response to an official American effort to engage China in stabilizing Afghanistan, the Chinese reaction was straightforward: 'This is your problem. You made the mess. In Afghanistan more war has made things worse, and in Pakistan things were not so bad before you started poking around.'[74] Though China's policy in Afghanistan is independent of Pakistan's approach to its neighbour, it is worth noting that Pakistan is still dubbed 'China's Israel' by Chinese diplomats, the implication being that China will continue to support Pakistan, no matter what it does.[75]

China is apparently least of all interested in the domestic political dynamics of Afghanistan, though destabilization of its Muslim-majority Xinjiang Province – a potential consequence of the rise of religious radicalism in the region – does seriously bother it.[76] A few dozen Chinese Uighurs joined Al-Qaeda and the Taliban forces in Afghanistan during the Taliban years, and some of them are now languishing in Guantanamo prison. It is the broader 'East Turkestan' movement that poses a real challenge to China. A massive riot in Urumqi, the capital of Xinjiang, in July 2009 led to around 200 deaths and resulted in the destruction of property. This was a wake-up call for China, and since then there has been a discernible shift in its policy. It is now more engaged in the security sector, even though it refused a British offer to join the ISAF forces in 2008. In September 2012, Zhou Yongkang, China's domestic security chief, became the most senior Chinese official to visit Afghanistan for almost 50 years.[77] The occasion was the signing of an agreement that provided for 300 Afghan police officers to be trained in China.

China's much-vaunted long-range approach, however, remains focused on the economic and energy sectors. Its biggest project – and the biggest foreign-investment project overall in Afghanistan – is the development of the Aynak copper mine. With a $4 billion investment over five years, this could provide a steady source of revenue generation for Afghanistan.[78] It is complemented by an additional $6 billion investment in the construction of a rail network and power stations.

China is also investing hugely in oil and gas exploration in the country. There has been some talk of a trilateral alliance between China, Afghanistan and Pakistan (called the Pamir Group, after the Pamir Mountains that abut all three countries). This is built around the ambitious agenda of reviving the ancient Silk Road and constructing a network of roads, energy pipelines and electric grids.[79] Of course, this idea was a response to the US-envisioned 'New Silk Road', mentioned earlier.

The acquisition of Gwadar port in Pakistan already provides China with a potentially vital energy and trading hub. It unsettles India but hardly surprises anyone. China is also likely to push more assertively for an expansion of the Shanghai Cooperation Organization to the whole region after the drawdown of US forces in Afghanistan.

At the Bonn II Conference in December 2011, Yang Jiechi, the Chinese minister of foreign affairs, emphasized the importance of an 'Afghan-led and Afghan-owned' peace and reconciliation process.[80] Basically, China will be prepared to work with whoever is at the helm in Kabul, so long as they allow China to pursue its economic interests.

As regards China's perceptions of the Taliban, Professor Zhao Huasheng, an accomplished Chinese scholar at Fudan University in Shanghai, sums things up well:

> China perceives the Taliban as more than a religious extremist group, but also as a real political force that could have a long-term presence in the Afghan political arena. China is unconvinced that the Taliban can be destroyed by military means.[81]

This statement will sound familiar to those who follow statements from Pakistan's Foreign Office. There is nothing wrong with that, but it does explain the convergence of interests.

Conclusion
Hubris and lack of vision versus hope and prospects for reform

The Taliban were the children of war, lawlessness and distorted religious education when they first emerged on the scene in the mid-1990s; but a wider range of factors caused their revival in Afghanistan a decade later. A reinforcement of Pashtun tribalism and a deep-rooted legacy of resistance to outsiders added more fury to the fire of the Taliban creed. The growing influence of criminal networks, the incompetence of international contractors and regional power politics created new avenues for the Taliban to acquire financial resources.

The ideological and political roots of the Pakistani Taliban are not much different but a separate, though linked, set of circumstances empowered them. The lack of the writ of the state in FATA, disproportionate use of force, and religious radicalization via Al-Qaeda strategists did the trick for them. To break the Taliban code, each of these contributing factors has to be tackled effectively. A stable political system that is enabled through good governance, investment in education and religious pluralism can combine to form an antidote to the extremist Taliban outlook and to build a better future for the Afghanistan–Pakistan region. Anything short of that is unlikely to dent the Taliban's vigour and momentum.

The Taliban in Pakistan and Afghanistan both pose a deadly but unique set of challenges. Similar in ideological mindset and military capability, they look in different directions. Today, in the context of Afghanistan, 'Taliban' is more of a loose term that covers old Taliban (many of them hiding in Pakistan), insurgent groups operating in various theatres across Afghanistan, and criminal networks that wear Taliban masks at night – even though for some of them the day job is to act as security contractors tasked with ensuring the safety of international forces' supply lines.

Increasing evidence suggests that most of the active fighters draw inspiration from being under occupation. They are not at all as organized as modern militaries are, but they are very committed to their cause. Financed by criminal activities and drug traffickers, their religious zeal continues to draw more recruits. Unemployment, illiteracy and high poverty rates further create a conducive environment for Taliban recruitment drives. The Afghan Taliban earnestly believe that they will return to Kabul in triumph, but they have little idea about what they will do next. They criticize the newly formed institutions of state, but they offer no alternative. They aspire to justice, but foolishly attack judges.

My research indicates that the old Taliban under Mullah Omar no longer directly control the insurgent activity in Afghanistan, though they obviously have influence and can potentially regain control of the narrative in future. A newer generation of militants operating in the field defines the ethos of the Taliban today; and it is more uncompromising than the older generation. The leadership of the older generation of the Taliban mostly resides in Pakistan, and many of them are conveniently becoming more pragmatic. Some of them are slowly moving back to Afghanistan – partly as a result of the Pakistan–Afghanistan dialogue – but it is not clear yet if they will be able to take charge of the various insurgent factions across Afghanistan. Despite all the fissures and divisions between hardline and relatively moderate Taliban leaders, overall the Afghan Taliban are largely concerned about the state of affairs in their homeland, Afghanistan.

The Pakistani Taliban, on the other hand, are more audacious and dangerous. They adopted the 'Taliban' title much later than their Afghan brethren, but in their case the foundations of the idea of Taliban are even more firmly held. The genesis of the Pakistani Taliban owes a great deal to the history of lawlessness, tribalism and Pakistan's perennial neglect of the Federally Administered Tribal Areas. Genuine political and economic grievances, coupled with Pakistan's controversial role in the 'war on terror' in Afghanistan, have turned out to be the defining impetus. Their fake claim to religious knowledge allows them to bend religion the way they want, and mixing Islam up with their tribal cultural values has made it a successful enterprise.

They, too, consider themselves to be reeling under occupation, as for them the Pakistani military is an outside force that is operating in their areas without sanction. Gradually, they have openly started challenging the very idea of Pakistan. It is not their goal to take over Islamabad and govern there: their preferred path is to make Waziristan the capital of their cherished Islamic Emirate.

There are yet other types of Taliban, too, ranging from those who operate in Punjab (mostly disgruntled elements of Kashmir-focused militant groups) to criminal gangs that are in this unholy game purely for the money.

The penetration of Al-Qaeda ideology into the Pakistani Taliban discourse further galvanized Taliban cadres in the country. The discourse of Syrian terror mastermind, Abu Musab Al-Suri, especially his writing *The Call to Global Islamic Resistance*, has greatly influenced the Pakistani Taliban. Though captured by Pakistan from Quetta in 2005, his philosophy – which advocates learning lessons from the past mistakes of Al-Qaeda and focusing on small-scale and independent operations as a survival strategy – reverberates throughout the training centres run by the Pakistani Taliban.[1]

Despite their capacity to conduct attacks anywhere in the country, including on the most sensitive of security targets, the Pakistani Taliban are not a mainstream force and are unable to develop into a wider political movement. While they face certain fractures due to the making and breaking of tribal alignments in FATA, their strength also lies in having foreign warriors, especially Arabs and Uzbeks, in their ranks. The Punjabi Taliban, which also recruit from among retired security

officials and educated urban professionals, have added a lethal capability to the Pakistani Taliban. The Pakistani Taliban fit perfectly into
the category of 'terrorist organization'. Joining the battlefield in Syria is
a new craze among its followers. They have little public support across
the country, and nearly half of all Pakistanis consider the Taliban to be
a very serious threat to the country.[2] The Afghan Taliban, in comparison, are more politically oriented and their moderate faction could
potentially transform itself into a political party in the future.

Despite some differences in approach and outlook, the various
Taliban factions in Pakistan and Afghanistan share information, logistics and (at times) manpower resources. They rent weapons to each
other and coordinate recruitment of suicide bombers. They also coordinate the targeting of those who challenge their ideas. Attacks on peace
jirgas and assassinations of progressive elements on both sides of the
Durand Line are now the norm in the area. Tribal ethos, Pashtun ethnic
chauvinism, radical religious doctrine and political-cum-economic
grievances provide a bond for this new generation of warriors.

The common thread running through the various Taliban factions is
their strategy, which relies heavily on the perception of inevitability and
a lack of time constraints. The funding streams of the Taliban – private
donors in the Gulf, the illicit drug economy and extortion rackets in
major economic hubs such as Karachi – provide them with a sustainable basis of support that not only enhances their capacity for insurgency and terror, but also connects them across the region.

The Taliban ideology never went unchallenged, either in Pakistan or
Afghanistan. Many modern and mainstream religious scholars – from
both the Sunni and the Shia traditions – have raised their voices against
the false Taliban teachings in Pakistan, especially Javed Ghamidi, a
Sunni scholar with Deobandi roots. In his analysis of the features of
Taliban philosophy, which he argues are built on anti-democratic norms
and the adoption of violent means, he maintains strongly that: 'I can say
with full confidence on the basis of my study of Islam that this [Taliban]
viewpoint and this strategy are not acceptable to the Qur'ān.'[3] Two other
important Pakistani Sunni Muslim scholars, Maulana Hasan Jan of

Peshawar and Dr Sarfraz Ahmed Naeemi of Lahore, went a step further and issued fatwas against Taliban suicide attacks. Unfortunately they had to pay for this valour with their lives, as the Taliban went after them.[4] The list of prominent Afghan clerics who have challenged the Taliban and been killed in response is very long; two recent examples are Maulvi Hekmatullah Hekmat and Maulvi Atta Muhammad.[5]

The leaders and strategists of the Taliban are apparently totally unaware of the rich Islamic literature dealing with governance issues, such as the famous letter of Ali ibne Abi Talib, the fourth caliph of Islam, to Malik Al-Ashtar, the designated governor of Egypt, effectively laying down the primary principles of governance. These include religious tolerance, the establishment of justice, the accountability of administrators, the welfare of the poor, and the selection of leaders on the basis of their knowledge and scholarship. Taliban functioning has been diametrically opposed to these guidelines.

Trends and mixed signals

Starting with Afghanistan, there is an emerging trend among international counterinsurgency experts to claim that Afghanistan was a 'mission impossible' in terms of nation-building endeavours. There is also a rising fear that, after the planned US withdrawal in 2014, a devastating civil war could be Afghanistan's fate, leading to another Taliban rise. Consequently, there is a tendency to accept war and conflict as a new norm in Afghanistan, which invites hopelessness. This unwarranted approach now directs the energies of various influential capitals of the world to think more in terms of 'crisis management', rather than 'conflict resolution' and 'peaceful settlement'. This attitude is not only counterproductive, but is also a recipe for disaster. A different and more positive end is still achievable in Afghanistan, provided the regional and international players involved there employ a more creative set of policies. Time is running out, but Talibanization trends in Afghanistan can be reversed. The realities on the ground in Afghanistan remain very challenging, but it is difficult to deny that progress has been made in various sectors.[6]

Many leading and resourceful political Afghans are moving their families and assets abroad (mostly to the UAE or the UK/USA) and the rise in applications for political asylum in the West is a reflection of this development. It is creating panic among those Afghans who moved back to their homeland to help rebuild the country. Still, there is a newly emerged middle class, mostly located in the urban centres of Afghanistan, who continue to have a big stake in the country's future – they are unlikely to give up hope easily. However, many of them want the international forces to stay longer in Afghanistan, in order to avoid the return of the Taliban and Al-Qaeda.[7]

The central government and provincial governors have established many new administrative offices, creating new legal and political structures. These will help the survival of the new constitutional system – at least in the north, west and centre of Afghanistan, though things remain highly unstable in the Pashtun-dominated regions. It is worth remembering that the Taliban's approach to swift justice – though crude and brutal – continues to appeal to the rural areas that have not benefited from the internationally funded development projects. At times, Afghans prefer to take their cases to Taliban courts because state-appointed judges are corrupt.

The Taliban at present are not in a position to overrun the major cities or to run a parallel government. In future, a lot depends on whether, after the drawdown of forces, the US continues to provide funds to sustain and develop the Afghan army and police (estimated at $6 billion a year). There is a strong likelihood that the flow of funds will continue, though the amount may gradually decrease. If the Afghan National Army survives for a couple of years after 2014, then Afghanistan will begin to stand on its own two feet. A successful political transition after the April 2014 presidential elections could also do wonders for Afghanistan. The quality of this election process is a sign of things to come.

Should international funds for Afghanistan dry up on account of some international development, and should the entire system collapse as a consequence, even then the Taliban are not expected to find Kabul a bed of roses: they will have to fight for control of Afghanistan against the competing interests of warlords, tribal militias and rival groups, and that will result in protracted conflict.

Corruption remains entrenched in the corridors of power in Kabul, as President Karzai has recreated patronage networks for his political survival. (Interestingly, a palatial building is being renovated for Karzai to move into after his term is over, just next door to the official residence of the Afghan president.) His successor is likely to continue this tradition, though the severe criticism of corrupt practices by the Afghan media is also a new reality and there is an increasing public awareness that corruption is a curse that must be overcome if governance is to improve. A growing and vibrant local media is a healthy addition to the Afghan scene.

A rise in the 'green on blue' or 'insider' attacks – targeting of US and NATO soldiers by Afghan forces – has seriously damaged trust between NATO and the Afghan security organizations. And while Taliban infiltration is a serious issue, defections due to economic reasons are also a potent factor. The situation is indeed troubling, but it is not beyond repair – a change in recruitment standards, better training and less intrusive monitoring of Afghan security operations could transform the dynamics in this context. Some Afghan experts worry that Tajik military officers in Afghanistan are likely to attempt a coup if Taliban success looks imminent in the aftermath of US withdrawal. Pashtun nationalism leading to more strength for Taliban insurgents or a virtual division of Afghanistan along ethnic lines will become a real possibility in such a case.

The regional players – China, Russia, Pakistan, India and Iran – are all asserting their national self-interest in Afghanistan in a manner that engenders instability. Many of the initiatives by regional states are constructive, but lack of coordination and cooperation between these players leads to mistrust, inefficiency and duplication. The drawdown of NATO and US forces scheduled for 2014 is often wrongly interpreted as a Western departure from Afghanistan. International financial support and NATO/US training and advising are likely to continue in Afghanistan for close to another decade, in an effort to help the country stand on its own two feet. However, better coordination between NATO components and US interagency harmony will be a prerequisite for making any significant contribution to strengthening Afghan nstitutions.

A few ideas for the Afghan government come from Bernard Bajolet, a recent French ambassador to Kabul who now heads the French foreign intelligence service. He provides some simple solutions: 'cut corruption, which discourages investment, deal with drugs and become fiscally self-reliant'.[8] Monsieur Bajolet certainly means well; one only wishes if it were as straightforward and easy to accomplish.

In Pakistan, the local Taliban and their affiliates pose an extreme threat to the idea of the country, as conceived by its founding father, Mohammad Ali Jinnah. Though Pakistan remains a democracy, and though its institutions are far more mature and established than those in Afghanistan, the deteriorating law and order situation across the country and the plight of its ethnic, sectarian and religious minorities do not bode well for its future cohesion. Rampant corruption in government bureaucracy, a high illiteracy rate and growing demographic challenges faced by the country are no secret. No amount of foreign aid can help a country whose leaders lack vision and a desire to reform.

In this age of tough global competitiveness, inadequate resourcing of education is a sure way for a state to become dysfunctional. People without good education are also more prone to believe in conspiracy theories. Pakistan has shown tremendous resilience in the face of growing security and economic challenges, but its foundations are not strong enough to bear the burden of insecurity for long, as that destroys its economic prospects.

Tehrik-i-Taliban Pakistan is neither a movement nor a political party. It is, in essence, a war machine, and its vision of society hinges on conflict. It exists only to fight, and hence it is unlikely that any peace agreement it might reach with the government of Pakistan (or with any of its institutions) will hold. It is also instructive that Mullah Omar has never issued a decree against Mullah Fazlullah, Baitullah Mehsud or Hakimullah Mehsud: this nullifies the notion of 'good Taliban' versus 'bad Taliban' that is entertained by some Pakistanis. In fact, Pakistani

Taliban leaders in their public declarations always pay their respects to Mullah Omar and claim to have his full support. No spokesman for the Afghan Taliban has ever contradicted this. Latest TTP propaganda videos show collaboration with the Afghan Taliban in conducting operations deep inside Afghanistan.[9]

For the sake of argument, if Taliban resurgence in Afghanistan succeeded in gaining active control of state institutions in Kabul, then that would encourage the Pakistani Taliban to aspire to the same ideal. The Durand Line would become even more of an irrelevance, and Pakistan would be in a deeper mess.

The outlook of Pakistan's security wizards is also a major hurdle in realizing the country's true potential. They are losing Pakistan in an effort to fulfil their misidentified interests in Afghanistan. Pakistan will have to find a balance between its security and its development needs if it wishes to escape its current downward spiral. The continuation of a democratic order – and here Pakistan could learn from the military–civilian transition in Turkey – could indeed bring change, leading to a harmonious civil–military relationship in future. Such a transition will also help the India–Pakistan peace process, without which the region simply cannot thrive economically. India must also realize that a stable Pakistan is in its best interests.

Can negotiations succeed?

In theory, a negotiated settlement with the insurgents is a necessary prerequisite for an end to the ongoing conflict in Afghanistan. But the million-dollar question is: at what cost? Reconciliation with the Taliban is an issue that affects more than just Afghanistan. It has regional implications: the interests of all neighbouring countries need to be taken into account before any major political adjustments can be made. The reality is that the Obama administration was initially very reluctant to pursue a negotiated settlement with the Afghan Taliban, though President Karzai had already reached out to them for 'reconciliation'. After 2008, Pakistani intelligence also made a case to its US counterparts for pursuing talks with the Afghan Taliban, and it even offered to mediate. On the ground in Afghanistan, there was an important initiative from German diplomats to talk to the Taliban in 2010.

The problem is that the Afghan Taliban are no longer a hierarchical organization, with leaders who are easily identifiable.[10] A range of localized insurgent groups with different agendas and grievances are operating in the field, as are criminal networks and organizations that are semi-independent Taliban affiliates, such as the Haqqani group, which uses Pakistan's tribal areas as a base from which to conduct and coordinate its activities in Afghanistan. American defence officials believe that 10–15 per cent of insurgent attacks inside Afghanistan are directly attributable to Haqqani group warriors. Pakistan is capable of bringing the Haqqani group to the table – and presumably others from the inner circle of Mullah Omar – but it is doubtful whether the Taliban sitting in Pakistan could negotiate on behalf of all Taliban insurgent leaders operating inside Afghanistan.

No major communication breakthrough with the Taliban leaders was in sight when former US Secretary of State Hillary Clinton delivered a major policy speech at the Asia Society in New York in February 2011, in which she set out three conditions for the Taliban if they wanted to come to the negotiating table – sever relations with Al-Qaeda, renounce violence and accept the Afghan constitution.[11] For the Taliban, this was a non-starter. But they had little inkling that Secretary of State Clinton was moving in this direction after having overcome stiff resistance from the other important power centres in Washington.[12] For Pakistan, it was a welcome development, though Islamabad believed in a slightly different approach, suggesting to the US that the three preconditions could be converted into the end goals of a negotiated deal. Washington agreed in principle, and Pakistan was given the go-ahead to play its part in making this happen.

At the time, Pakistan was itself under tremendous pressure from the TTP – the local faction of the Taliban – which was constantly on the offensive, targeting major military and intelligence infrastructure inside Pakistan. For Pakistan, an accommodation between the Taliban and Kabul would ease the pressure and also reinstate Pakistani influence in Afghanistan to balance the inroads India had made there.

Karzai, who was running his parallel reconciliation efforts via the 'High Peace Council', led by former President Burhanuddin Rabbani, wanted to control the process, but Pakistan was not inclined to trust him, and opted rather to communicate direct with the US in this regard. The Afghan approach – enshrined in a document entitled 'The Peace Process Roadmap to 2015' – emphasized an 'Afghan-led' and 'Afghan-owned' process that would ensure the freedoms and liberties of all Afghans.[13] The assassination of Rabbani at the hands of Taliban (whose spokesman claimed responsibility) in September 2011 was to be a blow to the Afghan reconciliation effort.

Meanwhile the bold US operation in the Pakistani city of Abbottabad in May 2011 to eliminate Osama bin Laden, followed in November 2011 by the death of 24 Pakistani soldiers and officers at the hands of NATO forces at Salala, a checkpoint on the Pakistan–Afghanistan border, changed the atmosphere in Pakistan and led to a deterioration in US–Pakistani relations that froze the planned negotiation initiative.

The situation only improved in mid-2012 after some 'give and take' that led to a resumption of Pakistani efforts to bring the Taliban to the negotiating table. Over two dozen Taliban militants languishing in Pakistani intelligence 'guest houses' (or in some cases in the 'protective custody' of local militant groups) were advised to return to Afghanistan. In official US-Pakistan discussions on the subject, Pakistani military and intelligence officials continued to emphasize that there were no 'guarantees' and that they only promised 'facilitation.'[14]

The opening of a Taliban office in Doha, Qatar, in June 2013 for talks with the US and the Afghan government was an important step. The initial agenda included the issue of Taliban prisoners at Guantanamo Bay and the removal of some Taliban leaders from the UN sanction lists.

The plan foundered, however, when the Taliban erected a plaque outside the office that read 'Political Office of the Islamic Emirate of Afghanistan' and hoisted the Taliban flag – despite a categorical objection from the US. According to an American insider, it was all a misjudgement on the part of the government of Qatar, which acceded to the Taliban request. Anyway, President Hamid Karzai was not amused. He conveyed his displeasure to Qatar, and that led to cancellation of the whole process.

The whole episode exposes a debilitating disconnect, caused by mutual apprehensions on the part of all the sides involved in this sensitive and controversial enterprise. Soon afterward, a senior Pakistani diplomat asked me: 'Are the Americans really serious in negotiating with the Taliban, or is this only a tactic to force Pakistan to show its hand?' The inference was that perhaps the US is indirectly attempting to drive a wedge between Pakistan and Afghan Taliban leaders. This perception explains Pakistani scepticism about US interests and its long-term commitment to the region.

The critics of reconciliation argue that the hard-core Taliban would never agree to a democratic order in Afghanistan, as they abhor the concept of citizens' rights and political freedom. Ethnic and sectarian minorities in the country are especially concerned about the reversal of the progress made by Afghanistan in these areas since 2001. A major terrorist attack in Kabul, which targeted a religious procession of Shia Muslims in December 2011 and killed 55 people, showed an increasing convergence between sectarian terrorists in Pakistan and Afghanistan.[15]

The Pakistani Taliban have been especially fond of such attacks, but the track record of the Afghan Taliban is equally tainted (think of the atrocities perpetrated on the Hazara community in Afghanistan during its time in office). The Shia Hazara living in Quetta, the capital of Pakistan's Balochistan Province, and Shia professionals across the country have faced a debilitating reign of terror in recent years. There has also been an unprecedented targeting of Sufi shrines in Pakistan.

It is intriguing why the Taliban and their affiliates should specifically target those who commemorate Hussain ibne Ali, the hero of the battle of Karbala in the year 680. This grandson of Prophet Mohammad faced the military might of the Muslim Empire (ruled then by a despot, Yazid ibn Mu'awiya) with only about 70 supporters, including many children.

Hussain had refused to abide by Yazid's tyrannical reign and had challenged the way he distorted Islamic principles in his hunger for power and territorial expansion in the name of Islam. Hussain was martyred in the most brutal fashion, along with many members of his family. For fourteen centuries both Shia and Sunni Muslims have revered his legacy; but a major chunk of the Taliban thinks differently.

Any political settlement in Afghanistan that does not provide guarantees to minority sects and ethnic groups is highly unlikely to resolve the looming crisis. Despite its flaws, the present Afghan constitution provides a balance whose essence is worth protecting. Some reconcilable elements of the Afghan insurgency are certainly aware of this reality, and many of them are prepared to work within the new system (with some adjustments); but Mullah Omar's take on the issue is different.

In a public message in August 2013, delivered on the occasion of the traditional Muslim Eid holiday, he took ownership of the Doha negotiation effort, proving that he was in close touch with Islamabad. But his statements sounded contradictory at best. Uncharacteristically, he asserted 'we [the Islamic Emirate] believe in reaching understanding with the Afghans regarding an Afghan-inclusive government'; but in the same breath he called the democratic process a 'deceiving drama' and distanced himself from the Afghan elections scheduled for 2014.[16]

Mullah Omar would like us to believe that he is moving towards the middle ground; but this choreographed message could well be a deception. He dreams of being crowned in Kabul once he sees the last American soldier departing from Afghanistan. And he holds out the prospect then of granting people rights as he deems fit, according to his perverted interpretation of Islam. But that is simply not going to happen. Though very shaky and lacking confidence in its future, Afghanistan has moved on and is unlikely meekly to accept a 1990s-style Taliban takeover.

Islamabad's attempts to negotiate with the Taliban remain fruitless, but the Sharif government is intransigently committed to keeping all the options open. General Raheel Sharif, the unassuming new army chief, however, convinced his political masters that a tit-for-tat response to terror attacks is a more sensible approach. The general can transform thinking in his own institution, too, but it is going to be a truly daunting task. Pakistan needs a strong and cohesive army that honestly adheres to democratic norms.

There are many lessons to be learnt from this seemingly unending saga by the US and its allies. Firstly, it never hurts to study the history and culture of a people you are attempting to engage and reform; ideally, it should precede any interaction. Secondly, civilian capacity-building is as critical as securing an area, and must be handled by trained and qualified professionals. The selection of local political partners is crucial to the building or destroying of the credibility of a project in the public eye. Lastly, as unwieldy as it may turn out to be, regional problems require regional solutions.

What can be done?

Without a stable and representative political order built on the foundations of the rule of law, economic and social development is likely to remain a distant dream for both Afghanistan and Pakistan. Legitimacy and power to implement decisions are the two pillars on which such an edifice can be built. There are several avenues available for initiating sustainable change in this direction.

First, a law enforcement model that focuses on enhancing the capabilities of the criminal justice system would be a critical factor in stabilizing the state and tackling militancy. Development of the capability for scientific investigation supported by modern forensics, the provision of high-quality training and the introduction of a witness protection system would go a long way towards building and strengthening the civilian law enforcement structures. A system where judges feel insecure and unsafe cannot deliver justice.

Secondly, it needs to be recognized that, without an independent revenue-generating capacity, Afghanistan cannot become a truly independent state. Ironically, the Taliban have developed sustainable streams of funding – largely from drugs and crime – but the Afghan state has little hope at the moment, aside from foreign aid. This must change if Afghanistan is to be transformed. Pakistan's tax-collection system also needs a major overhaul to ensure that its wealthy citizens play their due role in state-building. The economic lifeline provided by the IMF is only temporary, and without it the Pakistani economy could slide downward pretty quickly.

Religious harmony is the third crucial area that deserves attention. The degeneration of religious scholarship in Muslim states has dealt a severe blow to Islamic studies; as a consequence, sectarianism and intolerance have increased dramatically. A well-designed and well-resourced de-radicalization strategy involving religious centres of learning is the way forward. It is necessary to discredit the distortions projected by the Taliban and their like, in order to counter the retro-grade tendencies in both Afghanistan and Pakistan. This will be very difficult to accomplish unless the Shia and the Sunni are ready to join together in this endeavour. The teachings of the great Sufi saints of South Asia provide the bridge for such collaboration.

In parallel, it would be prudent to reach out to extremists and engage them in dialogue, but without compromising on principles. In Pakistan, the obstacles to such a path are far more cumbersome than in Afghanistan, but inclusiveness and an opening-up of the political process to every citizen would only strengthen the two countries' political systems. Forgiveness and compassion also helps to resolve conflicts peacefully, and Pashtuns are traditionally very amenable to such undertakings. To assume that the Taliban are incapable of reform is unwarranted. Mainstream and broadminded Pashtuns are quite capable of spearheading a meaningful effort to bring peace and freedom to their areas. With regards to Punjab Province, which according to noted scholar Ayesha Siddiqa is the source of the growing radicalization in Pakistan,[17] an intelligence-led police action could be more effective.

Another potential avenue for challenging the status quo, especially in Afghanistan, could be decentralization. This would open up more possibilities for wider public participation in governance, encouraging the sharing of responsibilities.[18] Pakistan also labours under the weight of over-centralization. Pakistan's democratic leaders, however, made major constitutional adjustments in 2010 to enhance provincial autonomy.[19] Afghanistan could draw some useful lessons.

When all is said and done, the time for short-term fixes is over: only an educated and aware population – Afghan and Pakistani – can tackle this multi-faceted challenge. The chances of success are infinitely greater if progressive elements and institutions were to be empowered, than if futile attempts continue to be made to buy loyalty and support.

While retaining a minimum local capacity to nip the trouble in the bud in case of an Al-Qaeda resurgence, the US will be better off if it restricts itself to supporting good governance in Afghanistan irrespective of who occupies the Afghan presidency. At least equally important, the international community must not abandon Afghanistan financially. In the case of Pakistan, a mere security-driven focus is unlikely to make a difference to the country's future. The best thing that the US has done in Pakistan is the relatively recent but massive expansion of the Fulbright Scholar Program. If continued, it will prove to be more effective than the controversial drone programme in defeating ignorance and bigotry, the two fundamental planks of the Taliban ideology.

The well-wishers of the region are advised to heed the words of the great South Asian poet–philosopher and reformer Muhammad Iqbal in the early years of the twentieth century:

Asia is a body built of clay and water
Afghanistan is the heart in this body!
If Afghanistan is in turmoil, the whole of Asia is in turmoil
If Afghanistan is in peace, the whole of Asia is in peace.[20]

Notes

1. Rahman Baba, Robert Sampson and Momin Khan, *The Poetry of Rahman Baba: Poet of the Pakhtuns*, University Book Agency, Peshawar, 2005.
2. Martin Luther King, Jr, Letter from Birmingham Jail, 16 April 1963.

Introduction

1. Interviews in April–May 2012 in Washington, DC.
2. Interviews in June 2010, Islamabad, Pakistan.

Chapter 1 'Intruders are always unwelcome'

1. Thomas J. Barfield, 'Weapons of the not so weak in Afghanistan: Pashtun agrarian structure and tribal organization for times of war and peace', 23 February 2007, at: http://www.yale.edu/agrarianstudies/colloqpapers/19weapons.pdf
2. Quoted in 'Ghani Khan works: Quotes and prose and tribute' at: http://www. ghanikhan.com/detail/books/
3. Rafay Mahmood, 'Ghani Khan: The rhythms of hope', *Express Tribune* (Karachi), 20 April 2011; Madeeha Syed, 'Soundcheck: The real world of music', *Dawn* (Karachi), 6 March 2011.
4. Olaf Caroe also maintains that Pashtuns are highly concerned with their origin, descent and genealogies. For details, see Olaf Caroe, *The Pathans, 550 B.C.–A.D. 1957*, Macmillan, London, 1957.
5. Syed Bahadur Shah Zafar Kakakhel, *Pashtun: Tarikh Key Aaiene Main* (Pashtuns in the light of history), trans. Syed Anwar ul Haq Jillani, University Book Agency, Peshawar, 2007, p. 23.
6. Joseph Pierre Ferrie, *History of the Afghans*, trans. Captain William Jesse, John Murray, London, 1858.
7. Kakakhel, *Pashtun*, p. 25.
8. Thomas Barfield, *Afghanistan: A cultural and political history*, Princeton University Press, 2010, pp. 90–92.
9. Peter Tomsen, *The Wars of Afghanistan: Messianic terrorism, tribal conflicts, and the failures of great powers*, Public Affairs, New York, 2011, p. 46.

236   Notes to pp. 14–26

10. 'Pushtunwali: Honour among them', *Economist*, 19 December 2006, at: http://www.economist.com/node/8345531
11. Hassan Abbas, 'Profile of Pakistan's seven tribal agencies', *Terrorism Monitor*, 4:20 (2006).
12. Hamid Hussain, 'Ethnic factor in Afghanistan', *Defense Journal* (Rawalpindi), March 2003.
13. Pashtun-dominated districts in Balochistan are in the south, and are generally border districts with Afghanistan, including Zhob, Qilla Saifullah, Pishin and Qilla Abdullah. Pashtun tribes living along the border with Afghanistan are Mohammad Khels, Noorzais, Achakzais, Kakars, Mandokhels and Suleyman Khels.
14. Amir Mateen, 'Eyewitness Balochistan–12: The two realities of Pashtuns and Baloch', *The News* (Lahore), 9 June 2012.
15. From personal notes based on interviews in Khyber agency, FATA, July 2011.
16. For details, see 'Afridi', Program for Cultural and Conflict Studies, Naval Postgraduate School, Monterey, CA, at: http://www.nps.edu/Programs/CCs/Docs/Pakistan/Tribes/Afridi_combo.pdf
17. For details, see Zia ur Rehman, 'Attacks on Sufi shrines signify new conflict in Pashtun lands', *Friday Times* (Lahore), 3–9 February 2012, at: http://www.thefridaytimes.com/beta2/tft/article.php?issue=20120203&page=3
18. 'Pushtunwali: Honour among them', *Economist*, 19 December 2006.
19. Hasan Faqeer, *North West Frontier Province (NWFP) Provincial Handbook: A guide to the people and the province*, ed. Nick Dowling and Amy Frumin, IDS International Government Services, Arlington, VA, 2009.
20. Sameera Rashid, 'Double jeopardy', *News on Sunday* (Lahore), 21 April 2013. For a detailed assessment, see Palwasha Kakar, 'Tribal law of Pashtunwali and women's legislative authority', Harvard Law School, undated, at: http://www.law.harvard.edu/programs/ilsp/research/kakar.pdf
21. Farhat Taj, *Taliban and Anti-Taliban*, Cambridge Scholars Publishing, Newcastle upon Tyne, 2011, pp. 1–5.
22. Paul Titus, 'Honor the Baloch, buy the Pushtun: Stereotypes, social organization and history in Western Pakistan', *Modern Asian Studies*, 32:3 (1998), p. 657.
23. Barfield, *Afghanistan*, pp. 54–65, 75–82.
24. Pervaiz Munir Alvi, 'Ahmad Shah Durrani: A king of high rank', Pak Tea House Blog, 25 November 2009, at: http://pakteahouse.net/2009/11/25/ahmad-shah-durrani-a-king-of-high-rank/
25. Hafiz A. Ghaffar Khan, 'Shah Waliullah (Qutb al-Din Ahmad Al-Rahim) (1703–62)', at: http://www.muslimphilosophy.com/ip/rep/H045
26. Naureen Durrani, 'Identity wars in the curriculum: Gender and the military in Pakistani national identity' in Fiona Leach and Mairead Dunne (eds), *Education, Conflict and Reconciliation: International perspectives*, Peter Lang, Bern, Switzerland, 2007, pp. 263–64.
27. 'Abdali missile tested', *Dawn* (Karachi), 6 March 2012.
28. Norimitsu Onishi, 'A nation challenged – a shrine – a tale of the mullah and Muhammad's amazing cloak', *New York Times*, 19 December 2001, at: http://www.nytimes.com/2001/12/19/world/a-nation-challenged-a-shrine-a-tale-of-the-mullah-and-muhammad-s-amazing-cloak.html
29. Dawood Azami, 'Kandahar: Assassination capital of Afghanistan', BBC News, 28 October 2012, at: http://www.bbc.co.uk/news/world-asia–19074921
30. Conversation with a visiting Afghan official, Boston, May 2007.
31. Joshua Foust, 'The myth of Taliban tribalism', Registan website, 15 July 2008, at: http://registan.net/2008/07/15/the-myth-of-taliban-tribalism/
32. Rashid Ahmad Khan, 'Political developments in FATA: A critical perspective' in Pervaiz Iqbal Cheema and Maqsudul Hasan Nuri (eds), *Tribal Areas of Pakistan: Challenges and responses*, Islamabad Policy Research Institute, 2005, p. 26.

33. For a brief overview, see Barnett Rubin, *The Fragmentation of Afghanistan*, Yale University Press, New Haven, CT, 2002, pp. 45–52.
34. Quoted in Satindar Kumar Lambah, 'The Durand Line', Aspen Institute India Policy Paper No. 4, at: http://www.aspenindia.org/pdf/durand.pdf
35. Thomas Barfield, 'The Durand Line: History, consequences and future', American Institute of Afghan Studies, Conference Report, 2007, at: http://www.bu.edu/aias/reports/durand_conference.pdf
36. Abdur Rahman, *The Life of Abdur Rahman*, ed. M.S.M.K. Munshi, London, J. Murray, 1900, vol. II, p. 251.
37. Barfield, *Afghanistan*, pp. 158–59.
38. Martin Evans, *Afghanistan: A new history*, Curzon Press, Richmond, Surrey, 2001, p. 95.
39. Ali Arqam, 'Taliban vs Pashtuns', *Viewpoint*, 160, 1 October 2010, via: http://www.europe-solidaire.org/spip.php?page=article_impr&id_article=18683
40. Olivier Roy, *Islam and Resistance in Afghanistan*, Cambridge University Press, 1990, pp. 69–70.
41. Christopher Andrew and Vasili Mitrokhin. *The World Was Going Our Way: The KGB and the battle for the third world*, Basic Books, New York, 2005, pp. 386–92.

Chapter 2 Enter at your own risk

1. Stanley Wolpert, *Shameful Flight: The last years of the British Empire in India*, Oxford University Press, New York, 2009.
2. Dennis Kux, *The United States and Pakistan, 1947–2000: Disenchanted allies*, Woodrow Wilson Center Press, Washington, DC, 2001, p. 57.
3. Text of Mohammad Ali Jinnah's first address to the Constituent Assembly of Pakistan, 11 August 1947, at: www.pakistani.org/pakistan/legislation/constituent_address_11aug1947.html
4. 'An engaging dictator who wants to stay that way', *Economist*, 12 December 1981.
5. Hassan Abbas, *Pakistan's Drift into Extremism: Allah, the army and America's war on terror*, M. E. Sharpe, New York, 2005, pp. 44–54.
6. For details, see George Crile, *Charlie Wilson's War: The extraordinary story of the largest covert operation in history*, Atlantic Inc., New York, 2003.
7. Khan, 'Political developments in FATA', p. 25.
8. Shaheen Sardar Ali and Javaid Rehman, *Indigenous People and Ethnic Minorities of Pakistan: Constitutional and legal perspectives*, Curzon Press, Richmond, Surrey, 2001, pp. 47–48.
9. 'The frontier policy of Pakistan: M.A. Jinnah's address to the tribal Jirga at Government House, Peshawar, 17 April 1948' in *Quaid-i-Azam Mohammad Ali Jinnah: Speeches and statements as Governor General of Pakistan 1947–48*, Ministry of Information and Broadcasting Directorate of Films and Publications, Islamabad, 1989, p. 239.
10. For instance, see Kakakhel, *Pashtun*, p. 614.
11. Sana Haroon, *Frontier of Faith: Islam in the Indo-Afghan borderland*, Columbia University Press, New York, 2007, p. 177.
12. Naveed Ahmed Shinwari, *Understanding FATA 2011*, vol. V, Islamabad, 2012, pp. 27–30, at: http://www.understandingfata.org
13. Interviews in Islamabad, Peshawar and Khyber agency, December 2011.
14. Human Rights Commission of Pakistan, *FCR: A bad law nobody can defend*, Lahore, 2005.
15. Imtiaz Gul, *The Most Dangerous Place: Pakistan's lawless frontier*, Viking, New York, 2009, p. 53.
16. Akbar S. Ahmed, *Religion and Politics in Muslim Society: Order and conflict in Pakistan*, Cambridge University Press, 1983, p. 36.
17. Historically, the decision of an independent *jirga* was binding on everyone, and for the implementation of a decision a *jirga* could constitute a *lashkar* (armed force), meant to

be a representative force raised by taking one or two members of each household/ family.

18. The political agent also approves the *majab* – an allowance paid to a tribe (as a whole and on a case-by-case basis) for its cooperation and loyalty.

19. Shuja Nawaz, *FATA: A most dangerous place*, Center for Strategic and International Studies, Washington, DC, 2009, p. 26.

20. Thomas Johnson and M. Chris Mason, 'No sign until the burst of fire: Understanding the Pakistan–Afghanistan frontier', *International Security*, 34:2 (Spring 2008), p. 73.

21. Quoted in Ziad Haider, 'Mainstreaming Pakistan's tribal belt: A human rights and security imperative', Belfer Centre Student Paper Series, Discussion Paper No. 09–01, Harvard Kennedy School, January 2009, p. 5.

22. Nawaz, *FATA: A most dangerous place*, p. 14.

23. Mohammad Ayub Khan, *Friends Not Masters: A political biography*, Oxford University Press, London, 1967, pp. 175–76.

24. Caroe, *The Pathans*, p. 437.

25. Hassan Abbas, 'Transforming Pakistan's Frontier Corps', *Terrorism Monitor*, 5:6 (2007).

26. Riaz Ahmed, 'The way of the gun: The legendary gunsmiths of Darra Adam Khel', *Express Tribune* (Karachi), 4 November 2012.

27. David Hart, *Qabila: Tribal profiles and tribe–state relations in Morocco and the Afghanistan–Pakistan frontier*, Het Spinhuis, Amsterdam, 2001, p. 162.

28. Abubakar Siddique, 'The Durand Line: Afghanistan's controversial, colonial-era border', *The Atlantic*, 25 October 2012.

29. Barfield, 'The Durand Line'.

30. 'Defence committee visit to Kabul breakthrough in ties: Mushahid', *Nation* (Pakistan), 13 September 2013.

31. Gul, *Most Dangerous Place*, p. 52.

32. World Development Indicators Database, World Bank, 1 July 2009.

33. World Food Programme, *Rapid Needs Assessment Report of FATA*, Pakistan, 13–19 February 2007, at: http://documents.wfp.org/stellent/groups/public/documents/ena/ wfp153748.pdf

34. 'Literacy in restive Fata in free fall', *Dawn* (Karachi), 23 April 2011.

35. Rahimullah Yusufzai, 'Analysis: Pakistan's tribal frontiers', BBC News, 14 December 2001.

Chapter 3 Holy warriors of an unholy war

1. For instance, see Crile, *Charlie Wilson's War*; Steve Coll, *Ghost Wars: The secret history of the CIA, Afghanistan, and bin Laden, from the Soviet invasion to September 10, 2001* Penguin, New York, 2004.

2. Peter Marsden, *The Taliban: War, religion and the new order in Afghanistan*, Oxford University Press, 1999, p. 34.

3. The Getty picture is available at: http://www.gettyimages.com/detail/news-photo/ afghan-chrmn-of-islamic-union-of-mujahedeen-mohammed-younis-news-photo/ 50361911

4. David B. Edwards, *Before Taliban: Genealogies of the Afghan Jihad*, University of California Press, Berkeley, 2002, p. 154.

5. For details of Iranian influence, see Niamatullah Ibrahimi, 'At the sources of factionalism and a civil war in Hazarajat', Crisis States Research Centre Working Paper, January 2009, at: http://www.dfid.gov.uk/r4d/PDF/Outputs/CrisisStates/ WP41.2.pdf

6. C.J. Dick, 'Mujahideen tactics in the Soviet–Afghan war', Conflict Studies Research Centre, Royal Military Academy, Sandhurst, UK, January 2002, at: http://edocs.nps. edu/AR/org/CSRC/csrc_jan_02.pdf

7. Hussain, 'Ethnic factor in Afghanistan'.

8. Mohammad Yousaf and Mark Adkin, *Afghanistan – The Bear Trap: The defeat of a superpower*, Casemate, Havertown, PA, 1992, p. 41.
9. ibid.
10. Edwards, *Before Taliban*, p. 153.
11. Robert Kaplan, 'Driven toward God', *Atlantic Monthly*, September 1988.
12. Abdul Salam Zaeef, *My Life with the Taliban*, C. Hurst & Co., London, 2010, p. 62.
13. ibid., p. 63.
14. Olivier Roy, 'Has Islamism a future in Afghanistan?' in William Maley (ed.), *Fundamentalism Reborn: Afghanistan and Taliban*, Vanguard Books, Lahore, 1998, p. 208.
15. Nushin Arbabzadah, 'The 1980s mujahideen, the Taliban and the shifting idea of jihad', *Guardian*, 28 April 2011, at: http://www.guardian.co.uk/commentisfree/2011/apr/28/afghanistan-mujahideen-taliban
16. Hussain, 'Ethnic factor in Afghanistan'.
17. See official biography of Ustad Mohammad Akbari, which mentions his joining the Taliban at: http://www.afghan-bios.info/index.php?option=com_afghanbios&id=113&task=view&total=2655&start=156&Itemid=2
18. Kamal Matinuddin, *The Taliban Phenomenon: Afghanistan 1994-1997*, Oxford University Press, Karachi, 1999, p. 94.
19. Alex Strick van Linschoten and Felix Kuehn, *An Enemy We Created: The myth of the Taliban–Al Qaeda merger in Afghanistan 1970-2010*, Hurst and Company, London, 2012, p. 46.
20. Sippi Azerbaijani Moghaddam, 'Northern exposure for the Taliban' in Antonio Giustozzi (ed.), *Decoding the New Taliban: Insights from the Afghan field*, Columbia University Press, New York, 2009, p. 251.
21. Barbara D. Metcalf, *Islamic Revival in British India: Deoband, 1860-1900*, Princeton University Press, 1982.
22. For background on this point, see Ahmed Rashid, *Taliban: Militant Islam, oil, and fundamentalism in Central Asia*, Yale University Press, New Haven, CT, 2000, pp. 88-94.
23. Matinuddin, *Taliban Phenomenon*, p. 14.
24. Barbara Metcalf, '"Traditionalist" Islamic activism: Deoband, Tablighis, and Talibs', Social Science Research Council, 2001, at: http://essays.ssrc.org/sept11/essays/metcalf.htm
25. Barfield, *Afghanistan*, p. 262.
26. Matinuddin, *Taliban Phenomenon*, p. 14.
27. Hamid Hussain, 'Afghanistan – Not so great games', *Defence Journal* (Rawalpindi), April 2002, at: http://www.defencejournal.com/2002/april/games.htm
28. Interview with Dr Mohammad Taqi, August 2012.
29. 'Pakistan: "The Taliban's godfather"?' in Barbara Elias (ed.), *National Security Archive Electronic Briefing Book No. 227*, 14 August 2007, at: http://www.gwu.edu/~nsarchiv/NSAEBB/NSAEBB227/
30. Rizwan Hussain, *Pakistan and the Emergence of Islamic Militancy in Afghanistan*, Routledge, London, 2005, p. 105.
31. 'The insurgency in Afghanistan's heartland', International Crisis Group Asia Report No. 207, 27 June 2011, at: http://www.crisisgroup.org/en/regions/asia/south-asia/afghanistan/207-the-insurgency-in-afghanistans-heartland.aspx
32. Ahmed Rashid, 'Soccer team pays penalty for bare legs on the field', *Daily Telegraph*, 18 July 2000.
33. S. Iftikhar Murshed, 'Meeting Mullah Omar', *The News* (Lahore), 2 December 2012, at: http://www.thenews.com.pk/Todays-News-9-146166-Meeting-Mullah-Omar
34. James Fergusson, *Taliban: The unknown enemy*, Da Capo Press, Cambridge, MA, 2010, pp. 315-16.
35. Neamatollah Nojoumi, *The Rise of the Taliban in Afghanistan: Mass mobilization, civil war, and the future of the region*, Palgrave, New York, 2002, pp. 136-42.

36. Gretchen Peters, *How Opium Profits the Taliban*, United States Institute of Peace, 2009, at: http://www.usip.org/files/resources/taliban_opium_1.pdf
37. UNDCP, *Afghanistan: Annual Opium Poppy Survey 2001*, at: http://www.unodc.org/pdf/publications/report_2001-10-16_1.pdf
38. William Sami and Charles Recknagel, 'Iran's war on drugs', *Transnational Organized Crime*, 5:2 (2002).
39. Fergusson, *Taliban*, p. 117.
40. Barfield, *Afghanistan*, p. 261.
41. Coll, *Ghost Wars*, p. 299.
42. 'Top US policymaker meets Taliban ambassador', Afghan News Service, 2 August 2001.
43. Fergusson, *Taliban*, p. 127.
44. 'Osama bin Laden v. the US: Edicts and statements', PBS *Frontline* website, at: http://www.pbs.org/wgbh/pages/frontline/shows/binladen/who/edicts.html
45. Alex Strick van Linschoten and Felix Kuehn, 'Separating the Taliban from al-Qaeda: The core of success in Afghanistan', New York University Centre on International Cooperation study, February 2011, at: http://cic.es.its.nyu.edu/sites/default/files/gregg_sep_tal_alqaeda.pdf

Chapter 4 Goodbye Taliban?

1. George Tenet, *At the Center of the Storm: My years at the CIA*, Harper Collins, New York, 2007, pp. 182–83.
2. Founded in 1926 by Maulana Ilyas in northern India, it has developed as a revivalist organization that eschews politics in its quest to reform society. It is known for its massive annual gathering at Raiwind near Lahore.
3. 'US threatened to bomb Pakistan', BBC News, 22 September 2006, at: http://news.bbc.co.uk/2/hi/south_asia/5369198.stm
4. Qaiser Butt, 'Taliban video solves two mysteries', *Express Tribune* (Karachi), 20 February 2011.
5. 'The MQM referendum', SA Global Affairs website, May 2011, at: http://www.saglobalaffairs.com/back-issues/906-the-mqm-referendum.html; 'Iran's gulf of understanding with US', BBC News, 25 September 2006, at: http://news.bbc.co.uk/2/hi/middle_east/5377914.stm
6. Bob Woodward, *Bush at War*, Simon & Schuster, New York, 2002, p. 237.
7. 'The fall of Kabul', PBS *Newshour*, 13 November 2001, transcript at: http://www.pbs.org/newshour/bb/asia/july-dec01/kabul_11-13.html
8. Hussain, 'Afghanistan – Not so great games'.
9. Fergusson, *Taliban*, p. 152.
10. James Risen, 'US inaction seen after Taliban POWs died', *New York Times*, 10 July 2009, at: http://www.nytimes.com/2009/07/11/world/asia/11afghan.html?pagewanted=all&_r=0
11. ibid.
12. For details see testimony to Senate Foreign Relations Committee of Peter Bergen, Director of the National Security Studies Program, 24 May 2011, at: http://www.foreign.senate.gov/imo/media/doc/Bergen_testimony.pdf
13. For a discussion of differences, see Strick van Linschoten and Kuehn, *An Enemy We Created*, pp. 159–88. For evidence of close cooperation, see Peter Bergen, *The Longest War: The enduring conflict between America and Al-Qaeda*, Free Press, New York, 2011.
14. Interview with a former Commander XI Corps, Rawalpindi, July 2009.
15. A conversation in March 2009, Washington, DC.
16. Ali Mohammad Jan Aurakzai et al., 'Situation in FATA: Causes, consequences and the way forward', *Policy Perspectives*, 6:1 (January–June 2009).
17. Ron Suskind, *The One Percent Doctrine: Deep inside America's pursuit of its enemies since 9/11*, Simon and Schuster, New York, 2006, p. 58.

18. 'The "Taliban Five" and the forgotten Afghan prisoners in Guantánamo', Andy Worthington website, 23 February 2012, at: http://www.andyworthington.co.uk/2012/03/23/the-taliban-five-and-the-forgotten-afghan-prisoners-in-guantanamo/

19. Anand Gopal, 'The Taliban in Kandahar' in Peter Bergen with Katherine Tiedemann (eds), *Talibanistan: Negotiating the borders between terror, politics and religion*, Oxford University Press, 2013, pp. 11–12.

20. See http://wikileaks.org/gitmo/pdf/ch/us9ch–000277dp.pdf

21. Terry McDermott and Josh Meyer, 'Inside the mission to catch Khalid Sheikh Mohammed', *The Atlantic*, 2 April 2012, at: http://www.theatlantic.com/international/archive/2012/04/inside-the-mission-to-catch-khalid-sheikh-mohammed/255319/

22. Interview with a US State Department official dealing with Afghan affairs at the time, October 2013, Washington, DC.

23. Interview with a US academic familiar with the debates taking place in the US State Department at the time, November 2013.

24. Barbara Crossette, 'Lakhdar Brahimi: Afghanistan's future', *The Nation* (New York), 9 March 2009, at: http://www.thenation.com/article/lakhdar-brahimi-afghanistans-future

25. For text of the Bonn Agreement, see: https://www.cimicweb.org/cmo/afg/Documents/Governance/CFC_Afghanistan_Agreements_June2012.pdf

26. Interview in Washington, DC, May 2013.

27. For instance, see an assessment about Dostum in Antonio Giustozzi, *Empires of Mud: Wars and warlords in Afghanistan*, Columbia University Press, New York, 2009, p. 190.

28. These were Ismail Khan in Herat; and Atta Mohammed Noor and Abdul Rashid Dostum in Balkh Province.

29. James Ingalls, 'The new Afghan constitution: A step backwards for democracy', Foreign Policy in Focus, 10 March 2004, at: http://www.fpif.org/articles/the_new_afghan_constitution_a_step_backwards_for_democracy

30. ibid.

31. Zalmay Khalilzad, 'Lessons from Afghanistan and Iraq', *Journal of Democracy*, 21:3 (2010), p. 43.

32. 'A big week for Afghanistan: The warlords are plotting a comeback', Human Rights Watch, 11 June 2002, at: http://www.hrw.org/news/2002/06/09/warlords-are-plotting-comeback

33. Giustozzi, *Empires of Mud*, p. 236.

34. Stephen Biddle, Fotini Christia and J. Alexander Thier, 'Defining success in Afghanistan', *Foreign Affairs*, July/August 2010, at: http://www.foreignaffairs.com/articles/66450/stephen-biddle-fotini-christia-and-j-alexander-thier/defining-success-in-afghanistan

35. The argument is also made by Rory Stewart, 'The irresistible illusion', *London Review of Books*, 31:13 (2009).

36. The last boundary changes occurred in 2007.

37. Interview with an ISAF official at NATO HQ, Heidelberg, Germany, November 2009.

38. 'Afghanistan: Exit vs engagement', International Crisis Group Asia Briefing No. 115, 28 November 2010, at: http://www.crisisgroup.org/~/media/Files/asia/south-asia/afghanistan/B115%20Afghanistan%20—%20Exit%20vs%20Engagement.pdf

39. Lakhdar Brahimi, 'Statebuilding in crisis and post-conflict countries', 7th Global Forum on Reinventing Government: Building Trust in Government, Vienna, 26–29 June 2007.

40. Details at: http://www.isaf.nato.int/history.html

41. Stephen Walt, 'Who was right about invading Iraq?', *Foreign Policy*, 6 March 2013, at: http://www.foreignpolicy.com/posts/2013/03/06/who_was_right_about_invading_iraq$hash.fEDaZkHZ.dpbs

42. Andrew Wilder, *Cops or Robbers? The struggle to reform the Afghan National Police*, Research and Evaluation Unit, Kabul, 2007.

43. David Rohde and David E. Sanger, 'How a "good war" in Afghanistan went bad', *New York Times*, 12 August 2007, at: http://www.nytimes.com/2007/08/12/world/asia/12 afghan.html?pagewanted=all

44. Robert Perito, 'Afghanistan's police: The weak link in the security sector reform', United States Institute of Peace, August 2009, at: http://www.usip.org/files/afghanistan_police. pdf

45. James K. Whither, 'Challenges of developing host nation police capacity', *PRISM* 3:4 (September 2012), at: http://cco.dodlive.mil/files/2013/08/prism3–4.pdf

46. 'Reforming Afghanistan's police', International Crisis Group Asia Report No. 138, 30 August 2007, at: http://www.crisisgroup.org/~/media/Files/asia/south-asia/afghanistan/ 138_reforming_afghanistan_s_police.pdf

47. See Afghanistan's Ministry of Education website at: http://www.moe.gov.af (data posted 10 April 2008).

48. 'In Afghanistan, out of conflict and into school', World Bank website, 11 November 2004, at: http://web.worldbank.org/WBSITE/EXTERNAL/TOPICS/EXTEDUCATION /0,,contentMDK:20279607~menuPK:617572~pagePK:148956~piPK:216618~theSi tePK:282386,00.html

49. Morten Sigsgaard, 'On the road to resilience: Capacity development with the ministry of education in Afghanistan', International Institute for Education Planning, UNESCO, 2011, at: http://www.iiep.unesco.org/fileadmin/user_upload/Info_Services_Publications/ pdf/2011/Afghanistan_Resilience.pdf.

50. Barry Bearak, 'Education in Afghanistan: A harrowing choice', *New York Times*, 9 July 2007, at: http://www.nytimes.com/2007/07/09/world/asia/09iht-afghan.4.6571860.html? pagewanted=all

51. ibid.

52. Figures taken from 'Afghanistan', UNDP, 23 March 2010, at: http://www.undp.org.af/ WhatWeDo/ee.htm

53. Barfield, *Afghanistan*, pp. 312–13.

54. Rohde and Sanger, 'How a "good war" in Afghanistan went bad'.

55. James Dobbins, 'Nation-building: The inescapable responsibility of the world's only superpower', RAND website, summer 2003, at: http://www.rand.org/pubs/periodicals/ rand-review/issues/summer2003/nation.html

56. ibid.

Chapter 5 Setting the stage for the Taliban revival in Afghanistan

1. 'Lashkar, Jaish, TJP, TNSM & SSP banned; ST under watch', *Dawn* (Karachi), 13 January 2002, at: http://www.dawn.com/news/14777/lashkar-jaish-tjp-tnsm-ssp-banned-st-under-watch

2. On 14 August 2001, Lashkar-e-Jhangvi and Sipah-e-Muhammad were banned and Sipah-e-Sahaba and Tehrik-e-Jafria Pakistan were placed under observation. In January 2002, Musharraf banned Sipah-e-Sahaba, Tehrik-e-Jafria Pakistan, Tehrik-e-Nifaz-e-Shariat-e-Mohammadi, Jaish-e-Mohammad and Lashkar-e-Taiba.

3. Quoted in A.R. Siddiqi, 'Commando complex', *The News* (Lahore), 11 July 2013, at: http://www.thenews.com.pk/Todays-News-9–189142-Commando-complex

4. According to *Nawa-e-Waqt* (18 October 2007), a popular right-wing Urdu newspaper, Mufti Shamzai issued the fatwa that when the Americans land in Pakistan, his followers should immediately take over the country's airports.

5. For details, see 'US embassy cables: Hillary Clinton says Saudi Arabia "a critical source of terrorist funding"', *Guardian*, 5 December 2010, at: http://www.theguardian.com/ world/us-embassy-cables-documents/242073

6. Paddy Docherty, *The Khyber Pass: A history of empire and invasion*, Union Square Press, New York, 2008, p. 115.

7. Teepu Mahabat Khan, *The Land of Khyber*, Sang-e-Meel Publications, Lahore, 2005, p. 31.
8. 'PPP challenges MMA's 2002 election symbol', *Daily Times* (Lahore), 9 December 2007.
9. According to official NWFP records (2006), out of an estimated 4,680 madrasas in NWFP, only 1,077 were registered – the rest either refused to register or ignored government instructions. Akhtar Amin, 'Only 22% of NWFP madrasas registered', *Daily Times* (Lahore), 24 March 2006.
10. 'Text of Hasba Bill', *Dawn* (Karachi), 16 July 2005, at: http://www.dawn.com/2005/07/16/ nat18.htm
11. 'His Majesty's loyal opposition?', Editorial, *Friday Times* (Lahore), 28 May 2004.
12. 'Pakistan's tribal areas: Appeasing the militants', International Crisis Group Asia Report No. 125, 11 December 2006, at: http://www.crisisgroup.org/~/media/Files/asia/south-asia/pakistan/125_pakistans_tribal_areas___appeasing_the_militants.pdf; 'Pakistan: The mullah and the military', International Crisis Group Asia Report No. 49, 20 March 2003, at: http://www.crisisgroup.org/en/regions/asia/south-asia/pakistan/049-pakistan-the-mullahs-and-the-military.aspx
13. Hasan Askari Rizvi, 'VIEW: Counter-terrorism: The missing links', *Daily Times* (Lahore), 4 March 2007.
14. For instance, see references in Hassan Abbas, 'From FATA to the NWFP: The Taliban spread their grip in Pakistan', *CTC Sentinel*, 1:10 (2008), pp. 3–5, at: http://www.hsdl. org/?abstract&did=235319&advanced=advanced
15. Between FATA and Khyber Pakhtunkhwa Province is another strip called the 'Frontier Regions' that acts as a transition zone between the tribal and the settled Pashtun areas. These regions are administered by officials of the KPK, but overall they fall under the jurisdiction of the FATA secretariat.
16. Johnson and Mason, 'No sign until the burst of fire', p. 51.
17. Seth G. Jones and C. Christine Fair, 'Counterinsurgency in Pakistan', RAND website, 2010, at: http://www.rand.org/content/dam/rand/pubs/monographs/2010/RAND_ MG982.pdf
18. Rahimullah Yusufzai, 'Fall of the last frontier?', *Newsline* (Pakistan), June 2002.
19. Tariq Mahmud Ashraf, 'Pakistan's Frontier Corps and the war against terrorism: Part two', *Terrorism Monitor*, 6:16 (2008).
20. Interview in May 2013, Washington, DC.
21. Amir Mohammad Khan, 'Spiraling into chaos', *Newsline* (Pakistan), March 2004.
22. Jones and Fair, 'Counterinsurgency in Pakistan', p. 43, fn. 26.
23. ibid. Also see Rohde and Sanger, 'How a "good war" in Afghanistan went bad'.
24. Rafaqat Ali, 'Dr Khan seeks pardon; Cabinet decision today; Meets Musharraf; Admits error of judgment', *Dawn* (Karachi), 5 February 2004, at: http://www.dawn.com/ 2004/02/05/top1.htm
25. 'A.Q. Khan "covered up" for Musharraf: Benazir', *Daily Times* (Lahore), 6 March 2004.
26. 'Pakistani govt not involved in proliferation: US', *Daily Times* (Lahore), 5 February 2004.
27. William Broad, David E. Sanger and Raymond Bonner, 'A tale of nuclear proliferation: How Pakistani built his network', *New York Times*, 12 February 2004, at: http://www. nytimes.com/2004/02/12/world/a-tale-of-nuclear-proliferation-how-pakistani-built-his-network.html?pagewanted=all&src=pm; for western views on the subject, see David Albright and Corey Hinderstein, 'Unraveling the A.Q. Khan and future proliferation networks', *Washington Quarterly*, 28:2 (2005), p. 117.
28. Ismail Khan, 'Four soldiers die in Wana attack', *Dawn* (Karachi), 10 January 2004, at: http://www.dawn.com/news/390791/four-soldiers-die-in-wana-attack; also Shabana Fayyaz, 'Towards a durable peace in Afghanistan', Pakistan Security Research Unit Brief No. 10, University of Bradford, 23 April 2007, at: https://www.dur.ac.uk/resources/ psru/briefings/archive/Brief10finalised.pdf

29. Ismail Khan, 'Operation in South Waziristan', *Dawn* (Karachi), 19 February 2004.
30. Owais Tohid, 'The new frontier', *Newsline* (Pakistan), April 2004.
31. Louis Dupree, *Afghanistan*, 2nd ed., Oxford University Press, 1980.
32. Justin Huggler, 'Rebel tribal leader is killed in Pakistan', *Independent*, 19 June 2004, at: http://www.independent.co.uk/news/world/asia/rebel-tribal-leader-is-killed-in-pakistan–6167146.html
33. Rohan Gunaratna and Syed Adnan Ali Shah Bukhari, 'Making peace with Pakistani Taliban to isolate Al-Qaeda: Successes and failures', *Peace and Security Review*, 1:2 (2008), at: http://www.pvtr.org/pdf/GlobalAnalysis/MakingPeaceWithTheTaliban.pdf
34. See Kadr family chronology, PBS *Frontline* website, at: http://www.pbs.org/wgbh/pages/frontline/shows/khadr/family/cron.html
35. Fayyaz, 'Towards a durable peace in Afghanistan'.
36. Rahimullah Yusufzai, 'All quiet on the north western front', *Newsline* (Karachi), May 2004.
37. 'Nek Mohammed', PBS *Frontline* website, at: http://www.pbs.org/wgbh/pages/frontline/taliban/militants/mohammed.html
38. Interview with Pir Zubair Shah, Washington, DC, November 2012.
39. Ismail Khan and Baqir Sajjad Syed, 'Airstrikes launched in Shakai', *Dawn* (Karachi), 12 June 2004.
40. 'Nek Mohammed', PBS *Frontline* website, at: http://www.pbs.org/wgbh/pages/frontline/taliban/militants/mohammed.html
41. Amir Mir, 'War and peace in Waziristan', *Asia Times*, 4 May 2005, at: http://www.atimes.com/atimes/South_Asia/GE04Df03.html
42. Iqbal Khattack, 'Shakai tribes will support govt against foreigners', *Daily Times* (Lahore), 6 July 2004.
43. Hasan Khan, 'Policy rethink needed', *Dawn* (Karachi), 9 October 2012, at http://dawn.com/2012/10/09/policy-rethink-needed/
44. 'Return of the Taliban', PBS *Frontline* website, 3 October 2006, at: http://www.pbs.org/wgbh/pages/frontline/taliban/militants/mehsud.html
45. Shamim Shahid, 'Baitullah, supporters lay down arms', *The Nation* (Lahore), 9 February 2005.
46. Shahid Saeed, 'Stockholm Syndrome-ed', *Dawn* (Karachi), 24 May 2011.
47. Personal interview with an official of the FATA Secretariat, Peshawar, 18 July 2009.
48. Mir, 'War and peace in Waziristan'.
49. 'Pakistan pays tribe al-Qaeda debt', BBC News, 9 February 2005, at: http://news.bbc.co.uk/2/hi/south_asia/4249525.stm
50. For Baitullah Mehsud's statement, see Haroon Rashid, 'Pakistan Taleban vow more violence', BBC News, 29 January 2007, at: http://news.bbc.co.uk/2/hi/south_asia/6292061.stm
51. Zulfiqar Ghumman, 'Taliban killed 150 pro-government maliks', *Daily Times* (Lahore), 18 April 2006.
52. Ismail Khan, 'Why the Waziristan deal is such a hard sell', *Dawn* (Karachi), 14 October 2006; Muhammad Amir Rana, 'Pitfalls in Miramshah peace deal', *Dawn* (Karachi), 30 September 2006.
53. 'Afridi claims Mullah Omar backed Waziristan truce', *The News* (Lahore), 28 September 2006.
54. 'Pakistan's tribal areas: Appeasing the militants', International Crisis Group Asia Report No. 125, 11 December 2006.
55. 'Back to Square One?', Editorial, *The News* (Lahore), 7 September 2006.
56. Sayed G.B. Shah Bokhari, 'How peace deals help only militants', *The News* (Lahore), 31 July 2008.
57. Asad Munir, 'How FATA was won by the Taliban', *Express Tribune* (Karachi), 21 June 2010.

58. For instance, columnists and writers such as Pervez Hoodbhoy, Rahimullah Yusufzai, Amir Rana and Ismail Khan regularly projected such scenarios in the *Daily Times, The News* and *Dawn* – Pakistan's three leading English-language newspapers.

59. Interview with an air force officer, Karachi, January 2012. The software (or some version of it) is now freely available in the US as it is no longer on the restricted list.

60. Steve Coll, 'War by other means', *New Yorker*, 24 May 2010, p. 44.

61. Strick van Linschoten and Kuehn, *An Enemy We Created*, p. 257.

62. Anand Gopal, 'The battle for Afghanistan: Militancy and conflict in Kandahar', New America Foundation website, 2010, p. 5, at: http://newamerica.net/sites/newamerica.net/files/policydocs/kandahar_0.pdf

63. Syed Saleem Shahzad, 'Secrets of the Taliban's success', *Asia Times*, 11 September 2008, at: http://www.atimes.com/atimes/South_Asia/JI11Df01.html

64. Thomas H. Johnson, 'Taliban adaptations and innovations', *Small Wars and Insurgencies*, 24:1 (2013), pp. 3–27.

65. 'Afghanistan's record of suicide bombings in 2006', Paktribune.com, 6 January 2007, at http://www.paktribune.com/news/print.php?id=165055; Brian Glyn Williams and Cathy Young, 'Cheney attack reveals Taliban suicide bombing patterns', *Terrorism Monitor*, 5:4 (2007).

66. Brian Glyn Williams, 'A report from the field: Gauging the impact of Taliban suicide bombing', *Terrorism Monitor*, 5:10 (2007).

67. Johnson, 'Taliban adaptations and innovations'.

68. Strick van Linschoten and Kuehn, *An Enemy We Created*, p. 279.

69. Astri Suhrke, *When More is Less: The international project in Afghanistan*, Columbia University Press, New York, 2011, pp. 55–56.

70. Hamid Mir, 'The Taliban's new face', Rediff.com, 27 September 2005, at: http://www.rediff.com/news/2005/sep/27spec4.htm

71. Aqeel Yusufzai, *Operation Natamam*, Nigarishat Publishers, Lahore, 2010, pp. 269–70.

72. 'Ahmed Rashid offers an update on the Taliban', NPR website, 17 February 2010, at: http://m.npr.org/news/Arts+%26+Life/123777455

73. Husain Nadim, 'The quiet rise of the Quetta Shura', *Foreign Policy*, 7 September 2012, at: http://southasia.foreignpolicy.com/posts/2012/08/14/the_quiet_rise_of_the_quetta_shura§hash.l0etvHqh.dpbs

74. Interview with an ISI officer, October 2008.

75. Shehzad H. Qazi, *The Neo-Taliban, Counterinsurgency and the American Endgame in Afghanistan*, Institute for Social Policy and Understanding, Washington, DC, 2011.

76. For instance, see assessment in Theo Farrell and Antonio Giustozzi, 'The Taliban at war: Inside the Helmand insurgency', *International Affairs* 89:4 (2013), pp. 845–71.

77. As regards expansion of the Taliban recruitment pattern, see Antonio Giustozzi, 'Negotiation with the Taliban: Issues and prospects', Century Foundation, New York, 2010, p. 5, at: http://tcf.org/assets/downloads/tcf-Giustozzi.pdf

78. Stefanie Nijssen, 'The Taliban's shadow government in Afghanistan', Civil Military Fusion Centre, September 2011, p. 5, at: https://www.cimicweb.org/Documents/CFC%20AFG%20Governance%20Archive/CFC_AFG_Shadow_Governance_September11.pdf

Chapter 6 Islamabad under siege

1. Quoted in *Weekly Independent* (Lahore), 11–17 October 2001.

2. Noreen Haider, 'Grabbing attention', *News on Sunday* (Lahore), 8 April 2007.

3. Hassan Abbas, 'The road to Lal Masjid and its aftermath', *Terrorism Monitor*, 5:14 (2007).

4. Kathleen Fenner Laird, 'Whose Islam? Pakistani women's political action groups speak out', PhD Dissertation, Department of Anthropology, Washington University, 2007, p. 136.

5. Amir Rana, 'Lal Mosque's terror links', Pakistan Institute of Peace Studies (PIPS), Islamabad, 25 May 2007.
6. 'Agencies blamed for Azam's murder', *Dawn* (Karachi), 8 October 2003.
7. Tariq Ali, 'Pakistan at sixty', *London Review of Books*, 29:19 (2007).
8. ibid.
9. Syed Saleem Shahzad, 'Pakistan: Trouble in the mosque', *Asia Times*, 12 April 2007, at: http://www.atimes.com/atimes/South_Asia/ID12Df03.html
10. Manjeet S. Pardesi, 'Battle for the soul of Pakistan in Islamabad's Red Mosque' in C. Christine Fair and Sumit Ganguly (eds), *Treading on Hallowed Ground: Counterinsurgency operations in sacred spaces*, Oxford University Press, New York, 2008, p. 97.
11. Syed Saleem Shahzad, 'The Taliban's brothers in alms', *Asia Times*, 14 March 2007, at: http://www.atimes.com/atimes/South_Asia/IC14Df01.html
12. As regards the involvement of Fazlur Rahman Khalil as a mediator, see 'Emergence of Harkat-ul-Mujahideen', *Express Tribune* (Karachi), 25 June 2011.
13. Ali, 'Pakistan at sixty'.
14. Interview with a senior army officer, Rawalpindi, February 2012.
15. For a detailed assessment, see Qandeel Siddique, 'The Red Mosque operation and its impact on the growth of the Pakistani Taliban', Norwegian Defence Research Establishment (FFI), 8 October 2008, at: http://www.ffi.no/no/Rapporter/08–01915. pdf
16. ibid.
17. Abbas, 'The road to Lal Masjid and its aftermath'.
18. Nicholas Schmidle, 'My buddy, the jihadi', *Washington Post*, 15 July 2007.
19. Hassan Abbas, 'Reforming Pakistan's police and law enforcement infrastructure', United States Institute of Peace, Washington, DC, 2011, at: http://www.usip.org/files/resources/sr266.pdf
20. 'Post-Lal Masjid suicide attacks claim 4,300 lives', *The News* (Lahore), 5 July 2008.
21. Syed Manzar Abbas Zaidi, 'Ghazi force: A threat to Pakistan's urban centers', *CTC Sentinel*, 3:7 (2010). Also see Kathy Gannon, 'The Ghazi force: Vengeful new militant group emerges in Pakistan', Associated Press, 1 July 2010.
22. Interview with former corps commander Karachi, Doha, Qatar, July 2010.
23. For details, see Steve Coll, 'The back channel: India and Pakistan's secret Kashmir talks', *New Yorker*, 2 March 2009.
24. Babar Dogar and Ranjan Roy, 'Kashmir solution just a signature away: Kasuri', Aman Ki Asha website, 24 April 2010, at: http://www.amankiasha.com/detail_news. asp?id=99
25. ibid. Also 'Musharraf offers Kashmir solution', *Guardian*, 5 December 2006, at: http://www.theguardian.com/world/2006/dec/05/pakistan.india
26. Interview with Athar Minullah, Islamabad, July 2009.
27. For instance, see Salman Masood and Carlotta Gall, 'After chief justice's return, court frees Musharraf critic', *New York Times*, 3 August 2007, at: http://www.nytimes. com/2007/08/04/world/asia/04islamabad.html
28. Interview in Washington, DC, May 2013.
29. Jane Perlez and David Rohde, 'Pakistan attempts to crush protests by lawyers', *New York Times*, 6 November 2007, at: http://www.nytimes.com/2007/11/06/world/asia/06pakistan. html?pagewanted=all
30. Hassan Abbas, 'Who tried to kill Benazir Bhutto?', *Terrorism Focus*, 4:34 (2007).
31. Email communication with Benazir Bhutto, 24 October 2007; also quoted partly in my op-ed entitled 'Benazir's sacrifice may yet save Pakistan', *Guardian*, 31 December 2007, at: http://www.guardian.co.uk/world/2008/jan/01/pakistan.comment
32. Incidentally, the park is named after Pakistan's first prime minister, Liaquat Ali Khan, who was assassinated there in 1951 while speaking to a large gathering.
33. For the statement, see 'Benazir meets Karzai', AAJ News Service, 27 December 2007, at: http://www.aaj.tv/2007/12/benazir-meets-karzai/

34. 'Bhutto said she'd blame Musharraf if killed', CNN website, 28 December 2007, at: http://www.cnn.com/2007/WORLD/asiapcf/12/27/bhutto.security/
35. Quoted in Yousaf Nazar, 'Why the Supreme Court never took interest in Benazir murder investigation?', State of Pakistan blog, 15 April 2010.
36. Owen Bennett Jones, 'Questions concerning the murder of Benazir Bhutto', *London Review of Books*, 34:23 (2012).
37. For text of the charter, see: http://www.dawn.com/news/192460/text-of-the-charter-of-democracy
38. Shahzad, 'Secrets of the Taliban's success'.
39. Steven A. Zyck, 'How to lose allies and finance your enemies: the economization of conflict termination in Afghanistan', *Conflict, Security & Development*, 12:3 (2012), p. 257.
40. Gaith Abdul-Ahad, 'Face to face with the Taliban', *Guardian*, 28 December 2008, at: http://www.theguardian.com/world/2008/dec/14/afghanistan-terrorism
41. Carlotta Gall, 'Taliban free 1,200 inmates in attack on Afghan prison', *New York Times*, 14 June 2008, at: http://www.nytimes.com/2008/06/14/world/asia/14kandahar.html
42. Eric Schmidt and Jared Cohen, *The New Digital Age: Reshaping the future of people, nations and business*, Knopf, New York, 2013, p. 159.
43. Strick van Linschoten and Kuehn, *An Enemy We Created*, pp. 275–76.
44. Fergusson, *Taliban*, pp. 184–85.

Chapter 7 The battle for the soul of Pakistan

1. Interview with a senior police official in Peshawar, NWFP, July 2009.
2. 'Vali Nasr interview: Conversations with history', Institute of International Studies, UC Berkeley, 2002, at: http://globetrotter.berkeley.edu/people2/Nasr/nasr-con4.html; for further details, see Seyyed Vali Reza Nasr, *The Vanguard of the Islamic Revolution: The Jamaat-i-Islami of Pakistan*, University of California Press, Berkeley, 1994.
3. For background and details, see Hassan Abbas, 'The black-turbaned brigade: The rise of TNSM in Pakistan', *Terrorism Monitor*, 4:23 (2006).
4. Dr Sultan–i-Rome, 'Administrative system of the princely state of Swat', 2006, at: http://www.valleyswat.net/literature/papers/Administrative_System_of_Swat.pdf
5. Quoted in Urdu newspaper *Daily Mashriq* (Lahore), 3 May 2001.
6. Shaheen Buneri, 'Pakistan's Swat Valley: Taliban gone but peace remains elusive', Pulitzer Centre website, 10 January 2012, at: http://pulitzercenter.org/reporting/pakistan-swat-valley-taliban-fazlullah-afghanistan-border-military
7. Riaz Khan, 'Inside rebel Pakistan cleric's domain', *USA Today*, 28 October 2007.
8. Zahid Hussain, *The Scorpion's Tail: The relentless rise of Islamic militants in Pakistan*, Simon and Schuster, New York, 2010, p. 100.
9. Quoted in Swat newspaper *Daily Azadi*, 21 October 2012.
10. Interview with a leading ANP leader, Peshawar, July 2008; also see forum discussion at: http://pkpolitics.com/2009/05/03/interview-of-sufi-mohammad-3-may-2009/
11. Delawar Jan, 'NWFP government, Swat militant strike ceasefire', *The News* (Lahore), 10 May 2008; 'US silent on visit of Asfandyar', *Dawn* (Karachi), 10 May 2008.
12. 'Hardtalk', *Daily Times* (Lahore), 2 February 2009.
13. For a useful analysis of the implications of this move, see Omar Waraich, 'Pakistan's Shari'a pact: Giving in to the Taliban?', *Time*, 17 February 2009, at: http://content.time.com/time/world/article/0,8599,1879820,00.html
14. Pervaiz Akhtar Zia, 'Exclusive interview of ANP President Asfandyar Wali Khan with Radio Pakistan', Radio Pakistan, 9 April 2013, at: http://www.radio.gov.pk/newsdetail-41893
15. 'Army official called Baitullah Mehsud, Fazlullah "patriots"', Pakistan News Service, 1 December 2008; also Hamid Mir, 'Army official called Baitullah Mehsud, Fazlullah patriots', *The News* ((Lahore), 1 December 2008.

16. Rahimullah Yusufzai, 'The man that is Sufi Mohammad', *The News* (Lahore), 5 May 2009; also 'Being photographed, video taped is un-Islamic: TNSM chief', *Daily Times* (Lahore), 4 May 2009.

17. 'Pakistan's IDP crisis: Challenges and opportunities', International Crisis Group Asia Briefing No. 93, 3 June 2009, at: http://www.crisisgroup.org/~/media/Files/asia/south-asia/pakistan/b93_pakistans_idp_crisis___challenges_and_opportunities

18. 'Fazlullah in Afghanistan', *Dawn* (Karachi), 19 October 2011.

19. 'Soldier killed in Pakistan militant attack', *Dawn* (Karachi), 26 July 2007; Haji Mujtiba, 'Militants threaten attacks in Pakistan's Waziristan', Reuters, 17 July 2007; 'North Waziristan clerics to launch "silent protest"', *Daily Times* (Lahore), 3 August 2007.

20. Comments made in TV programme *Jirga*, hosted by journalist Saleem Safi, Geo TV, 22 October 2009, at: http://www.pkaffairs.com/Play_Show_Jirga_-_22nd_October_2009_5938

21. Mushtaq Yusufzai, 'Militants seek end to military operations', *The News* (Lahore), 16 December 2007; 'Tribal areas under centralized control', *Daily Times* (Lahore), 16 December 2007.

22. Hassan Abbas, 'A profile of Tehrik-i-Taliban Pakistan', *CTC Sentinel*, 1:2 (2008). In February 2014, TTP appointed Aziz as a member of their negotiating team dealing with Islamabad.

23. 'Major incidents of terrorism-related violence in Pakistan, 2007', South Asia Terrorism Portal, at: http://www.satp.org/satporgtp/countries/pakistan/database/majorinci2007. htm

24. Aqeel Yusufzai, *Talibanization: Afghanistan Se FATA, Swat Aur Pakistan Tak*, Nigarishaat Publishers, Lahore, 2009, pp. 60, 73.

25. Speaking on the talkshow *Kamran Khan Kay Sath*, GEO TV, 4 May 2011.

26. Interview with Pir Zubair Shah, New York, 2 August 2013.

27. Rahimullah Yusufzai, 'Another Swat in the making', *The News* (Lahore), 2 January 2012.

28. Interview with Pir Zubair Shah, November 2012.

29. Anand Gopal, Mansur Khan Mahsud and Brian Fishman, 'The Taliban in North Waziristan' in Bergen with Tiedemann, *Talibanistan*, pp. 146–51.

30. For a detailed profile of Maulvi Nazir, see Chris Harnisch, 'Question mark of South Waziristan: Biography and analysis of Maulvi Nazir Ahmad', Critical Threats website, 17 July 2009, at: http://www.criticalthreats.org/pakistan/question-mark-south-waziristan-biography-and-analysis-maulvi-nazir-ahmad

31. Yusufzai, *Talibanization*, p. 72.

32. Iqbal Khattak, 'Local gangs assisting TTP in NWFP', *Daily Times* (Lahore), 26 November 2008.

33. Sohail Tajik, 'Insight into a suicide bomber training camp in Waziristan', *CTC Sentinel*, 3: 3 (2010).

34. Interviews with officials in the Ministry of Interior, Islamabad, July 2012. Also see Hassan Abbas, 'Defining the Punjabi Taliban network', *CTC Sentinel*, 2:4 (2009).

35. Sabrina Tavernise, Richard A. Oppel Jr and Eric Schmitt, 'United militants threaten Pakistan's populous heart', *New York Times*, 13 April 2009, at: http://www.nytimes.com/2009/04/14/world/asia/14punjab.html?pagewanted=all&_r=0

36. Sabrina Tavernise and Waqar Gillani, 'Pakistan produces suspect in cricket team attack', *New York Times*, 17 June 2009, at: http://www.nytimes.com/2009/06/18/world/asia/18pstan.html

37. For poll figures, see Julie Ray and Rajesh Srinivasan, 'Taliban increasingly unpopular in Pakistan', Gallup, 12 March 2010, at: http://www.gallup.com/poll/126602/taliban-increasingly-unpopular-pakistan.aspx

38. 'Pakistani public opinion ever more critical of US', Pew Research Global Attitudes Project website, 27 June 2012.

39. C. Christine Fair, 'Under the shrinking US security umbrella: India's end game in Afghanistan?', *Washington Quarterly*, 34:2 (2011), p. 184. Also Omar Farooq Khan,

'Lahore attack: Pak blame fails Waziristan circumcision test!', *Times of India*, 4 November 2009.

40. Amir Mir, 'Human bombs killed 5,243 in 896 attacks since 2002', *The News* (Lahore), 2 January 2013. See also: http://www.satp.org

41. Greg Miller, 'CIA pays for support in Pakistan', *Los Angeles Times*, 15 November 2009, at: http://articles.latimes.com/2009/nov/15/world/fg-cia-pakistan15

42. Mark Mazzetti and Jane Perlez, 'CIA and Pakistan work together, warily', *New York Times*, 14 February 2010, at: http://www.nytimes.com/2010/02/25/world/asia/25intel.html

43. Mansur Khan Mahsud, 'The Taliban in South Waziristan' in Bergen with Tiedemann, *Talibanistan*, pp. 191–93.

44. '2008: US tries to improve Pakistan's counterinsurgency capability', *Dawn* (Karachi), 1 June 2011, at: http://x.dawn.com/2011/06/01/2008-us-tries-to-improve-pakistans-counterinsurgency-capability/

45. Mahsud, 'The Taliban in South Waziristan', p. 192.

46. Nine interviews were conducted in 2011 and 2012 with the officers in Washington, DC, USA and Rawalpindi, Pakistan. Some of these were longer conversations, on the understanding that I would not quote anyone by name.

47. Interviews and discussions conducted during August–December 2011.

48. 'Remarks by the president on Osama bin Laden', White House website, 2 May 2011, at: http://www.whitehouse.gov/blog/2011/05/02/osama-bin-laden-dead

49. F.B. Ali, 'Osama bin Laden: The real story?', Sic Semper Tyrannis blog, 30 August 2011, at:http://turcopolier.typepad.com/sic_semper_tyrannis/2011/08/osama-bin-laden-the-real-story-fb-ali.html

50. Josh Rogin, 'Gates and Mullen: Stop leaking details of the bin Laden raid!', *Foreign Policy*, 18 May 2011, at: http://thecable.foreignpolicy.com/posts/2011/05/18/gates_and_mullen_stop_leaking_details_of_the_bin_laden_raid?utm_source—ondoweiss+List&utm_campaign=1792e8d558-RSS_EMAIL_CAMPAIGN&utm_medium=email#sthash.1NnVELEm.dpbs

51. Asad Hashim, 'Leaked report shows bin Laden's "hidden life"', Al Jazeera website, 8 July 2013, at: http://www.aljazeera.com/news/asia/2013/07/20137813412615531.html

52. Nelly Lahoud, Stuart Caudill, Liam Collins, Gabriel Koehler-Derrick, Don Rassler and Muhammad al-Ubaydi, *Letters from Abbottabad: Bin Laden sidelined?*, Combating Terrorism Center at West Point, 2012, at: http://www2.gwu.edu/~nsarchiv/NSAEBB/NSAEBB410/docs/UBLDocument16.pdf

53. Matthew Rosenberg, 'US disrupts Afghans' tack on militants', *New York Times*, 28 October 2013, at: http://www.nytimes.com/2013/10/29/world/asia/us-disrupts-afghans-tack-on-militants.html

54. Zahid Hussain, 'Kayani spells out terms for regional stability', *Dawn* (Karachi), 2 February 2010, at: http://www.dawn.com/news/517723/kayani-spells-out-terms-for-regional-stability

55. For military deployment figures, see Steve Inskeep, 'Pakistan, militants in deadly border fight', NPR website, 6 June 2011.

56. See Shehzad H. Qazi, 'An extended profile of the Pakistani Taliban', Institute for Social Policy and Understanding Policy Brief No. 44, Washington, DC, August 2011.

57. Owais Tohid, 'US drones are pounding Pakistan's North Waziristan. Here's why', *Christian Science Monitor*, 16 September 2010.

58. C. Christine Fair, 'Pakistan's own war on terror: What the Pakistani public thinks', *Journal of International Affairs*, 63 (Fall/Winter 2009), pp. 39–55.

59. Jayshree Bajoria, 'Shared goals for Pakistan's militants', Council on Foreign Relations website, 6 May 2010, at: http://www.cfr.org/pakistan/shared-goals-pakistans-militants/p22064

60. Jam Sajjad Hussain, 'Son-in-law of Gen Tariq wins freedom for Rs 300m', *The Nation* (Lahore), 16 March 2012.

61. Amir Mir, 'Usman Kurd, the man who caused fall of Raisani govt', *The News* (Lahore), 15 January 2013, at: http://www.thenews.com.pk/Todays-News-13-20265-Usman-Kurd,-the-man-who-caused-fall-of-Raisani-govt

62. Zahir Shah, 'Taliban release Bannu jailbreak video, vow to free more prisoners', *Dawn* (Karachi), 16 May 2012.

63. M. Ilyas Khan, 'Pakistan jailbreak: Taliban free 248 in Dera Ismail Khan', BBC News, 30 July 2013, at: http://www.bbc.co.uk/news/world-asia-23493323

64. Ismail Khan, 'Jailbreak: It wasn't an intelligence failure for once', *Dawn* (Karachi), 31 July 2013.

65. 'Public opinion in Pakistan's tribal regions', New America Foundation and Terror Free Tomorrow, September, 2010, at: http://www.newamerica.net/sites/newamerica.net/files/policydocs/FATApoll.pdf

66. Nadeem F. Paracha, 'Declaring sanity', *Dawn* (Karachi), 8 March 2012. Full text of the declaration is available at: http://rcanfield.blogspot.com/2010/03/full-text-of-peshawar-declaration.html

67. Nawaz, *FATA: A most dangerous place*, p. 18.

68. Patrick B. Johnston, 'Drone strikes keep pressure on al-Qaida', RAND blog, 22 August 2012, at: http://www.rand.org/blog/2012/08/drone-strikes-keep-pressure-on-al-qaida.html

69. 'Video shows Faisal Shahzad with Hakimullah Mehsud', *Express Tribune* (Karachi), 23 July 2010.

70. Mosharraf Zaidi, 'The Taliban will be defeated', *The News* (Lahore), 21 April 2009.

71. Zia ur Rahman, 'Taliban factions fight over Karachi turf', *Friday Times* (Lahore), 23 October 2013, at: http://www.thefridaytimes.com/tft/taliban-factions-fight-over-karachi-turf/

72. For a detailed article on her struggle, see Marie Brenner, 'Target', *Vanity Fair*, April 2013, at: http://www.vanityfair.com/politics/2013/04/malala-yousafzai-pakistan-profile#

Chapter 8 The political economy of Taliban resurgence in Afghanistan

1. US Department of Defense, *Report on Progress toward Security and Stability in Afghanistan*, June 2008, at: http://www.defenselink.mil/pubs/Report_on_Progress_toward_Security_and_Stability_in_Afghanistan_1230.pdf

2. 'Obama's remarks on Iraq and Afghanistan', *New York Times*, 15 July 2008, at: http://www.nytimes.com/2008/07/15/us/politics/15text-obama.html?pagewanted=all&_r=0

3. ibid.

4. 'Hillary Clinton puts conditions on US portion of $16b Afghanistan assistance pledge', CBS website, 9 July 2012, at: http://www.cbsnews.com/8301-505263_162-57468393/hillary-clinton-puts-conditions-on-u.s-portion-of-$16b-afghanistan-assistance-pledge/

5. 'COMISAF's initial assessment', 30 August 2009, available at: http://media.washingtonpost.com/wp-srv/politics/documents/Assessment_Redacted_092109.pdf

6. Steve Coll, 'Human terrain: Decoding the new Taliban', *The National*, 17 December 2009, at: http://www.thenational.ae/arts-culture/books/human-terrain-decoding-the-new-taliban#full

7. Barnett R. Rubin, *Afghanistan from the Cold War through the War on Terror*, Oxford University Press, New York, 2013, p. 107.

8. Not his real name, as per condition of the interview. He is now back in Afghanistan and the interview was conducted in January 2012.

9. Quil Lawrence, 'Afghan president pardons would-be suicide bombers', NPR website, 29 August 2011, at: http://www.npr.org/2011/08/29/140037111/afghan-president-pardons-would-be-suicide-bombers

10. Brian Williams, 'Suicide bombings in Afghanistan', *Jane's Islamic Affairs Analyst*, September 2007, at: http://www.brianglynwilliams.com/IAA%20suicide.pdf

11. Robert Pape, 'It's the occupation stupid', *Foreign Policy*, 18 October 2010, at: http://www.foreignpolicy.com/articles/2010/10/18/it_s_the_occupation_stupid
12. Fergusson, *Taliban*, p. 183.
13. Angelo Rasayanagam, *Afghanistan: A modern history*, I.B. Tauris, New York, 2003, p. 162.
14. Asia Foundation, 'Afghanistan in 2011: A survey of the Afghan people', at http://asia-foundation.org/country/afghanistan/2011-poll.php
15. UN Office on Drugs and Crime, *The Opium Economy in Afghanistan: An international problem*, 2003, at: http://www.unodc.org/pdf/publications/afg_opium_economy_www.pdf
16. 'Heroin funds Taliban revival in Afghanistan', Drugfree website, 31 May 2004, at: http://www.drugfree.org/join-together/legal/heroin-funds-taliban-revival
17. Peters, *How Opium Profits the Taliban*.
18. Peter Kenyon, 'Exploring the Taliban's complex, shadowy finance', NPR website, 19 March 2010, at: http://www.npr.org/templates/story/story.php?storyId=124821049
19. Alissa J. Rubin, 'Opium cultivation rose this year in Afghanistan, UN survey shows', *New York Times*, 20 November 2012, at: http://www.nytimes.com/2012/11/21/world/asia/afghan-opium-cultivation-rose-in-2012-un-says.html?_r=0
20. Peters, *How Opium Profits the Taliban*, pp. 5–6.
21. Dov S. Zakheim, *A Vulcan's Tale: How the Bush administration mismanaged the reconstruction of Afghanistan*, Brookings Institution, Washington, DC, 2011, pp. 267–68.
22. Ernesto Londoño, 'As US withdraws from Afghanistan, poppy trade it spent billions fighting still flourishes', *Washington Post*, 3 November 2013, at: http://www.washington-post.com/world/national-security/as-us-withdraws-from-afghanistan-poppy-trade-it-spent-billions-fighting-still-flourishes/2013/11/03/55cc99d6-4313-11e3-a751-f032898f2dbc_story.html
23. '1,900 gangs smuggling Afghan drugs to Russia – anti-narcotics agency', RIA Novosti website, 13 September 2013, at: http://en.ria.ru/russia/20130913/183405336/1900-Gangs-Smuggling-Afghan-Drugs-to-Russia—-Anti-Narcotics-Agency.html
24. Emma Graham-Harrison, 'Drug trade could splinter Afghanistan into fragmented criminal state – UN', *Guardian*, 5 January 2014, at: http://www.theguardian.com/world/2014/jan/05/drug-trade-afghanistan-fragmented-criminal-state
25. Phil Williams, 'Transnational criminal networks' in John Arquilla and David Ronfeldt (eds), *Networks and Netwars: The future of terror, crime and militancy*, RAND, Santa Monica, CA, 2001.
26. Robert Perito, 'Building civilian capacity for US stability operations: The rule of law component', United States Institute of Peace Special Report, 2004, at: http://www.usip.org/sites/default/files/sr118.pdf
27. Gretchen Peters, *Crime and Insurgency in the Tribal Areas of Afghanistan and Pakistan*, Combating Terrorism Center at West Point, 15 October 2010.
28. Kenyon, 'Exploring the Taliban's complex, shadowy finance'.
29. Dexter Filkins, 'US said to fund Afghan warlords to protect convoys', *New York Times*, 21 June 2010, at: http://www.nytimes.com/2010/06/22/world/asia/22contractors.html
30. Karen DeYoung, 'US indirectly paying Afghan warlords as part of security contract', *Washington Post*, 22 June 2010, at: http://www.washingtonpost.com/wp-dyn/content/article/2010/06/21/AR2010062104628.html
31. Antonio Giustozzi, 'Negotiating with the Taliban: Issues and prospects', Century Foundation Report, 2010, at: http://tcf.org/assets/downloads/tcf-Giustozzi.pdf
32. Khan Mohammad Danishju, 'Taleban try soft power', Institute for War and Peace Reporting website, 8 April 2011, at: http://iwpr.net/report-news/taleban-try-soft-power
33. Matiullah Achakzai, 'Taliban code of conduct seeks to win hearts, minds', Associated Press, 3 August 2010.
34. Suhrke, *When More is Less*, pp. 189–90.
35. ibid., p. 200.

36. ibid., p. 216.
37. 'Afghan women judges rise from Taliban terror to top of the class', USAID press release, 20 June 2012, at: http://www.usaid.gov/afghanistan/news-information/press-releases/afghan-women-judges-rise-taliban-terror-top-class
38. Farah Stockman, 'Three reasons for hope in Afghanistan', *Boston Globe*, 9 April 2013, at: http://www.bostonglobe.com/opinion/2013/04/08/gambling-pomegranates/dekCKppa3xT9QeEKGqEqlJ/story.html
39. Nahal Toosi, 'Taliban using sophisticated media network', *USA Today*, 24 July 2008, at: http://www.usatoday.com/news/world/2008-07-24-4143437049_x.htm
40. Thom Shanker, 'US plans a mission against Taliban's propaganda', *New York Times*, 15 August 2009, at: http://www.nytimes.com/2009/08/16/world/asia/16policy.html
41. 'The media activities of the Taliban Islamic movement', WorldAnalysis.net website, 17 January 2008, at: http://worldanalysis.net/postnuke/html/index.php?name–ews&file=article&sid=731
42. 'Extremist web sites are using US hosts', *Washington Post*, 9 April 2009, at: http://www.washingtonpost.com/wp-dyn/content/article/2009/04/08/AR2009040804378.html
43. Hamid Mir, 'The Taliban's new face', Rediff.com website, 27 September 2005, at: http://www.rediff.com/news/2005/sep/27spec4.htm
44. Michael Semple, 'The revival of the Afghan Taliban 2001–2011', *Orient*, II (2012), p. 58–67.
45. Seth Jones and Keith Crane, *Afghanistan after the Drawdown*, Council on Foreign Relations, November 2013, p. vii, at: http://www.cfr.org/afghanistan/afghanistan-after-drawdown/p31944
46. Sami Yousafzai and Ron Moreau, 'Viagrastan: An unorthodox play for Afghan hearts and minds', *Newsweek*, 12 February 2013, at: http://www.newsweek.com/viagrastan-unorthodox-play-afghan-hearts-and-minds-63261 See also Julian Borger, 'Ghost money from MI6 and CIA may fuel Afghan corruption, say diplomats', *Guardian*, 29 April 2013, at: http://www.theguardian.com/world/2013/apr/29/cia-mi6-afghan-corruption
47. Joshua Partlow, 'Afghanistan to need billions in aid for years, World Bank says', *Washington Post*, 22 November 2011, at: http://www.washingtonpost.com/world/asia_pacific/afghanistan-to-need-billions-in-aid-for-years-world-bank-says/2011/11/22/gIQA14zOlN_story.html
48. Special Inspector General for Afghanistan Reconstruction (SIGAR), *Quarterly Report to the United States Congress*, 30 January 2013, p. 6, available via: http://www.sigar.mil/quarterlyreports/
49. Rajiv Chandrasekaran, 'A brand-new US military headquarters in Afghanistan. And nobody to use it', *Washington Post*, 9 July 2013, at: http://www.washingtonpost.com/world/national-security/a-brand-new-us-military-headquarters-in-afghanistan-and-nobody-to-use-it/2013/07/09/2bb73728-e8cd-11e2-a301-ea5a8116d211_story.html
50. SIGAR, *Quarterly Report to the United States Congress*, 30 June 2013, p. 6, available via: http://www.sigar.mil/quarterlyreports/
51. Rajiv Chandrasekaran, 'US military, diplomats at odds over how to resolve Kandahar's electricity woes', *Washington Post*, 23 April 2010, at: http://www.washingtonpost.com/wp-dyn/content/article/2010/04/22/AR2010042206227.html
52. 'Kandahar's power department loses 20mn AFN every month', Wadsam website, 7 May 2013, at: http://www.wadsam.com/kandahars-power-department-loses-20mn-afn-every-month-788/; see also Katharine Houreld, 'Afghan electric company struggles to make powerful customers pay', Reuters, 15 April 2013, at: http://www.reuters.com/article/2013/04/15/us-afghanistan-electricity-idUSBRE93E15S20130415
53. Qasim A. Moini, 'US wanted closer scrutiny of "cash couriers" providing terror financing', *Dawn* (Karachi), 16 June 2011, at: http://x.dawn.com/2011/06/16/secret-us-cables-accessed-by-dawn-through-wikileaks-us-wanted-closer-scrutiny-of-cash-couriers-providing-terror-financing/

54. Ivan Watson, 'Holbrooke: Persian Gulf money key to Taliban insurgency', CNN website, 25 August 2009, at: http://edition.cnn.com/2009/WORLD/asiapcf/08/25/afghanistan. pakistan.holbrooke/

55. Sherard Cowper-Coles, *Cables from Kabul: The inside story of the west's Afghanistan campaign*, Harper Press, London, 2011, p. 78.

56. Matthew Rosenberg, 'An Afghan mystery: Why are large shipments of gold leaving the country?', *New York Times*, 15 December 2012, at: http://www.nytimes.com/2012/12/16/ world/asia/as-gold-is-spirited-out-of-afghanistan-officials-wonder-why.html

57. For instance, see Thomas Ruttig, 'How tribal are the Taleban?', Afghanistan Analysts Network website, 28 April 2010, at: http://www.afghanistan-analysts.org/publication/ how-tribal-are-the-taliban

58. Steve Coll, 'Let's hear from the spies', *New Yorker*, 24 November 2011, at: http://www. newyorker.com/online/blogs/comment/2011/11/steve-coll-afghanistan-national-intelligence-estimate.html

59. Johnson, 'Taliban adaptations and innovations'.

60. Ian S. Livingston and Michael O'Hanlon, 'Afghanistan index', Brookings Institution report, 31 October 2011, at: http://www.brookings.edu/~/media/Programs/foreign%20 policy/afghanistan%20index/index20111031.PDF

61. UNAMA, *Afghanistan: Annual Report 2010 protection of civilians in armed conflict*, p. 5, at: http://unama.unmissions.org/Portals/UNAMA/human%20rights/March%20 PoC%20Annual%20Report%20Final.pdf See also Ben Farmer, 'Afghan civilian deaths up 30 per cent as Taliban escalates assassination campaign', *Daily Telegraph*, 10 August 2010, at: http://www.telegraph.co.uk/news/worldnews/asia/afghanistan/7937027/ Afghan-civilian-deaths-up-30-per-cent-as-Taliban-escalates-assassination-campaign. html

62. Yaroslav Trofimov, 'Taliban gag Kandahar's clerics to keep grip on city', *Wall Street Journal*, 2 April 2010, at: http://online.wsj.com/news/articles/SB1000142405270230425 2704575156020308717184

63. ' "Afghan CIA bomber" shown vowing revenge', BBC News, 9 January 2010, at: http:// news.bbc.co.uk/2/hi/south_asia/8449789.stm

64. Mark Mazzetti, 'No firm plans for a US exit in Afghanistan', *New York Times*, 7 December 2009, at: http://www.nytimes.com/2009/12/07/world/asia/07afghan.html

65. Ian S. Livingston and Michael O'Hanlon, 'Afghanistan index', Brookings Institution, 27 August 2013, at: http://www.brookings.edu/~/media/Programs/foreign%20policy/ afghanistan%20index/index20130827.pdf

66. Dexter Filkins, 'Kabul attack shows resilience of Afghan militants', *New York Times*, 18 January 2010, at: http://www.nytimes.com/2010/01/19/world/asia/19afghan.html?page wanted=all

67. Jonathan S. Landay and Ali Safi, 'Taliban lead attacks on US bases and government sites across Afghanistan', McClatchy DC website, 15 April 2012, at: http://www.mcclatchydc. com/2012/04/15/145271/taliban-lead-attacks-on-us-bases.html

68. Azam Ahmed and Matthew Rosenberg, 'Attackers at US–Afghan base wore coalition uniforms', *New York Times*, 2 December 2012, at: http://www.nytimes.com/2012/12/03/ world/asia/taliban-bombers-attack-air-base-in-afghanistan.html

69. For instance, see Aref Karimi, 'Taliban ambush kills 15 police in Afghanistan', AFP, 29 August 2013, at: http://www.google.com/hostednews/afp/article/ALeqM5gnwC7Y566 kfLn0xIKJFqyoMyaxuw?docId=CNG.c7f3d5d86e44e790c679886c2e48d055.1061; Azam Ahmed and Sharifullah Sahak, 'Scores killed in 2 days of clashes between Afghan police and Taliban fighters', *New York Times*, 2 August 2013, at: http://www.nytimes. com/2013/08/03/world/asia/clashes-leave-scores-of-afghan-police-and-taliban-dead. html?_r=0

70. Open Society Foundations/Liaison Office, 'The cost of kill/capture: Impact of the night raid surge on Afghan civilians', 19 September 2011, p. 2, at: http://www.opensociety-foundations.org/sites/default/files/Night-Raids-Report-FINAL-092011.pdf

71. Matthias Gebauer, 'Afghanistan controversy: Karzai warns us over night raids', *Spiegel Online*, 5 December 2011, at: http://www.spiegel.de/international/world/afghanistan-controversy-karzai-warns-us-over-night-raids-a-801880.html

72. Alissa J. Rubin, 'US transfers control of night raids to Afghanistan', *New York Times*, 8 April 2012, at: http://www.nytimes.com/2012/04/09/world/asia/deal-reached-on-controversial-afghan-night-raids.html?pagewanted=all

73. For ANA figures, see Livingston and O'Hanlon, 'Afghanistan index', 27 August 2013, p. 7.

74. Vali Nasr, *The Dispensable Nation: American foreign policy in retreat*, Random House, New York, 2013, p. 11.

75. Dan Murphy, 'Karzai says Taliban no threat to women, NATO created "no gains" for Afghanistan', *Christian Science Monitor*, 7 October 2013, at: http://www.csmonitor.com/World/Security-Watch/Backchannels/2013/1007/Karzai-says-Taliban-no-threat-to-women-NATO-created-no-gains-for-Afghanistan

76. Jon Boone, 'UN report detailing Taliban fighter deaths warns of force's illicit funding', *Guardian*, 17 November 2013, at: http://www.theguardian.com/world/2013/nov/17/un-report-taliban-fighter-deaths

77. Mohammad Anwar, 'Afghan special forces commander defects with guns to insurgents', Reuters, 20 October 2013, at: http://uk.reuters.com/article/2013/10/20/uk-afghanistan-army-idUKBRE99J06T20131020

78. Sayed Rahmatullah Alizada, 'Afghan police in Taleban arms sales', Institute for War and Peace Reporting, website, 19 December 2013, at: http://iwpr.net/report-news/afghan-police-taleban-arms-sales

79. Rod Nordland, 'War deaths top 13,000 in Afghan security forces', *New York Times*, 3 March 2014.

Chapter 9 Empowering the Taliban revival?

1. 'Editorial: The terrorism threat and response', *Daily Times* (Lahore), 15 August 2013.

2. For instance, see Cyril Almeida, 'The demagogue in Khan', *Dawn* (Karachi), 10 October 2012, at: http://www.dawn.com/news/754841/the-demagogue-in-khan

3. Interview in May 2012 with a Pakistani security official who seized Taliban training manuals from a training center in South Waziristan in 2010.

4. This section borrows from Hassan Abbas and Shehzad H. Qazi, 'Rebellion, development and security in Pakistan's tribal areas', *CTC Sentinel*, 6:6 (2013), pp. 23–25.

5. 'Why development and diplomacy matter in national security', USAID IMPACT blog, 4 November 2011, at: http://blog.usaid.gov/2011/11/why-development-and-diplomacy-matter-in-national-security/

6. Ashfaq Yusufzai, 'School's out for Pakistan children trapped between militants and military', *Guardian*, 14 January 2013, at: http://www.theguardian.com/global-development/2013/jan/14/school-pakistan-children-militants-military; see also Michele Langevine Leiby, 'Pakistani schools targeted by militants', *Washington Post*, 21 May 2012, at: http://www.washingtonpost.com/world/asia_pacific/pakistani-schools-targeted-by-militants/2012/05/21/gIQAvDP1eU_story.html

7. Shehzad H. Qazi, 'Rebels of the frontier: Origins, organization and recruitment of the Pakistani Taliban', *Small Wars and Insurgencies*, 22:4 (2011).

8. Ismail Khan, 'Army close to winding up first phase of operation', *Dawn* (Karachi), 5 November 2009, at: http://archives.dawn.com/archives/42679

9. 'Tackling the other Taliban', *Economist*, 15 October 2009, at: http://www.economist.com/node/14660577

10. Owais Tohid, 'Pakistani teen tells of his recruitment, training as suicide bomber', *Christian Science Monitor*, 16 June 2011. at: http://www.csmonitor.com/World/Asia-South-Central/2011/0616/Pakistani-teen-tells-of-his-recruitment-training-as-suicide-bomber

11. Asad Qureshi and Ahmed Jamal, *Sabaoon: Umeed ki Aik Kiran* (A ray of hope) (2011). This is the Urdu-language version of the documentary *Defusing Human Bombs*.

12. 'Pakistani Taliban recruits via Facebook', *Express Tribune* (Karachi), 7 December 2012.
13. 'Expert: Afghan war needs new strategy', United Press International, 21 May 2007, at: http://www.upi.com/Business_News/Security-Industry/2007/05/21/Expert-Afghan-war-needs-new-strategy/UPI-48511179771824/
14. Aamir Latif, 'Taliban finds fertile recruiting ground in Pakistan's tribal refugee camps', *US News and World Report*, 9 February 2009, at: http://www.usnews.com/news/world/articles/2009/02/09/taliban-finds-fertile-recruiting-ground-in-pakistans-tribal-refugee-camps
15. Qazi, 'Rebels of the frontier'.
16. Based on interviews conducted in Pakistan during July 2012 and January 2013 with mid-ranking police and other law enforcement officials.
17. Declan Walsh, 'Taliban gaining more resources from kidnapping', *New York Times*, 19 February 2012, at: http://www.nytimes.com/2012/02/20/world/asia/pakistani-taliban-turn-to-kidnapping-to-finance-operations.html?pagewanted=all&_r=0
18. ibid.
19. Ashraf Ali, 'Pakistani criminals, Taliban find easy cash in kidnapping', *San Francisco Chronicle*, 13 July 2008, at: http://www.sfgate.com/crime/article/Pakistani-criminals-Taliban-find-easy-cash-in-3277254.php
20. Sami Yousafai, 'For the Taliban, a crime that pays', *Daily Beast*, 5 September 2008: http://www.thedailybeast.com/newsweek/2008/09/05/for-the-taliban-a-crime-that-pays.html
21. This section adapts material from the author's two articles on the subject published in *The Atlantic*: 'Are drone strikes killing terrorists or creating them?', *The Atlantic*, 31 March 2013, at: http://www.theatlantic.com/international/archive/2013/03/are-drone-strikes-killing-terrorists-or-creating-them/274499/; and 'How drones create more terrorists', *The Atlantic*, 23 August 2013, at: http://www.theatlantic.com/international/archive/2013/08/how-drones-create-more-terrorists/278743/
22. Owen Bowcott, 'Drone strikes threaten 50 years of international law, says UN rapporteur', *Guardian*, 21 June 2012, at: http://www.guardian.co.uk/world/2012/jun/21/drone-strikes-international-law-un
23. For instance, see: http://www.livingunderdrones.org
24. For data, see: http://www.thebureauinvestigates.com/2013/03/26/in-video-naming-the-dead
25. 'Analysis: The drone war in Pakistan', New America Foundation website, at: http://natsec.newamerica.net/drones/pakistan/analysis
26. Interviews with security officials in Islamabad, January 2013. See also New America Foundation list at: http://natsec.newamerica.net/drones/pakistan/leaders-killed
27. David Rohde, 'Obama's overdue step on drones', Reuters, 24 May 2013, at: http://blogs.reuters.com/david-rohde/2013/05/24/obamas-overdue-step-on-drones/
28. Mark Mazzetti, *The Way of the Knife: The CIA, a secret army, and a war at the ends of the earth*, Penguin Press, New York, 2013, p. 162.
29. For costs, see 'Understanding drones', FCNL website, at: http://fcnl.org/issues/foreign_policy/understanding_drones/; David Francis, 'Death by drones: Are they worth the cost?', *Fiscal Times*, 7 February 2013, at: http://www.thefiscaltimes.com/Articles/2013/02/07/Death-by-Drones-Are-They-Worth-the-Cost
30. Mureeb Mohmand, 'Education under siege: FATA's schools in dire straits', *Express Tribune* (Karachi), 9 September 2012, at: http://tribune.com.pk/story/433797/education-under-siege-fatas-schools-in-dire-straits/
31. 'Literacy in restive FATA in free fall', *Dawn* (Karachi), 23 April 2011, at: http://dawn.com/2011/04/23/literacy-in-restive-fata-in-free-fall-2/
32. Spencer Ackerman, 'US drone strikes more deadly to Afghan civilians than manned aircraft – adviser', *Guardian*, 2 July 2013, at: http://www.theguardian.com/world/2013/jul/02/us-drone-strikes-afghan-civilians

33. Spencer Ackerman, '2012 was the year of the drone in Afghanistan', *Wired*, 6 December 2012, at: http://www.wired.com/dangerroom/2012/12/2012-drones-afghanistan/; Beth Stebner, 'Revealed: US carried out 333 drone strikes in Afghanistan this year alone – more than the entire drone strikes in Pakistan over the past eight years COMBINED', *Daily Mail*, 20 December 2012, http://www.dailymail.co.uk/news/article-2251418/Revealed-U-S-carried-333-drone-strikes-Afghanistan-year—entire-drone-strikes-Pakistan-past-years-COMBINED.html

34. Jason Lyall, Graeme Blair and Kosuke Imai, 'Explaining support for combatants during wartime: A survey experiment in Afghanistan', *American Political Science Review*, 107:4 (2013).

35. Michael R. Gordon, 'Kerry in Pakistan, expresses optimism on ending drone strikes soon', *New York Times*, 1 August 2013, at: http://www.nytimes.com/2013/08/02/world/asia/kerry-in-pakistan-visit-sees-longer-us-role-in-afghanistan.html

36. Aryn Baker, 'The key to Afghanistan: India–Pakistan peace', *Time*, 11 November 2008, at: http://content.time.com/time/world/article/0,8599,1857953,00.html

37. Mark Sappenfield and Shahan Mufti, 'Is Kashmir key to Afghan peace?', *Christian Science Monitor*, 21 November 2008, at: http://www.csmonitor.com/World/Asia-South-Central/2008/1121/p01s01-wosc.html

38. Yaroslav Trofimov and Nathan Hodge, 'Afghanistan says Pakistan ties are fraying', *Wall Street Journal*, 27 March 2013, at: http://online.wsj.com/news/articles/SB100014241278 87324789504578384621832773616

39. Dana Priest, 'Pakistani militants hiding in Afghanistan', *Washington Post*, 6 November 2012, at: http://www.washingtonpost.com/world/national-security/pakistani-militants-hiding-in-afghanistan/2012/11/06/609cca82-2782-11e2-b4f2-8320a9f00869_story.html

40. ibid.

41. Declan Walsh, 'WikiLeaks cables reveal Afghan-Pakistani row over fugitive rebel', *Guardian*, 30 November 2010, at: http://www.theguardian.com/world/2010/nov/30/wikileaks-cables-afghan-pakistani-fugitive

42. Chidanand Rajghatta, 'US bails out India from Balochistan wrangle', *Times of India*, 31 July 2009.

43. Fair, 'Under the shrinking US security umbrella', p. 181.

44. Mark Perry, 'False flag', *Foreign Policy*, 13 January 2012, at: http://www.foreignpolicy.com/articles/2012/01/13/false_flag

45. Shanthie Mariet D'Souza, 'Indian-Afghan strategic partnership: Perceptions from the ground', *Foreign Policy*, 26 October 2011, at: http://southasia.foreignpolicy.com/posts/2011/10/26/indian_afghan_strategic_partnership_perceptions_from_the_ground

46. 'COMISAF's initial assessment'.

47. Shubhajit Roy, 'India financed Pak's problems in Afghanistan: Chuck Hagel', *Indian Express*, 27 February 2013.

48. Seth G. Jones, *In the Graveyard of Empires: America's war in Afghanistan*, W.W. Norton and Company, New York, 2009, p. 311.

49. Interview with a Pakistani major general visiting the US, Washington, DC, November 2012.

50. Don Rassler and Vahid Brown, *The Haqqani Nexus and the Evolution of Al-Qaida*, Combating Terrorism Centre at West Point, 2011, at: http://www.ctc.usma.edu/wp-content/uploads/2011/07/CTC-Haqqani-Report_Rassler-Brown-Final_Web.pdf

51. For a detailed analysis, see Thomas Ruttig, 'The Haqqani Network as an autonomous entity' in Giustozzi, *Decoding the New Taliban*.

52. Coll, 'Human terrain'.

53. James F. Dobbins, 'Time to deal with Iran', *Washington Post*, reproduced on the RAND website, at: http://www.rand.org/commentary/2004/05/06/WP.html

54. Muhammad Tahir, 'Gulbuddin Hekmatyar's return to the Afghan insurgency', *Terrorism Monitor*, 29 May 2008.

55. Nasr, *The Dispensable Nation*, pp. 50–53.

56. Mohsen Milani, 'Iran and Afghanistan' in Robin Wright (ed.) *The Iran Primer*, United States Institute of Peace, 2010, at: http://iranprimer.usip.org/resource/iran-and-afghanistan
57. Kevjn Lim, 'Iran's outreach to Afghanistan, Tajikistan faces obstacles', *World Politics Review*, 5 June 2013, at: http://www.worldpoliticsreview.com/articles/12998/iran-s-outreach-to-afghanistan-tajikistan-faces-obstacles
58. Quoted on Tolo TV, Afghanistan, 26 December 2010.
59. 'India hands over Zaranj–Delaram highway to Afghanistan', *Times of India*, 22 January 2009.
60. Mohammad Ali Khan, 'The shift in Afghan transit trade', *Dawn* (Karachi), 2 February 2009, at: http://www.dawn.com/news/839023/the-shift-in-afghan-transit-trade
61. George Gavrilis, 'Harnessing Iran's role in Afghanistan', Council on Foreign Relations website, 5 June 2009, at: http://www.cfr.org/iran/harnessing-irans-role-afghanistan/p19562
62. Zakheim, *A Vulcan's Tale*, p. 267.
63. UN Office on Drugs and Crime, *Afghanistan: Opium winter assessment*, 2009, at: http://www.unodc.org/documents/crop-monitoring/ORA_report_2009.pdf
64. United States Department of State, *2009 International Narcotics Control Strategy Report*, US Department of State, 2009.
65. Amir A. Afkhami, 'How Iran won the war on drugs: Lessons for fighting the Afghan narcotics trade', *Foreign Affairs*, 2 April 2013, at: http://www.foreignaffairs.com/articles/139095/amir-a-afkhami/how-iran-won-the-war-on-drugs. For Iran's anti-narcotics budget figure, see Seyed Hossein Mousavian, 'Engage with Iran in Afghanistan', *National Interest*, 30 May 2013, at: http://nationalinterest.org/commentary/engage-iran-afghanistan-8528
66. Janne Bjerre Christensen, *Strained Alliances: Iran's troubled relations to Afghanistan and Pakistan*, Danish Institute of International Relations, 2011, pp. 20–23.
67. Amir Bagherpour and Asad Farhad, 'The Iranian influence in Afghanistan', PBS *Frontline* website, 9 August 2010, at: http://www.pbs.org/wgbh/pages/frontline/tehran-bureau/2010/08/the-iranian-influence-in-afghanistan.html
68. Amie Ferris-Rotman, 'Insight: Iran's "great game" in Afghanistan', Reuters, 24 May 2012, at: http://www.reuters.com/article/2012/05/24/us-afghanistan-iran-media-idUSBRE84N0CB20120524
69. Emma Graham-Harrison, 'Saudi Arabia funding $100m Kabul mosque and education centre', *Guardian*, 2 November 2012, at: http://www.theguardian.com/world/2012/nov/02/saudi-arabia-funding-kabul-mosque
70. Maria Abi-Habib, 'Iranians build up Afghan clout', *Wall Street Journal*, 26 October 2012, at: http://online.wsj.com/news/articles/SB10001424052970204076204578078564022815472
71. For instance, see Jacob Zenn, 'The IMU expansion in Afghanistan's Takhar province: Jumping off point to Central Asia?', *Eurasia Daily Monitor*, 10:79 (2013). Also see, Carlotta Gall, 'Taliban open northern front in Afghanistan', *New York Times*, 26 November 2009, at: http://www.nytimes.com/2009/11/27/world/asia/27kunduz.html?pagewanted=all
72. Bernard A. Gelb, 'Caspian oil and gas: Production and prospects', Congressional Research Service Report, Library of Congress, 9 April 2002.
73. Hillary R. Clinton, 'Secretary of State Hillary Rodham Clinton speaks on India and the United States: A vision for the 21st century', Speech at Anna Centenary Library, Chennai Consulate General of the United States, US Department of State, 20 July 2011, at: http://newdelhi.usembassy.gov/remarks72112.html
74. Nasr, *The Dispensable Nation*, p. 13.
75. Christina Lin, 'China's Silk Road strategy in AfPAk: The Shanghai Cooperation Organization', Institute for Strategic, Political, Security and Economic Consultancy, Germany, 2011. Also see Peter Young, 'Pakistan is our Israel', *Daily Times* (Lahore), 19 September 2011.

76. Zhao Huasheng, *China and Afghanistan: China's interests, stances and perspectives*, CSIS Russia and Eurasia Program Report, March 2012.
77. 'China and Afghanistan sign economic and security deals', BBC News, 23 September 2012, at: http://www.bbc.co.uk/news/world-asia-china-19693005
78. Zhao Huasheng, *China and Afghanistan*.
79. Li Xiguang, 'New Silk Road could revitalize war-torn Afghanistan', *Global Times*, 6 June 2011, at: http://www.globaltimes.cn/opinion/commentary/2011-06/662377.html
80. 'Yang Jiechi attends the international Afghanistan conference', Ministry of Foreign Affairs of the People's Republic of China, 6 December 2011, at: http://www.fmprc.gov.cn/eng/topics/yjc_afh_dg/t884908.shtml
81. Zhao Huasheng, *China and Afghanistan*, pp. 8–9.

Conclusion

1. Jim Lacey (ed.), *A Terrorist's Call to Global Jihad: Deciphering Abu Musab Al-Suri's Islamic Jihad Manifesto*, Naval Institute Press, Annapolis, MD, 2008. See also Jason Burke, '"Premature" to declare Al-Qaeda's defeat', *Dawn* (Karachi), 4 June 2008, at: http://dawn.com/news/305847/
2. 'On eve of elections, a dismal public mood in Pakistan: Rising concerns about Taliban', Pew Research Global Attitudes Project website, 7 May 2013, at: http://www.pewglobal.org/2013/05/07/on-eve-of-elections-a-dismal-public-mood-in-pakistan/
3. Javed Ahmed Ghamidi, 'Islam and Taliban', trans. Asif Iftikhar, *Renaissance*, available at: http://www.monthly-renaissance.com/issue/content.aspx?id=1158
4. Hasan Jan was assassinated in September 2007 and Sarfraz Naeemi in June 2009. For details, see Mushfiq Murshed, 'United against militant ideology', *Dawn* (Karachi), 3 May 2009; Ashraf Javed, 'Sarfraz Naeemi killed in suicide hit', *The Nation* (Lahore), 13 June 2009.
5. Maulvi Hekmatullah Hekmat was killed in July 2011 (while he was in a mosque praying for the deceased Wali Karzai) and Maulvi Atta Muhammad in November 2013. For more details, see Dawood Azami, 'The dissenting clerics killed in Afghanistan', BBC News, 18 November 2013, at: http://www.bbc.co.uk/news/world-asia-22885170
6. For latest figures and details, see Kenneth Katzman, 'Afghanistan: Post-Taliban governance, security and US policy', Congressional Research Service report, 8 August 2013, at: http://www.fas.org/sgp/crs/row/RL30588.pdf
7. For instance, see Mark Nicol, 'Top commander: If UK leaves Afghanistan, Taliban will return to launch global jihad', *Daily Mail*, 2 February 2013, at: http://www.dailymail.co.uk/news/article-2272585/Top-commander-If-UK-leaves-Afghanistan-Taliban-return-launch-global-jihad.html
8. Alissa J. Rubin, 'Departing French envoy has frank words on Afghanistan', *New York Times*, 27 April 2013, at: http://www.nytimes.com/2013/04/28/world/asia/bernard-bajolet-leaving-afghanistan-has-his-say.html
9. Amir Mir, 'TTP joins Afghan Taliban to wage spring offensive', *The News* (Lahore), 29 April 2013.
10. For background on the points, see Graeme Smith, 'Talking to the Taliban', *Globe and Mail* (Canada), 22 March 2008, at: http://v1.theglobeandmail.com/talkingtothetaliban/
11. 'Remarks at the launch of the Asia Society's series of Richard C. Holbrooke memorial addresses', 18 February 2011, at: http://www.state.gov/secretary/rm/2011/02/156815.htm
12. Nasr, *The Dispensable Nation*, p. 42.
13. Available at: http://www.foreignpolicy.com/files/121213_Peace_Process_Roadmap_to_2015.pdf
14. Based on interviews with Pakistani, Afghan and American officials in 2013.
15. Jon Boone and Saeed Shah, 'At least 55 dead in Kabul suicide attack on Shia pilgrims', *Guardian*, 6 December 2011, at: http://www.theguardian.com/world/2011/dec/06/55-dead-kabul-suicide-shia

16. Tahir Khan, 'Eid message: Mullah Omar blames US for Qatar dialogue deadlock', *Express Tribune* (Karachi), 6 August 2013, at: http://tribune.com.pk/story/587191/eid-message-mullah-omar-blames-us-for-qatar-dialogue-deadlock/

17. For details, see Ayesha Siddiqa, 'The new frontiers: Militancy and radicalism in Punjab', Center for International and Strategic Analysis report, 4 February 2013.

18. For a detailed assessment of this idea, see an excellent paper by Michael Semple, 'Power to the periphery? The elusive consensus on how to decentralize Afghanistan', CIDOB Policy Research Project, July 2012.

19. Colin Cookman, 'The 18th amendment and Pakistan's political transitions', Center for American Progress website, 19 April 2010, at: http://www.americanprogress.org/issues/security/news/2010/04/19/7587/the-18th-amendment-and-pakistans-political-transitions/

20. My translation; another is available at: http://islamicartdb.com/calligraphy-poem-iqbal/

Bibliography

Abbas, Hassan. *Pakistan's Drift into Extremism: Allah, the army and America's war on terror*, M. E. Sharpe, New York, 2005.

Ahmed, Akbar S. *Religion and Politics in Muslim Society: Order and conflict in Pakistan*, Cambridge University Press, 1983.

Ahmed, Akbar S. *The Thistle and the Drone: How America's war on terror became a global war on tribal Islam*, Brookings Institution, Washington, DC, 2013.

Andrew, Christopher and Vasili Mitrokhin. *The World Was Going Our Way: The KGB and the battle for the third world*, Basic Books, New York, 2005.

Barfield, Thomas. *Afghanistan: A cultural and political history*, Princeton University Press, 2010.

Bergen, Peter with Katherine Tiedemann (eds). *Talibanistan: Negotiating the borders between terror, politics and religion*, Oxford University Press, 2013.

Caroe, Olaf. *The Pathans, 550 B.C.–A.D. 1957*, Macmillan, London, 1957.

Chandrasekaran, Rajiv. *Little America: The war within the war for Afghanistan*, Alfred A. Knopf, New York, 2012.

Coll, Steve. *Ghost Wars: The secret history of the CIA, Afghanistan, and bin Laden, from the Soviet invasion to September 10, 2001*, Penguin, New York, 2004.

Cowper-Coles, Sherard. *Cables from Kabul: The inside story of the west's Afghanistan campaign*, Harper Press, London, 2011.

Crile, George. *Charlie Wilson's War: The extraordinary story of how the wildest man in Congress and a rogue CIA agent changed the history of our times*, Grove Press, New York, 2003.

Edwards, David B. *Before Taliban: Genealogies of the Afghan Jihad*, University of California Press, Berkeley, 2002.

Evans, Martin. *Afghanistan: A new history*, Curzon Press, Richmond, Surrey, 2001.

Fair, C. Christine. 'Pakistan's own war on terror: What the Pakistani public thinks', *Journal of International Affairs*, 63 (Fall/Winter 2009), pp. 39–55.

Fergusson, James. *Taliban: The unknown enemy*, Da Capo Press, Cambridge, MA, 2010.

Ferrie, Joseph Pierre. *History of the Afghans*, trans. Captain William Jesse, John Murray, London, 1858.

Ganon, Kathy. *I is for Infidel . . . J is for Jihad, K is for Kalashnikov: From holy war to holy terror in Afghanistan*, Public Affairs, New York, 2005.

Giustozzi, Antonio (ed.). *Decoding the New Taliban: Insights from the Afghan field*, Columbia University Press, New York, 2009.

Giustozzi, Antonio. *Empires of Mud: Wars and warlords in Afghanistan*, Columbia University Press, New York, 2009.

Gul, Imtiaz. *The Most Dangerous Place: Pakistan's lawless frontier*, Viking, New York, 2009.

Haroon, Sana. *Frontier of Faith: Islam in the Indo-Afghan borderland*, Columbia University Press, New York, 2007.

Hussain, Mujahid. *Punjabi Taliban: Driving extremism in Pakistan*, Pentagon Press, New Delhi, 2012.

Hussain, Rizwan. *Pakistan and the Emergence of Islamic Militancy in Afghanistan*, Routledge, London, 2005.

Hussain, Zahid. *The Scorpion's Tail: The relentless rise of Islamic militants in Pakistan*, Simon and Schuster, New York, 2010.

Jalal, Ayesha. *Partisans of Allah: Jihad in South Asia*, Harvard University Press, Cambridge, MA, 2008.

Johnson, Thomas H. 'Taliban adaptations and innovations', *Small Wars and Insurgencies*, 24:1 (2013), pp. 3–27.

Johnson, Thomas and M. Chris Mason. 'No sign until the burst of fire: Understanding the Pakistan–Afghanistan frontier', *International Security*, 34:2 (Spring 2008), pp. 41–77.

Jones, Seth G. *In the Graveyard of Empires: America's war in Afghanistan*, W.W. Norton and Company, New York, 2009.

Kakakhel, Syed Bahadur Shah Zafar. *Pashtun: Tarikh Key Aaiene Main [Pashtuns in the Light of History] 550 to 1964*, trans. Syed Anwar ul Haq Jillani, University Book Agency, Peshawar, 2007.

Khalilzad, Zalmay. 'Lessons from Afghanistan and Iraq', *Journal of Democracy*, 21:3 (2010), pp. 41–49.

Kux, Dennis. *The United States and Pakistan, 1947–2000: Disenchanted allies*, Woodrow Wilson Center Press, Washington, DC, 2001.

Linschoten, Alex Strick van and Felix Kuehn. *An Enemy We Created: The myth of the Taliban–Al Qaeda merger in Afghanistan 1970–2010*, Hurst and Company, London, 2012.

Maley, William (ed.). *Fundamentalism Reborn: Afghanistan and Taliban*, Vanguard Books, Lahore, 1998.

Marten, Kimberly. 'The danger of tribal militias in Afghanistan: Learning from the British Empire', *Journal of International Affairs*, 63 (Fall–Winter 2009), pp. 157–74.

Marsden, Peter. *The Taliban: War, religion and the new order in Afghanistan*, Oxford University Press, 1999.

Matinuddin, Kamal. *The Taliban Phenomenon: Afghanistan 1994–1997*, Oxford University Press, Karachi, 1999.

Mazzetti, Mark. *The Way of the Knife: The CIA, a secret army, and a war at the ends of the earth*, Penguin Press, New York, 2013.

Metcalf, Barbara D. *Islamic Revival in British India: Deoband, 1860–1900*, Princeton University Press, 1982.

Nasr, Seyyed Vali Reza. *The Vanguard of the Islamic Revolution: The Jamaat-i-Islami of Pakistan*, University of California Press, Berkeley, 1994.

Nasr, Vali. *The Dispensable Nation: American foreign policy in retreat*, Random House, New York, 2013.

Nojoumi, Neamatollah. *The Rise of the Taliban in Afghanistan: Mass mobilization, civil war, and the future of the region*, Palgrave, New York, 2002.

Pervaiz Iqbal Cheema and Maqsudul Hasan Nuri (eds). *Tribal Areas of Pakistan: Challenges and responses*, Islamabad Policy Research Institute, 2005.

Rana, Muhammad Amir, Safdar Sial and Abdul Basit. *Dynamics of Taliban Insurgency in FATA*, Pakistan Institute of Peace Studies, Islamabad, 2010.

Rasayanagam, Angelo. *Afghanistan: A modern history*, I.B. Tauris, New York, 2003.

Rashid, Ahmed. *Taliban: Militant Islam, oil, and fundamentalism in Central Asia*, Yale University Press, New Haven, CT, 2000.

Roy, Olivier. *Islam and Resistance in Afghanistan*, Cambridge University Press, 1990.

Rubin, Barnett. *The Fragmentation of Afghanistan*, Yale University Press, New Haven, CT, 2002.

Rubin, Barnett R. *Afghanistan from the Cold War through the War on Terror*, Oxford University Press, New York, 2013.

Spain, James W. *The Pathan Borderland*, Mouton, The Hague, 1963.

Suhrke, Astri. *When More is Less: The international project in Afghanistan*, Columbia University Press, New York, 2011.

Taj, Farhat. *Taliban and Anti-Taliban*, Cambridge Scholars Publishing, Newcastle upon Tyne, 2011.

Sagar, Tariq Ismail. *Pase Parda Haqaiq: Lal Masjid – Operation Silence*, Tahir Sons Publishers, Lahore, 2007.

Tenet, George. *At the Center of the Storm: My years at the CIA*, Harper Collins, New York, 2007.

Titus, Paul. 'Honor the Baloch, buy the Pushtun: Stereotypes, social organization and history in Western Pakistan', *Modern Asian Studies*, 32:3 (1998), pp. 657–87.

Tomsen, Peter. *The Wars of Afghanistan: Messianic terrorism, tribal conflicts, and the failures of great powers*, Public Affairs, New York, 2011.

Wolpert, Stanley. *Shameful Flight: The last years of the British Empire in India*, Oxford University Press, New York, 2009.

Woodward, Bob. *Bush at War*, Simon and Schuster, New York, 2002.

Woodward, Bob. *Obama's Wars*, Simon and Schuster, New York, 2010.

Yousaf, Mohammad and Mark Adkin. *Afghanistan – The Bear Trap: The defeat of a super-power*, Casemate, Havertown, PA, 1992.

Zaeef, Abdul Salam. *My Life with the Taliban*, C. Hurst & Co., London, 2010.

Zakheim, Dov S. *A Vulcan's Tale: How the Bush administration mismanaged the reconstruction of Afghanistan*, Brookings Institution, Washington, DC, 2011.

List of Illustrations

Acknowledgments

I cannot thank enough my professors and colleagues at my alma mater, the Fletcher School of Law and Diplomacy at Tufts University, and at Harvard University's Belfer Center for Science and International Affairs, who helped me tremendously in trying to understand the issues discussed in the book. My students at Columbia University in New York and the National Defense University (NDU) in Washington, DC, have enlightened and intrigued me with their brilliant questions and analysis. I am proud that many of my students are serving in Afghanistan and Pakistan today as journalists, bureaucrats, civil society activists and security officials. In all honesty, I have learnt a great deal from my students, many of whom are accomplished practitioners in their own right.

My association with the Asia Society in New York has also given me many opportunities to travel around the world and pursue my research interests. It would be remiss of me not to mention the kind offers I received from the Jamestown Foundation, the New America Foundation, the United States Institute of Peace, the Brookings Institution, the Council on Foreign Relations, the Institute for Social Policy and Understanding, Oxford Analytica and *CTC Sentinel* at West Point to write and speak on issues related to South Asia and security sector developments. The articles that I researched and wrote for them over the years greatly helped my comprehension of the issues that I cover in this book.

From these rich experiences, I have learnt that asking the right question is often the most important key to resolving a puzzle. That is what I wish to do for my readers – contribute by raising the questions that really matter and help them with some necessary and relevant facts to reach their own judgement. I write this book in my role as an educator. The modern history of the Taliban is presented in a chronological fashion for the ease of the general reader. The goal is to present a realistic and honest picture of the present trends – both in the political and the security arena. My cultural roots and religious experience possibly influence my 'take' on the subject, but I have expressed my personal views upfront where relevant. In my scholarly pursuits, academic freedom and objectivity are both very dear to me.

I owe a debt of gratitude to those without whom this book might never have seen the light of day. My loving wife Benish remained a constant source of motivation, and her feedback on the drafts and her editing tips helped me enormously. I also benefited greatly from the very thoughtful and detailed comments of three colleagues who read the whole manuscript – Nafisa Hoodbhoy, an accomplished Pakistani journalist and writer; Dr Geoffrey Gresh, a bright academic with great expertise on Central Asia; and Professor Christopher Candland, an outstanding scholar of South Asian studies. Discussions about Afghanistan with my colleagues Kenneth Baker, Paul D. Miller, Jeffrey Meiser and Michael Koffman at the National Defense University in Washington were also very useful. I am very thankful to Dr Michael Bell, chancellor of NDU's College of International Security Affairs, for his tremendous support and kindness while I was pursuing this project. I salute many unnamed military and intelligence officials – including my students – from Pakistan, India, Afghanistan and the United States who have shared their perspectives with me, thus enriching my understanding of the region.

Phoebe Clapham, my brilliant editor at Yale University Press, deserves credit for conceiving the idea for this book. Her clarity of thought, patience and marvellous editing skills are a true reflection of her professional excellence. Great support from Heather McCallum and Rachael Lonsdale at Yale, and from my copy-editor Clive Liddiard, is also highly appreciated. I am also especially grateful to Pir Zubair Shah, Peter Lavoy, Nasim Zehra, Imtiaz Ali, Ambassador C. Steven McGann, Brigadier Zubair Khan, Hamid Hussein, Raseema Alam, Mujib Mashal, Richard Deasy, Nosheen Abbas, Arshad Sharif and Wajahat Khan for sharing their valuable insights and in some cases also for their help in acquiring other materials for this book.

Index